EVERYDAY *crafting*

Crochet
FOR KIDS

IRA ROTT, TINE NIELSEN &
CAROLINA GUZMAN BENITEZ

sewandso

www.sewandso.co.uk

Contents

Little Happy Circus 258

Index 335

Crochet Animal Rugs

IRA ROTT

Get creative and transform your child's room into a magical modern bedroom inspired by animals!

Crochet rugs are the perfect place for your children to read and play. They make a great conversation piece with a unique style. This collection of animal rugs includes adorable matching pillows and other coordinating accessories that will bring any home to life.

You can decorate your craft room or nursery with items from this section and spend only a few evenings making each piece. So no need to wait, just get your hooks and yarn ready to begin a fun crochet adventure!

HOW TO USE THIS SECTION

SKILL LEVELS

Each pattern in this section has been assigned a skill level, ranging from beginner to challenging. To get comfortable with a project, pick a pattern that suits your skill level and then move up to the next level as you learn new stitches and techniques.

Beginner – Best choice for novice crocheters. These patterns are written using basic stitches and techniques, with minimal shaping and simple assembly.

Moderate – These patterns include basic and moderate stitches, such as treble crochet (tr), popcorn stitch (PC), reverse single crochet (rsc) and picot. There are simple color changes and shaping with repetitive stitch patterns. Easy assembly might involve hand-sewing and blocking.

Challenging – Be ready for some challenging step-by-step assembly and more complex pattern repeats. These patterns may include basic lace, irregular curves, unique shapes and techniques. Increased level of concentration might be required for some parts of these patterns.

SIZE AND GAUGE

Every pattern specifies the finished size based on the gauge, yarn weight and hook size. The gauge is the number of stitches and rows per 4in x 4in (10cm x 10cm) square. This number might be crucial for some patterns and forgiving for others.

Checking the gauge is always beneficial for the final measurements. For instance, if you are using the suggested yarn weight and hook size, but crochet too tight, then the number of stitches and rows per 4in x 4in (10cm x 10cm) square will be greater and your finished item will be smaller. The opposite effect will occur if you crochet too loose. To calibrate the gauge, use a larger or smaller size hook.

If the size is not important, you can use any yarn with any suitable size hook and your finished measurements will vary depending on the gauge. For example, you can make a doily or a wall decoration from a rug pattern by using thin yarn instead of thick yarn (see General Techniques: Wall Decoration).

TIPS

- If you are new to crochet, start with a beginner-level pattern. For example, make a beginner-level pillow base (see Common Shapes) and then choose a moderate-level pillow pattern to finish the remaining parts.

- Try a moderate-level rug pattern before attempting to make a challenging rug.

- Ensure that you are familiar with stitches and techniques listed for each pattern before starting (see Useful Information, Crochet Techniques and General Techniques).

- If you are a left-handed crocheter, please refer to the tips in the Crochet Techniques section (see Crochet Techniques: Left-Handed Crochet).

READING PATTERNS

Crochet patterns in this book are written using American (US) terminology. This means that if you follow UK terminology then you need to convert the terms to British (UK) terminology (see Useful Information: Crochet Terminology).

- "Work in rows" means – crochet a row of stitches as indicated in the pattern, then turn your work to begin the next row. The pattern will specify which rows are on right side (RS) and wrong side (WS).

- "Work in the round" means – begin with a magic ring/foundation ring or work along both sides of the foundation chain (see Crochet Techniques). Crochet each round as indicated in the pattern without turning, then join the last stitch to the first stitch. Always work with right side (RS) facing, unless otherwise indicated.

- "Work in spiral rounds" means – begin with a magic ring/foundation ring or work across both sides of the foundation chain (see Crochet Techniques). Crochet the first round as indicated in the pattern without turning and without joining. Work the beginning stitch of each round into first stitch of the previous round; never join rounds. Work spiral rounds with right side (RS) facing, unless otherwise indicated.

- The total stitch count is indicated after the equal sign (=) at the end of each row/round. The beginning chain(s) might be counted as stitch(es) or not, as marked at the beginning of the rows/rounds. Some instructions apply to multiple rows/rounds, for example Ch 1 (doesn't count as a st now and throughout).

READING CHARTS

A crochet chart is an illustration featuring special symbols to represent stitches. Charts help to visualize patterns before you start crocheting. The beginning of the work is marked with a small black arrow. Different colors indicate each row/round along with the row/round number. If the chart has more than 2 colors, a color key will be provided. To understand a chart, refer to the symbol key (see Useful Information: Abbreviations).

The use of charts is optional. You can choose to follow a chart or the pattern text, or even use both.

The charts shown in this section are for right-handed crochet and show your work on the right side (RS). If the chart begins on the left, the first row is on the wrong side (WS).

TOOLS AND MATERIALS

CROCHET HOOKS

Various sizes of crochet hooks are required for these projects. We have listed the metric and US sizes with the project instructions, but you can use this conversion chart for reference to quickly find the correct size for your region.

Metric	US letter	US number	Canada/UK
3.75mm	F	5	9
4mm/4.5mm	G	6/7	8/7
5mm	H	8	6
5.5mm	I	9	5
6mm	J	10	4
6.5mm	K	10.5	3
9mm	M/N	13	00

YARN

All of these projects are made using medium weight yarn (weight 4). However, you'll notice instructions for using 1, 2 or 3 strands throughout the section. See Crochet Techniques for tips on how to work with several strands of yarn at once.

If you struggle working with multiple strands, simply substitute 2 strands of medium yarn (weight 4) with 1 strand of bulky yarn (weight 5), or 3 strands of medium yarn (weight 4) with 1 strand of super bulky yarn (weight 6).

US	UK	Australia	Meters per 100g
Medium (4)	Aran	10-ply	150-199
Bulky (5)	Chunky	12-ply	100-149
Super Bulky (6)	Super Chunky	14-ply	60-99

The amount of yarn is given in yards/meters for each color of medium weight yarn (weight 4). "Small amount" means less than 93yd (85m) of yarn.

Please keep in mind that the finished size and the total yarn length may vary depending on the materials used and the gauge.

Yarn weight is the thickness of yarn, which may vary from country to country. Use the conversion chart provided to find the correct yarn for your region.

OTHER EQUIPMENT

You'll also need the following equipment to create the projects in this section:

- Stitch markers – for marking stitches and indicating the start of the round
- Spray bottle – useful for wet blocking
- Tapestry needle(s) or latch hook – for sewing and weaving in ends
- Scissors
- Blocking board or interlocking play mat – for wet blocking
- Polyester stuffing or bed pillow filler
- Clips – for holding pieces in place while sewing

RUG LINING

I recommend adding a non-slip lining to crochet rugs to ensure that they stay in place. To do this, you'll require the following additional equipment:

- Basic straight stitch sewing machine
- Non-adhesive shelf liner with grip or rug gripper pad
- Hook and loop tape (strip with hooks only) – 1in (2.5cm) wide
- All-purpose sewing thread

WALL HANGING

To transform your crocheted designs into wall art, you'll require the following equipment:

- Size 10 crochet thread – approximately 875yd (800m)
- 1.9mm (US size 5) steel hook
- Wall frame or poster frame at least 3in (7.6cm) larger than the finished wall decoration on each side
- Matboard backing that fits in frame
- Matboard edging that fits in frame
- Chenille needle with sharp point
- Finger guard (thimble)
- Fabric stiffener or corn starch
- Rust-proof straight pins
- Scotch tape or packing tape

JEFFERY THE ELEPHANT

Rug, Pillow, and Stool Cover

Jeffery is my most favorite animal creation! His amazing curved trunk reminds me of hooks and inspires me to crochet. It's not surprising that I chose to make this elephant collection to decorate my craft studio – the combination of texture, lace, and chunkiness brings my workspace to life!

After making Jeffery in gray yarn, I just had to make a colorful friend for him! So I crocheted Josefina in a pretty pink yarn with a purple bow. Choose your favorite (or make both) and, once you've completed the rug, crochet a coordinating elephant pillow and a sweet stool cover to decorate your room.

ELEPHANT RUG

SKILL LEVEL

FINISHED SIZE
52in x 31½in (132cm x 80cm)

HOOKS
5.5mm (I), 6.5mm (K), 9mm (M/N)

YARN WEIGHT
4

NUMBER OF STRANDS
1, 2, and 3

**GAUGE WITH 3 STRANDS
AND 9MM (M/N) HOOK**
9 dc x 4.5 rows = 4in x 4in (10cm x 10cm)

STITCH SUMMARY
Ch, sl st, sc, sc2tog, hdc, dc, dc2tog, tr,
picot, PC, beg PC, crest, shell, arch, join

SKILLS
Working in rows and in the round,
raw edge finishing, working across
the bottom of the foundation chain,
blocking, sewing

LEFT-HANDED CROCHET
See Crochet Techniques:
Left-Handed Crochet

YARN

Abbreviation	Color	Amount
MC	Gray or Pink	2187-2515yd (2000-2300m)
CC1	Black	Small amount
CC2	White	Small amount
CC3	Lilac or Pink (optional)	93-109yd (85-100m)

HEAD AND TRUNK

Make 1. Begin by working in the round with a 9mm (M/N) hook and 3 strands of **MC**.

STEP 1 - HEAD

To beg: Ch 3, sl st in third ch from hook to form a ring (or start with a magic ring)

Rnd 1: Ch 2 (doesn't count as a st from now to Rnd 11), 12 dc in ring; join = 12 sts

Rnd 2: Ch 2, 2 dc in same st as join, 2 dc in next 11 sts; join = 24 sts

Rnd 3: Ch 2, dc in same st as join, 2 dc in next st, [dc in next st, 2 dc in next st] 11 times; join = 36 sts

Rnd 4: Ch 2, 2 dc in same st as join, dc in next 2 sts, [2 dc in next st, dc in next 2 sts] 11 times; join = 48 sts

Rnd 5: Ch 2, dc in same st as join, dc in next 2 sts, 2 dc in next st, [dc in next 3 sts, 2 dc in next st] 11 times; join = 60 sts

Rnd 6: Ch 2, 2 dc in same st as join, dc in next 4 sts, [2 dc in next st, dc in next 4 sts] 11 times; join = 72 sts

Rnd 7: Ch 2, dc in same st as join, dc in next 4 sts, 2 dc in next st, [dc in next 5 sts, 2 dc in next st] 11 times; join = 84 sts

Rnd 8: Ch 2, 2 dc in same st as join, dc in next 6 sts, [2 dc in next st, dc in next 6 sts] 11 times; join = 96 sts

Rnd 9: Ch 2, dc in same st as join, dc in next 6 sts, 2 dc in next st, [dc in next 7 sts, 2 dc in next st] 11 times; join = 108 sts

Rnd 10: Ch 2, 2 dc in same st as join, dc in next 8 sts, [2 dc in next st, dc in next 8 sts] 11 times; join = 120 sts

Rnd 11: Ch 2, dc in same st as join, dc in next 8 sts, 2 dc in next st, [dc in next 9 sts, 2 dc in next st] 11 times; join = 132 sts

Don't break off yarn. Continue to work **Step 2** in rows.

HEAD AND TRUNK CHART

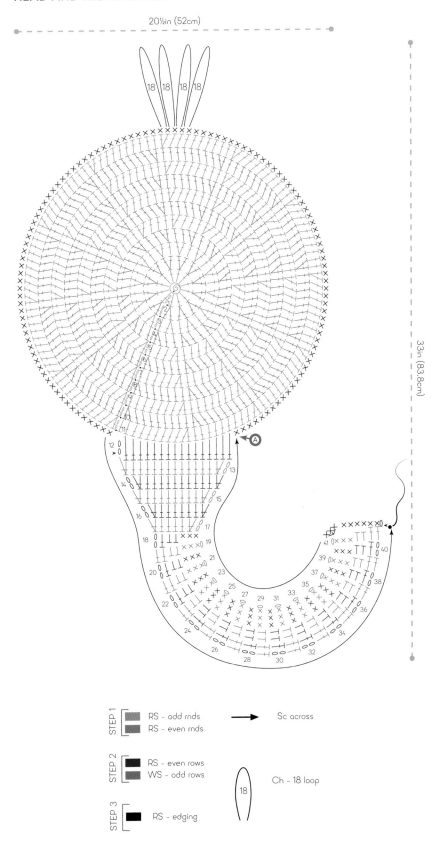

20½in (52cm)

33in (83.8cm)

STEP 1		RS - odd rnds	→	Sc across
STEP 1		RS - even rnds		
STEP 2		RS - even rows		
STEP 2		WS - odd rows		Ch - 18 loop
STEP 3		RS - edging		

STEP 2 - TRUNK

Row 12: (RS) Ch 2 (counts as first dc now and throughout), skip st with join, dc in next 16 sts, place **Marker A** in next st; turn = 17 sts

Row 13: (WS) Ch 2, skip first st, dc2tog, dc in next 12 sts, dc2tog; turn = 15 sts

Row 14: (RS) Ch 2, skip first st, dc2tog, dc in next 10 sts, dc2tog; turn = 13 sts

Row 15: (WS) Ch 2, skip first st, dc2tog, dc in next 8 sts, dc2tog; turn = 11 sts

Row 16: (RS) Ch 2, skip first st, dc2tog, dc in next 6 sts, dc2tog; turn = 9 sts

Row 17: (WS) Ch 2, skip first st, dc2tog, dc in next 4 sts, dc2tog; turn = 7 sts

Row 18: (RS) Ch 2, skip first st, dc in next st, hdc in next 2 sts, sc in next 3 sts; turn = 7 sts

Row 19: (WS) Ch 1 (doesn't count as a st), sc in first st, sc in next 2 sts, hdc in next 2 sts, dc in next 2 sts; turn = 7 sts

Rows 20-41: Repeat Rows 18 and 19 in established pattern, ending on WS

Turn and work **Step 3** on RS.

STEP 3 - EDGING

With RS facing, ch 1 (doesn't count as a st), sc in first st, sc in next 5 sts, 3 sc in next st, sc evenly across the concave edge of the trunk, sc in st with **Marker A** and remove the marker, sc in next 55 sts, [ch 18, sc in next st] 4 times, sc in next 55 sts, sc evenly across the convex edge of the trunk; join (1)

Fasten off, leaving a long single strand of **MC** for sewing. Weave in the other ends.

LEFT EAR CHART

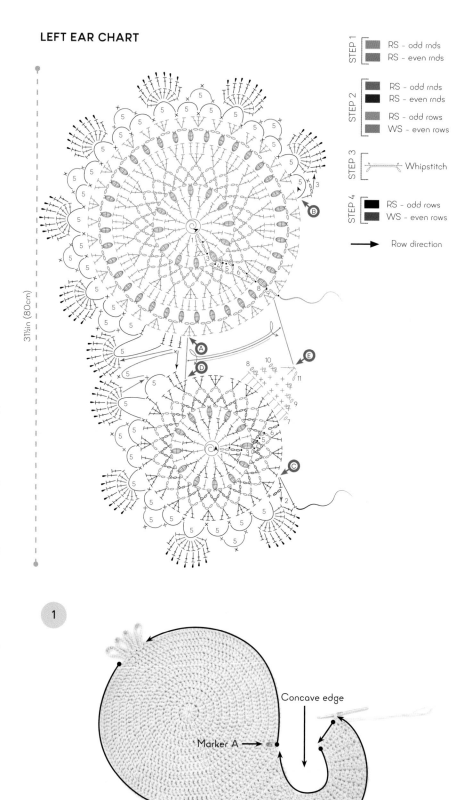

31½in (80cm)

STEP 1

RS - odd rnds
RS - even rnds

STEP 2

RS - odd rnds
RS - even rnds
RS - odd rows
WS - even rows

STEP 3

Whipstitch

STEP 4

RS - odd rows
WS - even rows

Row direction

1

Concave edge

Marker A

Convex edge

LEFT EAR

Make 1. Work with a 9mm (M/N) hook and 3 strands of **MC**.

STEP 1 - BIG CIRCLE

Work in the round to make 1 big circle.

To beg: Ch 3, sl st in third ch from hook to form a ring (or start with a magic ring)

Rnd 1: Ch 2 (doesn't count as a st now and throughout), 12 dc in ring; join = 12 sts

Rnd 2: Ch 2, 2 dc in same st as join, 2 dc in next 11 sts; join = 24 sts

Rnd 3: Beg PC in same st as join, ch 1, dc in next st, ch 1, [PC in next st, ch 1, dc in next st, ch 1] 11 times; join = 12 PC and 12 dc

Rnd 4: Ch 1 (doesn't count as a st now and throughout), [skip PC, sc in next ch-1 sp, ch 3, skip dc, sc in next ch-1 sp, ch 3] 12 times; join = 24 arches

Rnd 5: Sl st in first ch of the first arch, ch 1, sc in same arch, [ch 3, sc in next arch] 23 times, ch 3; join = 24 arches

Rnd 6: Ch 2, [3 dc in next arch, 2 dc in next arch] 12 times; join = 60 sts

Rnd 7: Ch 2, dc in same st as join, dc in next 3 sts, 2 dc in next st, [dc in next 4 sts, 2 dc in next st] 11 times; join = 72 sts

Rnd 8: Beg PC in same st as join, ch 2, skip st, [PC in next st, ch 2, skip st] 35 times; join = 36 PC

Rnd 9: Ch 2, [skip PC, 3 dc in next ch-2 sp, skip PC, 2 dc in next ch-2 sp] 18 times, place **Marker A** in 14th st to the right, place **Marker B** in 14th st to the left; join = 90 sts

Fasten off, leaving a long single strand of **MC** for sewing. Weave in the other ends.

STEP 2 - SMALL CIRCLE

Make 1 small circle by following the instructions for the big circle from the beginning to Rnd 6 (see Left Ear: Step 1 - Big Circle). Place **Marker C** in 7th st to the right and continue to work the tip in rows as follows:

Row 7: (RS) Ch 1 (doesn't count as a st now and throughout), hdc in same st as join, hdc in next 8 sts, place **Marker D** in 7th st to the left; turn = 9 sts

Row 8: (WS) Ch 1, don't skip first st, sc2tog, sc in next 5 sts, sc2tog; turn = 7 sts

Row 9: (RS) Ch 1, don't skip first st, sc2tog, sc in next 3 sts, sc2tog; turn = 5 sts

Row 10: (WS) Ch 1, don't skip first st, sc2tog, sc in next st, sc2tog; turn = 3 sts

Row 11: (RS) Ch 2 (counts as first dc), skip first st, dc2tog, place **Marker E** in st just made = 2 sts

Fasten off and weave in the ends.

STEP 3 - ASSEMBLING CIRCLES

With RS of both circles facing you, place the small circle right up against the big circle with **Marker D** below **Marker A** and **Marker E** below the long tail of the big circle (2). Using the long tail from the big circle, whipstitch towards **Marker A** to join the small circle from **Marker E** to **Marker D** (3). Turn to WS and whipstitch across the same edges. Weave in the end. Don't remove markers.

STEP 4 - EDGING

With RS of the ear facing you, join yarn in st with **Marker B** of the big circle.

Row 1: (RS) Working from **Marker B** towards **Marker A**, [ch 5, skip 2 sts, sc in next st] 18 times, ch 5, skip 2 sts, dc in next st, ch 5, skip 2 sts, tr in next 3 sts, skip **Marker A** and **Marker D**, tr in next 2 sts of small circle, ch 5, skip 2 sts, dc in next st, [ch 5, skip 2 sts, sc in next st] 10 times, ch 2, skip 2 sts, dc in st with **Marker C** (counts as last arch); turn = 32 arches (4)

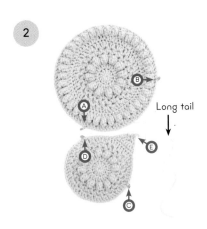

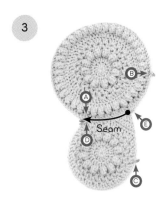

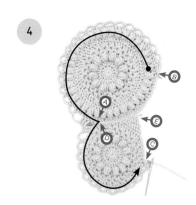

15

Row 2: (WS) Skip ch-2 sp, [9 dc in next arch, sc in next arch, ch 5, sc in next arch] 3 times, 9 dc in next arch, sc in next arch, ch 5, skip 2 tr, sc in next tr, skip 2 tr, [9 dc in next arch, sc in next arch, ch 5, sc in next arch] 6 times, 9 dc in next arch, sc in next arch, ch 2, dc in st with **Marker B** (counts as last arch); turn = 11 shells and 11 arches

Row 3: (RS) Skip ch-2 sp, [crest across next shell, sc in next arch] 10 times, crest across next shell, dc in st with **Marker C** = 11 crests

Fasten off, leaving a long single strand of **MC** for sewing. Weave in the other ends. Remove all markers. Spray block the shell edge or wet block the entire ear if necessary (see General Techniques: Blocking).

RIGHT EAR

Make 1. Work with a 9mm (M/N) hook and 3 strands of **MC**.

STEP 1 - BIG CIRCLE

Follow the instructions for the big circle from the Left Ear (see Left Ear: Step 1 - Big Circle).

STEP 2 - SMALL CIRCLE

Follow the instructions for the small circle from the Left Ear (see Left Ear: Step 2 - Small Circle).

STEP 3 - ASSEMBLING CIRCLES

With RS of both circles facing you, place the small circle right up against the big circle with **Marker C** below **Marker B**, and **Marker E** below the long tail of the big circle (5). Using the long tail from the big circle, whipstitch towards **Marker B** to join the small circle from **Marker E** to **Marker C** (6). Turn to WS and whipstitch across the same edges. Weave in the ends. Don't remove markers.

STEP 4 - EDGING

With RS of the ear facing you, join yarn in st with **Marker D** of the small circle.

Row 1: (RS) Working from **Marker D** towards **Marker C**, [ch 5, skip 2 sts, sc in next st] 10 times, ch 5, skip 2 sts, dc in next st, ch 5, skip 2 sts, tr in next 2 sts, skip **Marker C** and **Marker B**, tr in next 3 sts of big circle, ch 5, skip 2 sts, dc in next st, [ch 5, skip 2 sts, sc in next st] 18 times, ch 2, skip 2 sts, dc in st with **Marker A** (counts as last arch); turn = 32 arches (7)

Row 2: (WS) Skip ch-2 sp, [9 dc in next arch, sc in next arch, ch 5, sc in next arch] 6 times, 9 dc in next arch, skip 2 tr, sc in next tr, ch 5, skip 2 tr, sc in next arch, [9 dc in next arch, sc in next arch, ch 5, sc in next arch] 3 times, 9 dc in next arch, sc in next arch, ch 2, dc in st with **Marker D** (counts as last arch); turn = 11 shells and 11 arches

Row 3: (RS) Skip ch-2 sp, [crest across next shell, sc in next arch] 10 times, crest across next shell, dc in st with **Marker A** = 11 crests

Fasten off, leaving a long single strand of **MC** for sewing. Weave in the other ends. Remove all markers. Spray block the shell edge or wet block the entire ear if necessary (see General Techniques: Blocking).

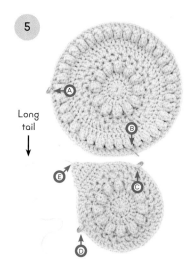

5

Long tail

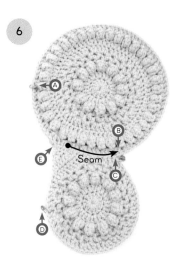

6

Seam

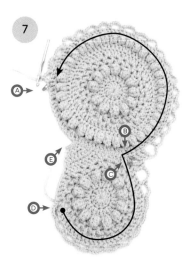

7

EYES

Make 2. Follow the instructions for the basic eyes (see Common Shapes: Basic Eyes). Use 2 strands of **CC1** with a 9mm (M/N) hook for the pupils and 1 strand of **CC2** with a 5.5mm (I) hook for the highlights.

TUSKS (OPTIONAL)

Make 2. Work in rows with a 6.5mm (K) hook and 2 strands of **CC2**.

To beg: Ch 11

Row 1: (WS) Sl st in second ch from hook (the skipped ch doesn't count as a st), sc in next 2 chs, hdc in next 3 chs, dc in next 4 chs; turn = 10 sts

Row 2: (RS) Ch 1 (doesn't count as a st), sc in next 10 sts, 2 sc in end ch, continuing working across the bottom of the foundation ch, sc in next 10 sts = 22 sts

Fasten off, leaving a long single strand of **CC2** for sewing. Weave in the other ends.

BOW (OPTIONAL)

Make 1. Follow the instructions for the big bow (see Common Shapes: Big Bow). Use 3 strands of **CC3** with a 9mm (M/N) hook.

RIGHT EAR CHART

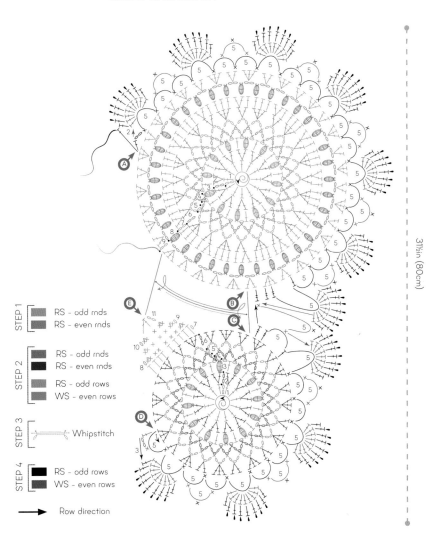

STEP 1		RS – odd rnds
		RS – even rnds
STEP 2		RS – odd rnds
		RS – even rnds
		RS – odd rows
		WS – even rows
STEP 3		Whipstitch
STEP 4		RS – odd rows
		WS – even rows

→ Row direction

31½in (80cm)

TUSK CHART

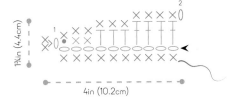

1¾in (4.4cm)

4in (10.2cm)

ASSEMBLING RUG

Place the eyes approximately 3 rounds above the edge on each side of the head (8).

To position the eyebrows (optional), cut 2 x 5in (12.7cm) lengths of any color yarn and place them above the eyes to reflect a facial expression. Place a marker on each end of both yarn guides (8).

Backstitch the eyes around the edge using the long **CC1** tail from the eyes. Thread the needle with a double strand of **CC1** and chain stitch the eyebrows between the markers (9), removing markers as you go.

If using, place the tusks on each side of the trunk and whipstitch across RS and WS using the long **CC2** tail from the tusks (10).

With RS facing, place the ears right up against the head, 8-9 stitches apart from the top loops on each side. Using the long **MC** tail from the ears, whipstitch across the inner edge of the ears on RS (11) and WS (12).

The tip of the curved trunk should overlap onto the ear, but don't worry if it doesn't as everyone crochets differently. Leave the trunk unattached or whipstitch the corner of the trunk to the ear on RS and WS using the long MC tail from the trunk (11 and 12).

For Josefina, place the bow onto the head and backstitch around the center with 1 strand of **CC3** (13). Leave the side edges of the bow unattached or whipstitch the corners to keep them in place.

If desired, make a removable non-slip lining (see General Techniques: Non-Slip Lining).

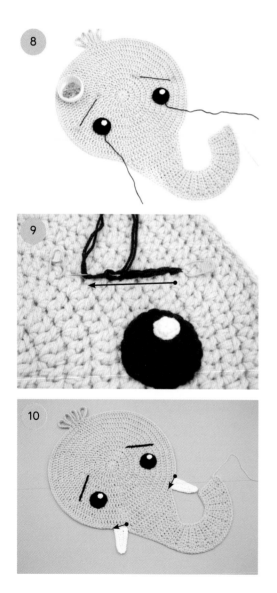

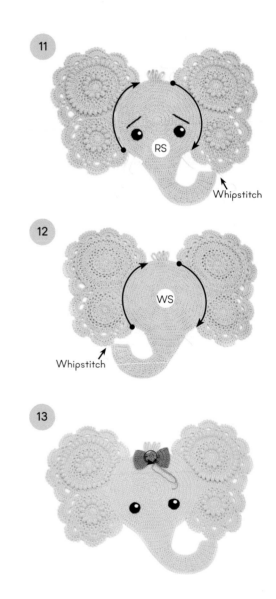

Use light
pink yarn
to create
Josefina.

ELEPHANT PILLOW

SKILL LEVEL

FINISHED SIZE
26in x 17½in (66cm x 44.5cm)

HOOKS
3.75mm (F), 4mm (G), 5.5mm (I)

YARN WEIGHT
4

NUMBER OF STRANDS
1

**GAUGE WITH 1 STRAND
AND 5.5MM (I) HOOK**
14 sc x 16 rows = 4in x 4in (10cm x 10cm)

STITCH SUMMARY
Ch, sl st, sc, sc3tog, bpsc, hdc, dc,
dc2tog, dc3tog, picot, PC, beg PC, join

SKILLS
Working in rows and in the round,
raw edge finishing, sewing

LEFT-HANDED CROCHET
Fully compatible

YARN

Abbreviation	Color	Amount
MC	Light Gray	842-930yd (770-850m)

Contrasting colors are the same as for the
Elephant Rug (small amount of each).

HEAD PILLOW BASE

Make 1 front and 1 back using 1 strand of **MC** with a 5.5mm
(I) hook. Follow the instructions for the round pillow base
(see Common Shapes: Round Pillow Base). Fasten off
after finishing the back piece, but don't break off yarn after
finishing the front piece.

Holding the front and the back pieces together with WS
facing each other, work the joining round through both
pieces of fabric at the same time using the working yarn
from the front piece.

Rnd 26: Ch 1 (doesn't count as a st), sc in same st as
previous sl st, sc in next 75 sts, [ch 18, sc in next st] 5 times,
sc in next 60 sts, stuff the pillow (I), sc in next 15 sts; join =
156 sts and 5 loops

Fasten off and weave in the ends.

EYES

Make 2. Follow the instructions for the basic eyes (see Common Shapes: Basic Eyes). Work with a 4mm (G) hook using 1 strand of **CC1** for the pupils and 1 strand of **CC2** for the highlights.

BOW (OPTIONAL)

Make 1. Follow the instructions for the small bow (see Common Shapes: Small Bow). Use 1 strand of **CC3** with a 3.75mm (F) hook.

EARS

Make 2 front and 2 back pieces following the same instructions. Work in rows with a 5.5mm (I) hook and 1 strand of **MC**.

STEP 1 - FRONT AND BACK

To beg: Ch 39

Row 1: (RS) Sc in second ch from hook (the skipped ch doesn't count as a st), place **Marker A** in skipped ch, sc in next 11 sts, [2 sc in next st, sc in next 12 sts] 2 times; turn = 40 sts

Row 2: (WS) Ch 3 (counts as first dc now and throughout), dc in first st, dc in next 19 sts, 2 dc in next st, dc in next 18 sts, 2 dc in next st; turn = 43 sts

Row 3: (RS) Ch 3, skip first st, dc in next st, [ch 2, skip st, PC in next st] 19 times, ch 2, skip st, dc in next 2 sts; turn = 19 PC and 4 dc

Row 4: (WS) Ch 3, skip first st, dc in next st, 2 dc in next ch-2 sp, skip PC, 2 dc in next ch-2 sp, [skip PC, 3 dc in next ch-2 sp, skip PC, 2 dc in next ch-2 sp] 9 times, dc in next 2 sts; turn = 53 sts

Row 5: (RS) Ch 3, skip first st, dc in next st, [ch 2, skip st, PC in next st] 24 times, ch 2, skip st, dc in next 2 sts; turn = 24 PC and 4 dc

Row 6: (WS) Ch 3, skip first st, dc in next st, *3 dc in next ch-2 sp, skip PC, [2 dc in next ch-2 sp, skip PC] 2 times**, repeat 7 more times from * to **, 3 dc in next ch-2 sp, dc in next 2 sts; turn = 63 sts

Row 7: (RS) Ch 3, skip first st, dc in next st, [ch 2, skip st, PC in next st] 29 times, ch 2, skip st, dc in next 2 sts; turn = 29 PC and 4 dc

Row 8: (WS) Ch 3, skip first st, dc in next st, [2 dc in next ch-2 sp, skip PC] 29 times, 2 dc in next ch-2 sp, dc in next 2 sts; turn = 64 sts

Row 9: (RS) Ch 3, skip first st, dc2tog, PC in next st, [ch 2, skip st, PC in next st] 12 times, dc in next st, dc3tog, place **Marker B** in next st; turn = 13 PC and 4 dc

Row 10: (WS) Ch 3, skip first st, dc in next st, [skip PC, 2 dc in next ch-2 sp] 12 times, skip PC, dc2tog; turn = 27 sts

Row 11: (RS) Ch 3, skip first st, dc2tog, skip st, PC in next st, [ch 2, skip st, PC in next st] 9 times, skip st, dc in next st, dc2tog; turn = 10 PC and 4 dc

Row 12: (WS) Ch 3, skip first st, dc in next st, [skip PC, 2 dc in next ch-2 sp] 9 times, skip PC, dc2tog = 21 sts

Fasten off and weave in the ends.

STEP 2 - FRONT AND BACK

With RS facing, join **MC** in stitch with **Marker B** and work the next row across the remaining stitches of Row 8 as follows:

Row 9: (RS) Ch 3, skip st with **Marker B**, dc3tog, PC in next st, [ch 2, skip st, PC in next st] 12 times, dc in next st, dc2tog; turn = 13 PC and 4 dc

Rows 10-12: Repeat Rows 10-12 of the front and back (see Ears: Step 1 - Front and Back).

Fasten off and weave in the ends.

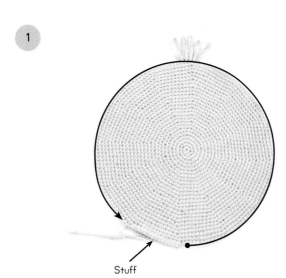

Stuff

STEP 3 - ASSEMBLING EARS

Place the front and the back pieces of each ear together with WS facing each other. Use clips to hold the layers of fabric in place for joining (2). Don't use straight basting pins as they can easily get lost in the pillow.

To join the layers, work around the outer edge of the ear with 1 strand of **MC** and a 5.5mm (I) hook, inserting the hook through both pieces of fabric at the same time. Join yarn in stitch with **Marker A** of front piece, ch 1 to beg, [2 sc, picot] repeat evenly around the edge working towards **Marker B** of both pieces, then towards **Marker A** of back piece (3). Don't join the inner edge of the ear.

Fasten off, leaving a long tail for sewing. Remove all markers.

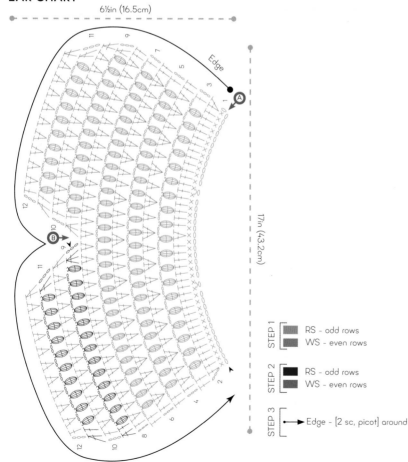

EAR CHART

TRUNK

Make 1. Work in the round with a 4mm (G) hook and 1 strand of **MC**. Stuff the trunk as you go, using a moderate amount of polyester stuffing (don't over-stuff, as stuffing may show through the stitches).

To beg: Ch 3, sl st in third ch from hook to form a ring (or start with a magic ring)

Rnd 1: Ch 1, (doesn't count as a st now and throughout), 6 sc in ring; join = 6 sts

Rnd 2: Ch 1, 2 sc in same st as join, 2 sc in next 5 sts; join = 12 sts

Rnd 3: Ch 1, 2 sc in same st as join, 2 sc in next 11 sts; join = 24 sts

Rnd 4: Ch 1, bpsc in same st as join, bpsc in next 23 sts; join = 24 sts

Rnds 5-24: Ch 1, sc in same st as join, sc in next 3 sts, hdc in next 4 sts, dc in next 8 sts, hdc in next 4 sts, sc in next 4 sts; join = 24 sts

Rnd 25: Ch 1, hdc in same st as join, 2 hdc in next st, [hdc in next st, 2 hdc in next st] 11 times; join = 36 sts

Rnd 26: Ch 1, sc in same st as join, sc in next 5 sts, hdc in next 6 sts, dc in next 12 sts, hdc in next 6 sts, sc in next 6 sts; join = 36 sts

Rnd 27: Ch 1, hdc in same st as join, hdc in next st, 2 hdc in next st, [hdc in next 2 sts, 2 hdc in next st] 11 times; join = 48 sts

Rnd 28: Ch 1, hdc in same st as join, hdc in next 47 sts; join = 48 sts

Fasten off, leaving a long tail for sewing.

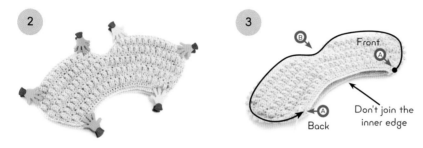

	STEP 1	RS - odd rows
		WS - even rows
	STEP 2	RS - odd rows
		WS - even rows
	STEP 3	→ Edge - [2 sc, picot] around

ASSEMBLING PILLOW

Place the ears right up against the head on each side, approximately 10 stitches apart from the top loops. Using the long **MC** tail from the ears, whipstitch around entire edge, sandwiching the pillow edge in between the layers of the ears (4 and 5).

Place the trunk 4-5 rounds below the center of the head and whipstitch around the edge using the long **MC** tail from the trunk (6).

Whipstitch the tip of the trunk to the head using **MC** to keep it in place (7).

Place the eyes on each side above the trunk and backstitch around the edge using the long **CC1** tail from the eyes (8).

To position the eyebrows (optional), cut 2 x 3in (7.6cm) lengths of any color yarn and place them above the eyes to reflect a facial expression. Place a marker on each end of both yarn guides. Thread the needle with **CC1** and chain stitch the eyebrows between the markers (8), removing markers as you go. Jeffery is now completed.

For Josefina, place the bow onto the head and backstitch around the center using the long **CC3** tail from the bow (9).

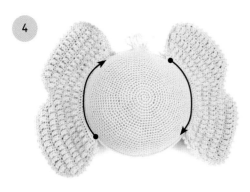

ELEPHANT STOOL COVER

SKILL LEVEL

FINISHED SIZE
12in-13½in (30.5cm-34.3cm) diameter

HOOK
9mm (M/N)

YARN WEIGHT
4

NUMBER OF STRANDS
3

GAUGE WITH 3 STRANDS AND 9MM (M/N) HOOK
9 dc x 4.5 rows = 4in x 4in (10cm x 10cm)

STITCH SUMMARY
Ch, sl st, sc, dc, PC, beg PC, arch, join

SKILLS
Working in the round

LEFT-HANDED CROCHET
Fully compatible

STOOL COVER

Make 1. Work in the round with a 9mm (M/N) hook and 3 strands of **MC**. Follow the instructions for the big circle of the Elephant Rug from the beginning to Rnd 6 (see Left Ear: Step 1 - Big Circle). Work the remaining rounds as follows:

Rnd 7: Beg PC in same st as join, ch 2, skip st, [PC in next st, ch 2, skip st] 29 times; join = 30 PC

Rnd 8: Ch 1, skip beg PC, sc in next ch-2 sp, ch 3, [sc in next ch-2 sp, ch 3] 29 times; join = 30 arches

Rnds 9-11: Sl st in first ch of the first arch, ch 1, sc in same arch, [ch 3, sc in next arch] 29 times, ch 3; join = 30 arches

Fasten off and weave in the ends.

DRAWSTRING

Make 1. Work with a 9mm (M/N) hook and 3 strands of **MC**.

To beg: Ch 4

Row 1: (RS) *2 dc in fourth ch from hook (3 skipped chs count as first dc), ch 3 (counts as dc), sl st in same ch as previous dc**, ch 179, repeat once from * to ** = 175 chs with 4 dc on each end

Fasten off and weave in the ends.

ASSEMBLING STOOL COVER

Using a crochet hook, thread the drawstring through the arches of the final round of stool cover (1) and tie when ready to use.

YARN

Abbreviation	Color	Amount
MC	Light Gray	361-394yd (330-360m)

Repeat
Rnds 9-11 if
alterations
are needed.

RUSTY THE GIRAFFE

Rug, Pillow, and Security Blanket

Africa's tallest freckled mammals roam the Savannah – they are truly gentle giants. Giraffes are enchanting creatures, so interesting to watch and admire. You don't have to travel to Africa when you can have a safari in your own room.

This precious collection of a rug, a pillow, and a security blanket will make any nursery room fun and adorable! A complex appearance of colorwork in the giraffe skin print is created by simply changing the colors for alternate rows. You'll be amazed by how effortless this beautiful texture is.

GIRAFFE RUG

SKILL LEVEL

FINISHED SIZE
38in x 40in (96.5cm x 101.6cm)

HOOK
9mm (M/N)

YARN WEIGHT
4

NUMBER OF STRANDS
2 and 3

GAUGE WITH 3 STRANDS AND 9MM (M/N) HOOK
9 dc x 4.5 rows = 4in x 4in (10cm x 10cm)

STITCH SUMMARY
Ch, sl st, sc, rsc, hdc, dc, dc3tog, tr, PC, beg PC, FDC, OS, shell, OS over shell, arch, join

SKILLS
Working in rows and in the round, raw edge finishing, working across the bottom of the foundation chain, changing colors, blocking, sewing

LEFT-HANDED CROCHET
See Crochet Techniques: Left-Handed Crochet

YARN

Abbreviation	Color	Amount
MC	Yellow	710-820yd (650-750m)
CC1	Warm Brown	710-820yd (650-750m)
CC2	Oatmeal	710-820yd (650-750m)
CC3	Black	Small amount
CC4	White	Small amount
CC5	Any color for bow (optional)	93-109yd (85-100m)

EARS

Make 2. Work in rows with a 9mm (M/N) hook and 3 strands of **MC**.

To beg: Ch 7

Row 1: (WS) OS in fourth ch from hook (3 skipped chs count as dc), skip ch, OS in next ch, place **Marker A** in last ch, dc in same ch with marker; turn = 2 OS and 2 dc

Row 2: (RS) Ch 3 (counts as first dc now and throughout), OS over shell, (dc, ch 1, dc) in sp between shells, OS over shell, dc in last st; turn = 2 OS and 4 dc

Row 3: (WS) Ch 3, OS over shell, ch 2, skip dc, OS in next ch-1 sp, ch 2, skip dc, OS over shell, dc in last st; turn = 3 OS and 2 dc

Row 4: (RS) Ch 3, OS over shell, ch 2, 9 dc in center of next shell, ch 2, OS over shell, dc in last st; turn = 2 OS, 1 shell and 2 dc

Row 5: (WS) Ch 3, OS over shell, ch 1, work across the next shell [dc in next st, ch 1] 9 times, OS over shell, dc in last st; turn = 2 OS and 11 dc

Row 6: (RS) Ch 3, OS over shell, [ch 3, skip dc, sc in next ch-1 sp] 8 times, ch 3, skip dc, OS over shell, dc in last st; turn = 2 OS, 9 arches and 2 dc

Row 7: (WS) Ch 3, OS over shell, ch 3, skip arch, [sc in next arch, ch 3] 7 times, skip arch, OS over shell, dc in last st; turn = 2 OS, 8 arches and 2 dc

Row 8: (RS) Ch 3, OS over shell, ch 3, skip arch, [sc in next arch, ch 3] 6 times, skip arch, OS over shell, dc in last st; turn = 2 OS, 7 arches and 2 dc

Row 9: (WS) Ch 3, OS over shell, ch 3, skip arch, [sc in next arch, ch 3] 5 times, skip arch, OS over shell, dc in last st; turn = 2 OS, 6 arches and 2 dc

Row 10: (RS) Ch 3, OS over shell, ch 3, skip arch, [sc in next arch, ch 3] 4 times, skip arch, OS over shell, dc in last st; turn = 2 OS, 5 arches and 2 dc

Row 11: (WS) Ch 3, OS over shell, ch 3, skip arch, [sc in next arch, ch 3] 3 times, skip arch, OS over shell, dc in last st; turn = 2 OS, 4 arches and 2 dc

Row 12: (RS) Ch 3, OS over shell, ch 3, skip arch, [sc in next arch, ch 3] 2 times, skip arch, OS over shell, dc in last st; turn = 2 OS, 3 arches and 2 dc

Row 13: (WS) Ch 3, OS over shell, ch 3, skip arch, sc in next arch, ch 3, skip arch, OS over shell, dc in last st; turn = 2 OS, 2 arches and 2 dc

Row 14: (RS) Ch 3, OS over shell, skip 2 arches, OS over shell, dc in last st; turn = 2 OS and 2 dc

Row 15: (WS) Ch 3, 2 dc in center of next OS, ch 1, 2 dc in center of next OS, dc in last st; turn = 6 sts

Row 16: (RS) Skip 3 dc, OS in next ch-1 sp, skip 2 dc, sl st in last st = 1 OS and 1 sl st

Fasten off and weave in the ends.

Edge: Use the same yarn and hook as for the ears. Join yarn in st with **Marker A** and remove the marker. Ch 1 (doesn't count as a st), sc evenly across the edge towards the top corner, 3 sc in top corner, sc evenly across the remaining edge. Don't work across the bottom edge.

Fasten off, leaving a long single strand of **MC** for sewing. Weave in the other ends. Spray block the ears (see General Techniques: Blocking).

EAR CHART

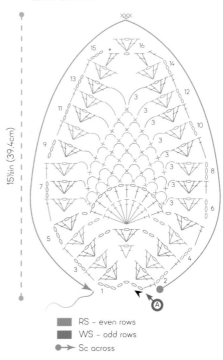

15½in (39.4cm)

▨ RS – even rows
▨ WS – odd rows
●→ Sc across

HEAD

Make 1. Work in rows with a 9mm (M/N) hook and 3 strands of yarn, changing colors (**MC** and **CC1**) as indicated in the pattern.

NOTE: Ch-2 sps are not included in the total stitch count.

To beg: With **CC1**, ch 59

Row 1: (WS) Sc in second ch from hook (the skipped ch doesn't count as a st), hdc in next ch, dc in next 2 chs, tr in next 2 chs, dc in next 2 chs, hdc in next ch, sc in next ch, [ch 2, skip 2 chs, sc in next ch, hdc in next ch, dc in next 2 chs, tr in next 2 chs, dc in next 2 chs, hdc in next ch, sc in next ch] 4 times; change to **MC** and turn = 50 sts

Row 2: (RS) With **MC**, Ch 1 (doesn't count as a st now and throughout), sc in first st, sc in next 9 sts, [dc in next 2 chs of the foundation row below, sc in next 10 sts] 4 times; turn = 58 sts

Row 3: (WS) Ch 1, sc in first st, sc in next 57 sts; change to **CC1** and turn = 58 sts

Row 4: (RS) With **CC1**, ch 3 (counts as first dc now and throughout), skip first st, dc in next st, hdc in next st, sc in next st, [ch 2, skip 2 sts, sc in next st, hdc in next st, dc in next 2 sts, tr in next 2 sts, dc in next 2 sts, hdc in next st, sc in next st] 4 times, ch 2, skip 2 sts, sc in next st, hdc in next st, dc in next 2 sts; turn = 48 sts

Row 5: (WS) Ch 3, skip first st, dc in next st, hdc in next st, sc in next st, [ch 2, skip ch-2 sp, sc in next st, hdc in next st, dc in next 2 sts, tr in next 2 sts, dc in next 2 sts, hdc in next st, sc in next st] 4 times, ch 2, skip ch-2 sp, sc in next st, hdc in next st, dc in next 2 sts; change to **MC** and turn = 48 sts

Row 6: (RS) With **MC**, ch 1, sc in first st, sc in next 3 sts, *[FDC in next sc two rows below] 2 times, skip ch-2 sp, sc in next 10 sts**, repeat 3 more times from * to **, [FDC in next sc two rows below] 2 times, skip ch-2 sp, sc in next 4 sts; turn = 58 sts

Row 7: (WS) Ch 1, sc in first st, sc in next 57 sts; change to **CC1** and turn = 58 sts

Row 8: (RS) With **CC1**, ch 1, sc in first st, hdc in next st, dc in next 2 sts, tr in next 2 sts, dc in next 2 sts, hdc in next st, sc in next st, [ch 2, skip 2 sts, sc in next st, hdc in next st, dc in next 2 sts, tr in next 2 sts, dc in next 2 sts, hdc in next st, sc in next st] 4 times; turn = 50 sts

Row 9: (WS) Ch 1, sc in first st, hdc in next st, dc in next 2 sts, tr in next 2 sts, dc in next 2 sts, hdc in next st, sc in next st, [ch 2, skip ch-2 sp, sc in next st, hdc in next st, dc in next 2 sts, tr in next 2 sts, dc in next 2 sts, hdc in next st, sc in next st] 4 times; change to **MC** and turn = 50 sts

Row 10: (RS) With **MC**, ch 1, sc in first st, sc in next 9 sts, *[FDC in next sc two rows below] 2 times, skip ch-2 sp, sc in next 10 sts**, repeat 3 more times from * to **; turn = 58 sts

Row 11: (WS) Ch 1, sc in first st, sc in next 57 sts; change to **CC1** and turn = 58 sts

Rows 12-19: Repeat Rows 4-11

Rows 20-25: Repeat Rows 4-9

Row 26: (RS) Repeat Row 10, carrying **CC1** across 6 sts at the beg of the row

Row 27: (WS) Sl st in first st, sl st in next 5 sts, ch 1, sc in next 46 sts; change to **CC1** and turn = 52 sts

Row 28: (RS) With **CC1**, ch 1, sc in first st, hdc in next st, dc in next 2 sts, tr in next 2 sts, dc in next 2 sts, hdc in next st, sc in next st, [ch 2, skip 2 sts, sc in next st, hdc in next st, dc in next 2 sts, tr in next 2 sts, dc in next 2 sts, hdc in next st, sc in next st] 3 times; turn = 40 sts

Row 29: (WS) Ch 1, sc in first st, hdc in next st, dc in next 2 sts, tr in next 2 sts, dc in next 2 sts, hdc in next st, sc in next st, [ch 2, skip ch-2 sp, sc in next st, hdc in next st, dc in next 2 sts, tr in next 2 sts, dc in next 2 sts, hdc in next st, sc in next st] 3 times; change to **MC** and turn = 40 sts

Row 30: (RS) With **MC**, ch 1, carrying **CC1** across 6 sts at the beg of the row, sc in first st, sc in next 9 sts, *[FDC in next sc two rows below] 2 times, skip ch-2 sp, sc in next 10 sts**, repeat 2 more times from * to **; turn = 46 sts

Row 31: (WS) Sl st in first st, sl st in next 5 sts, ch 1, sc in next 34 sts; change to **CC1** and turn = 40 sts

Row 32: (RS) With **CC1**, ch 1, sc in first st, hdc in next st, dc in next 2 sts, tr in next 2 sts, dc in next 2 sts, hdc in next st, sc in next st, [ch 2, skip 2 sts, sc in next st, hdc in next st, dc in next 2 sts, tr in next 2 sts, dc in next 2 sts, hdc in next st, sc in next st] 2 times; turn = 30 sts

Row 33: (WS) Ch 1, sc in first st, hdc in next st, dc in next 2 sts, tr in next 2 sts, dc in next 2 sts, hdc in next st, sc in next st, [ch 2, skip ch-2 sp, sc in next st, hdc in next st, dc in next 2 sts, tr in next 2 sts, dc in next 2 sts, hdc in next st, sc in next st] 2 times; change to **MC**, break off **CC1** and turn = 30 sts

Row 34: (RS) With **MC**, ch 1, sc in first st, sc in next 9 sts, *[FDC in next sc two rows below] 2 times, skip ch-2 sp, sc in next 10 sts**, repeat one more time from * to ** = 34 sts

Fasten off and weave in the ends.

ASSEMBLING HEAD

STEP 1 - SC EDGING

Work with a 9mm (M/N) hook and 3 strands of **MC**. With RS facing, begin working from the bottom right corner. Beg sc evenly around the edge towards the bottom left corner, placing 3 sc in each top corner for increasing. Don't work across the bottom edge.

Enlarge the last loop temporarily to secure the work from unraveling, but don't fasten off. Spray block the head (see General Techniques: Blocking).

STEP 2 - SEWING EARS

Place the ears right up against the top corners of the head. Whipstitch around the edge on RS and WS using the long **MC** tail from the ears (1).

STEP 3 - RSC EDGING

With RS facing, insert the hook through the large loop at the bottom left corner and reduce the size of the loop to normal. Working with a 9mm (M/N) hook and using the attached yarn, ch 1, rsc around the head and the ears towards the bottom right corner (2). Fasten off and weave in the ends.

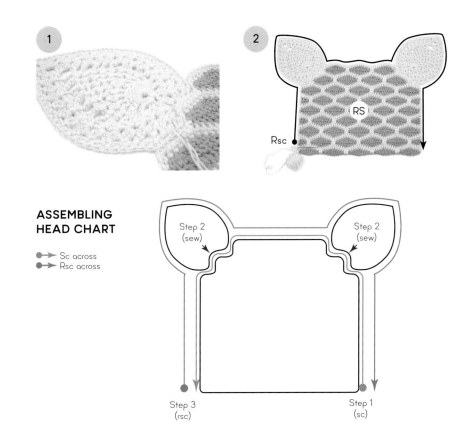

ASSEMBLING HEAD CHART

➥ Sc across
➥ Rsc across

HEAD CHART

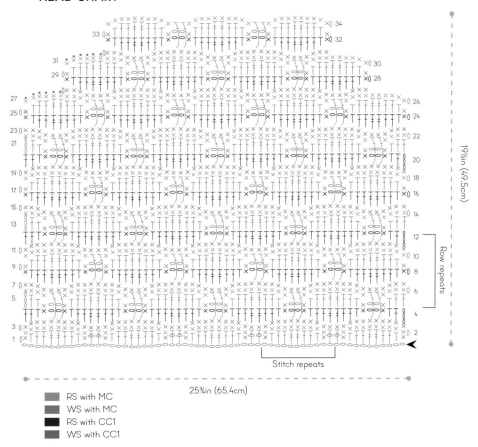

19¾in (49.5cm)

Row repeats

Stitch repeats

25¾in (65.4cm)

RS with MC
WS with MC
RS with CC1
WS with CC1

MUZZLE

Make 1. Work in the round with a 9mm (M/N) hook and 3 strands of **CC2**.

To beg: Ch 53

Rnd 1: Dc in third ch from hook (2 skipped chs don't count as a st), dc in next 49 chs, 6 dc in last ch, continue working across the bottom of the foundation ch, dc in next 49 chs, 5 dc in last ch; join = 110 sts

Rnd 2: Ch 2 (doesn't count as a st now and throughout), 2 dc in same st as join, dc in next 24 sts, 3 dc in next st (**bottom point**), dc in next 24 sts, 2 dc in next 6 sts, dc in next 23 sts, dc3tog (**center top**), dc in next 23 sts, 2 dc in next 5 sts; join = 122 sts

Rnd 3: Ch 2, 2 dc in same st as join, dc in next 26 sts, 3 dc in next st (**bottom point**), dc in next 26 sts, 2 dc in next st, [dc in next st, 2 dc in next st] 5 times, dc in next 22 sts, dc3tog (**center top**), dc in next 22 sts, [2 dc in next st, dc in next st] 5 times; join = 134 sts

Rnd 4: Ch 2, dc in same st as join, dc in next st, 2 dc in next st, dc in next 26 sts, 3 dc in next st (**bottom point**), dc in next 26 sts, [2 dc in next st, dc in next 2 sts] 6 times, dc in next 21 sts, dc3tog (**center top**), dc in next 23 sts, 2 dc in next st, [dc in next 2 sts, 2 dc in next st] 4 times; join = 146 sts

Rnd 5: Ch 2, 2 dc in same st as join, dc in next 30 sts, 3 dc in next st (**bottom point**), dc in next 30 sts, 2 dc in next st, [dc in next 3 sts, 2 dc in next st] 5 times, dc in next 20 sts, dc3tog (**center top**), dc in next 20 sts, [2 dc in next st, dc in next 3 sts] 5 times; join = 158 sts

Rnd 6: Ch 2, dc in same st as join, dc in next 3 sts, 2 dc in next st, dc in next 28 sts, 3 dc in next st (**bottom point**), dc in next 28 sts, [2 dc in next st, dc in next 4 sts] 6 times, dc in next 19 sts, dc3tog (**center top**), dc in next 23 sts, 2 dc in next st, [dc in next 4 sts, 2 dc in next st] 4 times; join = 170 sts

Use stitch markers as you go to mark the **bottom point** and the **center top** stitches.

Rnd 7: Ch 2, 2 dc in same st as join, dc in next 34 sts, 3 dc in next st (**bottom point**), dc in next 34 sts, 2 dc in next st, [dc in next 5 sts, 2 dc in next st] 5 times, dc in next 18 sts, dc3tog (**center top**), dc in next 18 sts, [2 dc in next st, dc in next 5 sts] 5 times; join = 182 sts

Fasten off and weave in the ends. Block the muzzle if shaping is necessary (see General Techniques: Blocking).

MUZZLE CHART

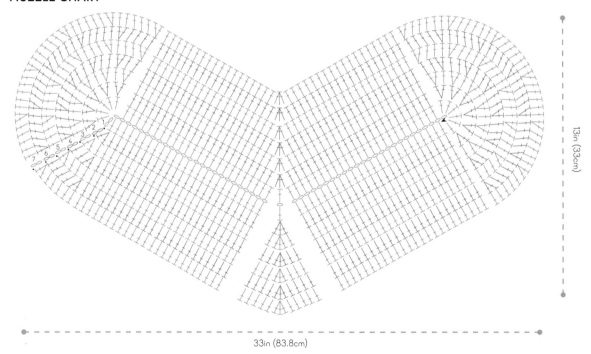

33in (83.8cm)

13in (33cm)

HORN CHART

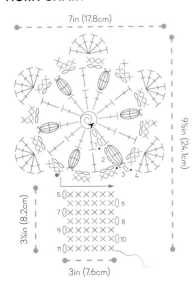

7in (17.8cm)

9½in (24.1cm)

3¼in (8.2cm)

3in (7.6cm)

EYE CHART

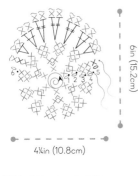

6in (15.2cm)

4¼in (10.8cm)

- Odd rnds with CC3
- Even rnds with CC3
- Odd rows with CC2
- Even rows with CC2

NOSTRIL CHART

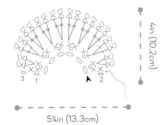

4in (10.2cm)

5¼in (13.3cm)

HORNS

Make 2. Begin by working in the round with a 9mm (M/N) hook and 3 strands of **CC1**.

To beg: Ch 3, sl st in third ch from hook to form a ring (or start with a magic ring)

Rnd 1: Ch 2 (doesn't count as a st) 12 dc in ring; join = 12 sts

Rnd 2: Beg PC in same st as join, ch 2, dc in next st, ch 2, [PC in next st, ch 2, dc in next st, ch 2] 5 times; join = 12 sts

Rnd 3: Ch 1 (doesn't count as a st now and throughout), skip beg PC, [3 sc in next ch-2 sp, skip st] 12 times; join = 36 sts

Rnd 4: Skip st with join, skip next st, 6 dc in next st, [skip 2 sts, sc in next st, skip 2 sts, 6 dc in next st] 4 times, skip 2 sts, sl st in next st = 5 shells

Continue to work in rows.

Rows 5-11: Ch 1, sc in next 6 sts; turn = 6 sts

Fasten off, leaving a long single strand of **CC1** for sewing. Weave in the other ends.

EYES

OUTER EYES

Make 2. Begin by working in the round with a 9mm (M/N) hook and 3 strands of **CC3**.

To beg: Ch 3, sl st in third ch from hook to form a ring (or start with a magic ring)

Rnd 1: Ch 1 (doesn't count as a st now and throughout), 6 sc in ring; join = 6 sts

Rnd 2: Ch 1, 2 sc in same st as join, 2 sc in next 5 sts; join = 12 sts

Rnd 3: Ch 1, 2 sc in same st as join, 2 sc in next 11 sts; join = 24 sts

Rnd 4: Ch 1, sc in same st as join, sc in next 23 sts; change to **CC2** and join = 24 sts

Break off **CC3**, leaving a long single strand for sewing. Continue to work in rows with **CC2**.

Row 5: (RS) Ch 1, skip st with join, sc in next st, 2 hdc in next st, 2 dc in next st, [2 tr in next st] 3 times, 2 dc in next st, 2 hdc in next st, sc in next st, sl st in next st; don't turn = 17 sts

Row 6: (RS) Ch 1, skip first sl st, rsc in next 15 sts, sl st in last st = 16 sts

Fasten off, leaving a long single strand of **CC2** for sewing. Weave in the other ends.

HIGHLIGHTS

Make 2 (see Common Shapes: Basic Eyes). Work with a 9mm (M/N) hook and 2 strands of **CC4**.

ASSEMBLING EYES

Place the highlights on top of the outer eyes and backstitch around, using the long tail from the highlight.

NOSTRILS

Make 2. Work in rows with a 9mm (M/N) hook and 2 strands of **CC2**.

To beg: Ch 7

Row 1: (WS) 2 sc in second ch from hook (the skipped ch doesn't count as a st), 2 sc in next 5 sts; turn = 12 sts

Row 2: (RS) Ch 1 (doesn't count as a st now and throughout), sc in first st, 2 hdc in next st, 2 dc in next st, 2 tr in next 6 sts, 2 dc in next st, 2 hdc in next st, sc in last st; don't turn = 22 sts

Row 3: (RS) Ch 1, skip first st, rsc in next 20 sts, sl st in last st = 21 sts

Fasten off, leaving a long single strand of **CC2** for sewing. Weave in the other ends.

BOW (OPTIONAL)

Make 1. Follow the instructions for the big bow (see Common Shapes: Big Bow). Use 3 strands of **CC5** with a 9mm (M/N) hook.

ASSEMBLING RUG

With RS facing, place the horns on the top of the head slightly under the head edge.

Place the muzzle to cover the bottom edge of the head.

Using the corresponding colors of yarn, backstitch across the overlapped edges of all pieces on RS (3).

Flip the rug to WS and whipstitch across the overlapped edges using the corresponding colors of yarn (4).

Position the eyes and the nostrils to create a facial expression (5).

Backstitch around the edge of each pupil using the long **CC3** tail and backstitch under the edge of the eyelids using the long **CC2** tail (6).

Using the long **CC2** tail from each nostril, backstitch below the rsc edge and whipstitch along the bottom edge (7).

If using, position the bow by the ear or under the muzzle and backstitch along the overlapping edge (8) or around the center.

If desired, make a removable non-slip lining (see General Techniques: Non-Slip Lining).

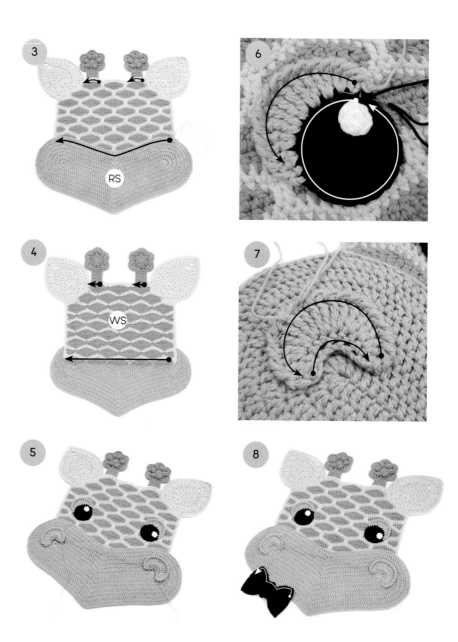

GIRAFFE PILLOW

SKILL LEVEL

FINISHED SIZE
14in x 20in (35.5cm x 50.8cm)

HOOKS
3.75mm (F), 4mm (G),
5mm (H), 5.5mm (I)

YARN WEIGHT
4

NUMBER OF STRANDS
1

GAUGE WITH 1 STRAND
AND 5.5MM (I) HOOK
14 sc x 16 rows = 4in x 4in (10cm x 10cm)

STITCH SUMMARY
Ch, sl st, sc, beg sc, sc2tog, rsc, hdc,
dc, dc3tog, tr, PC, beg PC, FDC, join

SKILLS
Working in rows and in the round,
raw edge finishing, working across
the bottom of the foundation chain,
changing colors, blocking, sewing

LEFT-HANDED CROCHET
See Crochet Techniques:
Left-Handed Crochet

YARN

Abbreviation	Color	Amount
CC5	Turquoise or Orange	350-415yd (320-380m)
CC6	Green and/or Orange	Small amount

All other colors are the same as for the
Giraffe Rug (small amount of each).

HEAD PILLOW BASE

Make 1 front and 1 back using 1 strand of **CC5** with a 5.5mm (I) hook. Follow the instructions for the oval pillow base (see Common Shapes: Oval Pillow Base). Fasten off after finishing each piece.

Holding the front and the back pieces together with WS facing each other, work the joining round through both pieces of fabric at the same time using a 5.5mm (I) hook and 1 strand of **CC6**.

Rnd 26: Beg sc in same st as previous sl st, sc in next 180 sts, stuff the pillow, sc in next 15 sts; join = 196 sts

Rnd 27: [Ch 3, 2 dc in same st, skip 2 sts, sl st in next st] 65 times = 65 points

Fasten off and weave in the ends.

HEAD

Make 1. Work in rows with a 5mm (H) hook and 1 strand of yarn, changing colors (**MC** and **CC1**) as indicated in the pattern.

NOTE: Ch-2 sps are not included in the total stitch count.

To beg: With **CC1**, ch 35

Row 1: (WS) Sc in second ch from hook (the skipped ch doesn't count as a st), hdc in next ch, dc in next 2 chs, tr in next 2 chs, dc in next 2 chs, hdc in next ch, sc in next ch, [ch 2, skip 2 chs, sc in next ch, hdc in next ch, dc in next 2 chs, tr in next 2 chs, dc in next 2 chs, hdc in next ch, sc in next ch] 2 times; change to **MC** and turn = 30 sts

HEAD CHART

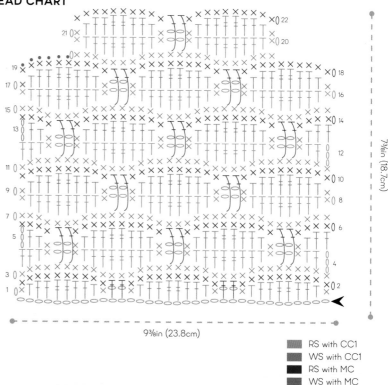

9⅜in (23.8cm)

7⅜in (18.7cm)

- RS with CC1
- WS with CC1
- RS with MC
- WS with MC

MUZZLE CHART

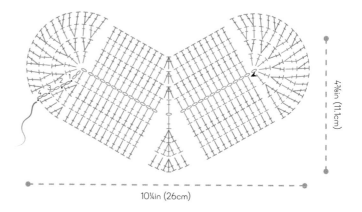

10¼in (26cm)

4⅜in (11.1cm)

Use stitch markers to mark the **bottom point** and the **center top** stitches of the muzzle.

Row 2: (RS) With **MC**, ch 1 (doesn't count as a st now and throughout), sc in first st, sc in next 9 sts, [dc in next 2 chs of the foundation row below, sc in next 10 sts] 2 times; turn = 34 sts

Row 3: (WS) Ch 1, sc in first st, sc in next 33 sts; change to **CC1** and turn = 34 sts

Row 4: (RS) With **CC1**, ch 3 (counts as first dc now and throughout), skip first st, dc in next st, hdc in next st, sc in next st, [ch 2, skip 2 sts, sc in next st, hdc in next st, dc in next 2 sts, tr in next 2 sts, dc in next 2 sts, hdc in next st, sc in next st] 2 times, ch 2, skip 2 sts, sc in next st, hdc in next st, dc in next 2 sts; turn = 28 sts

Row 5: (WS) Ch 3, skip first st, dc in next st, hdc in next st, sc in next st, [ch 2, skip ch-2 sp, sc in next st, hdc in next st, dc in next 2 sts, tr in next 2 sts, dc in next 2 sts, hdc in next st, sc in next st] 2 times, ch 2, skip ch-2 sp, sc in next st, hdc in next st, dc in next 2 sts; change to **MC** and turn = 28 sts

Row 6: (RS) With **MC**, ch 1, sc in first st, sc in next 3 sts, *[FDC in next sc two rows below] 2 times, skip ch-2 sp, sc in next 10 sts**, repeat 1 more time from * to **, [FDC in next sc two rows below] 2 times, skip ch-2 sp, sc in next 4 sts; turn = 34 sts

Row 7: (WS) Ch 1, sc in first st, sc in next 33 sts; change to **CC1** and turn = 34 sts

Row 8: (RS) With **CC1**, ch 1, sc in first st, hdc in next st, dc in next 2 sts, tr in next 2 sts, dc in next 2 sts, hdc in next st, sc in next st, [ch 2, skip 2 sts, sc in next st, hdc in next st, dc in next 2 sts, tr in next 2 sts, dc in next 2 sts, hdc in next st, sc in next st] 2 times; turn = 30 sts

Row 9: (WS) Ch 1, sc in first st, hdc in next st, dc in next 2 sts, tr in next 2 sts, dc in next 2 sts, hdc in next st, sc in next st, [ch 2, skip ch-2 sp, sc in next st, hdc in next st, dc in next 2 sts, tr in next 2 sts, dc in next 2 sts, hdc in next st, sc in next st] 2 times; change to **MC** and turn = 30 sts

Row 10: (RS) With **MC**, ch 1, sc in first st, sc in next 9 sts, *[FDC in next sc two rows below] 2 times, skip ch-2 sp, sc in next 10 sts**, repeat 1 more time from * to **; turn = 34 sts

Row 11: (WS) Ch 1, sc in first st, sc in next 33 sts; change to **CC1** and turn = 34 sts

Rows 12-17: Repeat Rows 4-9

Row 18: (RS) Repeat Row 10, carrying **CC1** across 6 sts at the beg of the row

Row 19: (WS) Sl st in first st, sl st in next 5 sts, ch 1, sc next 22 sts; change to **CC1** and turn = 28 sts

Row 20: (RS) With **CC1**, ch 1, sc in first st, hdc in next st, dc in next 2 sts, tr in next 2 sts, dc in next 2 sts, hdc in next st, sc in next st, ch 2, skip 2 sts, sc in next st, hdc in next st, dc in next 2 sts, tr in next 2 sts, dc in next 2 sts, hdc in next st, sc in next st; turn = 20 sts

Row 21: (WS) Ch 1, sc in first st, hdc in next st, dc in next 2 sts, tr in next 2 sts, dc in next 2 sts, hdc in next st, sc in next st, ch 2, skip ch-2 sp, sc in next st, hdc in next st, dc in next 2 sts, tr in next 2 sts, dc in next 2 sts, hdc in next st, sc in next st; change to **MC**, break off **CC1** and turn = 20 sts

Row 22: (RS) With **MC**, ch 1, sc in first st, sc in next 9 sts, [FDC in next sc two rows below] 2 times, skip ch-2 sp, sc in next 10 sts = 22 sts

Fasten off and weave in the ends.

EDGING

With RS facing, begin working from the bottom right corner, using a 5.5mm (I) hook and 1 strand of **MC**.

Row 1: (RS) Beg sc, sc evenly around the edge towards the bottom left corner, placing 3 sc in each top corner for increasing. Don't work across the bottom edge and don't turn.

Row 2: (RS) Ch 1, rsc around the head towards the bottom right corner.

Fasten off, leaving a long tail for sewing. Wet block the head (see General Techniques: Blocking)

MUZZLE

Make 1. Work in the round with a 5mm (H) hook and 1 strand of **MC**.

To beg: Ch 29

Rnd 1: Dc in third ch from hook (2 skipped chs don't count as a st), dc in next 25 chs, 6 dc in last ch, continue working across the bottom of the foundation ch, dc in next 25 chs, 5 dc in last ch; join = 62 sts

Rnd 2: Ch 2 (doesn't count as a st now and throughout), 2 dc in same st as join, dc in next 12 sts, 3 dc in next st (**bottom point**), dc in next 12 sts, 2 dc in next 6 sts, dc in next 11 sts, dc3tog (**center top**), dc in next 11 sts, 2 dc in next 5 sts; join = 74 sts

Rnd 3: Ch 2, 2 dc in same st as join, dc in next 14 sts, 3 dc in next st (**bottom point**), dc in next 13 sts, [dc in next st, 2 dc in next st] 6 times, dc in next 10 sts, dc3tog (**center top**), dc in next 10 sts, [2 dc in next st, dc in next st] 5 times; join = 86 sts

Rnd 4: Ch 2, dc in same st as join, dc in next st, 2 dc in next st, dc in next 14 sts, 3 dc in next st (**bottom point**), dc in next 14 sts, [2 dc in next st, dc in next 2 sts] 6 times, dc in next 9 sts, dc3tog (**center top**), dc in next 9 sts, [dc in next 2 sts, 2 dc in next st] 5 times; join = 98 sts

Fasten off, leaving a long tail for sewing.

HORNS

Make 2. Begin by working in the round with a 5mm (H) hook and 1 strand of **CC1**.

To beg: Ch 3, sl st in third ch from hook to form a ring (or start with a magic ring)

Rnd 1: Ch 1 (doesn't count as a st now and throughout), 6 sc in ring; join = 6 sts

Rnd 2: Beg PC in same st as join, ch 2, [PC in next st, ch 2] 5 times; join = 6 sts

Rnd 3: Ch 1, skip beg PC, 3 sc in next ch-2 sp, [skip next PC, 3 sc in next ch-2 sp] 5 times; join = 18 sts

Rnd 4: [Ch 2, 2 dc in same st, skip st, sl st in next st] 7 times = 7 points

Continue to work in rows.

Row 5: Ch 1, sc in same st as previous sl st, sc in next 3 sts; turn = 4 sts

Rows 6-9: Ch 1, sc in each st across; turn = 4 sts

Fasten off, leaving a long tail for sewing.

EARS

Make 2. Work in spiral rounds with a 5.5mm (I) hook and 1 strand of **MC**.

Use a stitch marker to mark the beginning of each round as you go.

To beg: Ch 3, sl st in third ch from hook to form a ring (or start with a magic ring)

Rnd 1: Ch 1 (doesn't count as a st), 6 sc in ring; don't join now and throughout = 6 sts

Rnd 2: Sc in first st of previous rnd, sc in next 5 sts = 6 sts

Rnd 3: 2 sc in each st around = 12 sts

Rnd 4: Sc in each st around = 12 sts

Rnd 5: [Sc in next st, 2 sc in next st] 6 times = 18 sts

Rnd 6: Sc in each st around = 18 sts

Rnd 7: [Sc in next 2 sts, 2 sc in next st] 6 times = 24 sts

Rnd 8: Sc in each st around = 24 sts

Rnd 9: [Sc in next 3 sts, 2 sc in next st] 6 times = 30 sts

Rnds 10-16: Sc in each st around = 30 sts

Rnd 17: [Sc in next 3 sts, sc2tog] 6 times = 24 sts

Rnd 18: [Sc in next 2 sts, sc2tog] 6 times = 18 sts

Rnd 19: [Sc in next st, sc2tog] 6 times = 12 sts

Fasten off, leaving a long tail for sewing.

Holding the edge flat, whipstitch the opening; don't break off **MC**.

HORN CHART

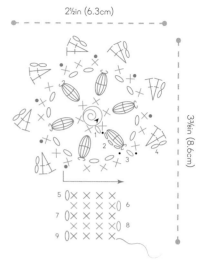

2½in (6.3cm)

3⅜in (8.6cm)

EYES

Make 2. Follow the instructions for the basic eyes (see Common Shapes: Basic Eyes). For the pupils, use 1 strand of **CC3** with a 4mm (G) hook and for the highlights use 1 strand of **CC4**.

BOW (OPTIONAL)

Make 1. Follow the instructions for the small bow (see Common Shapes: Small Bow). Use **CC6**.

ASSEMBLING PILLOW

Place the head onto the front of the pillow. Backstitch around the rsc edge and whipstitch across the straight bottom edge using the long **MC** tail from the head. Place the muzzle to cover the bottom edge of the head and backstitch around using the long **MC** tail from the muzzle (1).

Position the ears on each side of the head (2).

Using the long tail from each ear, whipstitch across the corresponding edge of the head, then bring the needle to the midpoint on the back side of the ear and whipstitch to secure (3 and 4).

Place the horns right up against the top of the head, evenly spaced between the ears, and backstitch around using the long **CC1** tail from the horns (5).

Place the eyes on each side right up against the muzzle and backstitch around using the long **CC3** tail from the eyes (6).

A double-sided pillow would look just as adorable if you make the giraffes slightly different on each side. Finish both sides in the same manner; position the bow by the ear on one side and under the muzzle on the other side, and backstitch around the center of the bows.

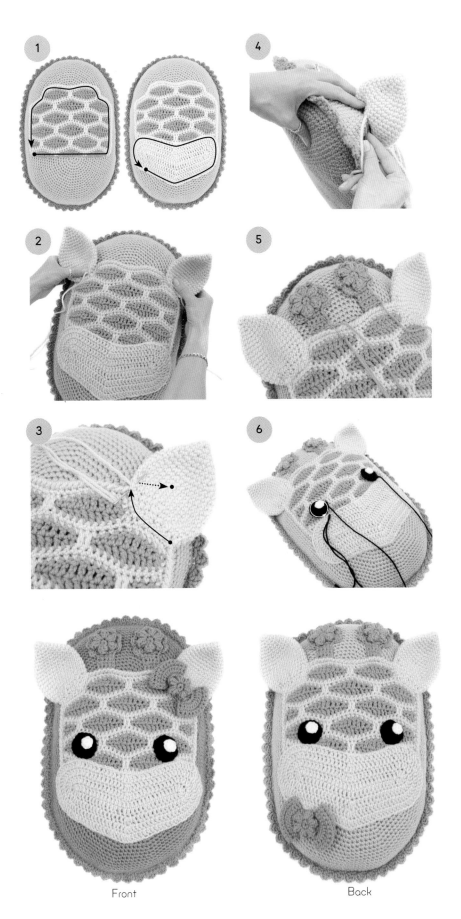

Front

Back

GIRAFFE SECURITY BLANKET

SKILL LEVEL

FINISHED SIZE
19½in x 19½in (49.5cm x 49.5cm)

HOOKS
3.75mm (F), 5mm (H)

YARN WEIGHT
4

NUMBER OF STRANDS
1

GAUGE WITH 1 STRAND AND 5MM (H) HOOK
15 dc x 8 rows = 4in x 4in (10cm x 10cm)

STITCH SUMMARY
Ch, sl st, sc, sc2tog, bpsc, hdc, dc, tr, FDC, picot, join

SKILLS
Working in rows and in the round, raw edge finishing, working across the bottom of the foundation chain, changing colors, blocking, sewing

LEFT-HANDED CROCHET
Fully compatible

YARN

Abbreviation	Color	Amount
MC	Yellow	208-240yd (190-220m)
CC1	Warm Brown	252-284yd (230-260m)
CC2	Coffee	Small amount

BLANKET

Make 1. Work in rows with a 5mm (H) hook and 1 strand of yarn, changing colors (**MC** and **CC1**) as indicated in the pattern.

NOTE: Ch-2 sps are not included in the total stitch count.

To beg: With **MC**, ch 71

Row 1: (WS) Sc in second ch from hook (the skipped ch doesn't count as a st), sc in next 69 chs; change to **CC1** and turn = 70 sts

Row 2: (RS) With **CC1**, ch 1 (doesn't count as a st now and throughout), sc in first st, hdc in next st, dc in next 2 sts, tr in next 2 sts, dc in next 2 sts, hdc in next st, sc in next st, [ch 2, skip 2 sts, sc in next st, hdc in next st, dc in next 2 sts, tr in next 2 sts, dc in next 2 sts, hdc in next st, sc in next st] 5 times; turn = 60 sts

Row 3: (WS) Ch 1, sc in first st, hdc in next st, dc in next 2 sts, tr in next 2 sts, dc in next 2 sts, hdc in next st, sc in next st, [ch 2, skip ch-2 sp, sc in next st, hdc in next st, dc in next 2 sts, tr in next 2 sts, dc in next 2 sts, hdc in next st, sc in next st] 5 times; change to **MC** and turn = 60 sts

Row 4: (RS) With **MC**, ch 1, sc in first st, sc in next 9 sts, *[FDC in next sc two rows below] 2 times, skip ch-2 sp, sc in next 10 sts**, repeat 4 more times from * to **; turn = 70 sts

Row 5: (WS) Ch 1, sc in first st, sc in next 69 sts; change to **CC1** and turn = 70 sts

Row 6: (RS) With **CC1**, ch 3 (counts as first dc now and throughout), skip first st, dc in next st, hdc in next st, sc in next st, [ch 2, skip 2 sts, sc in next st, hdc in next st, dc in next 2 sts, tr in next 2 sts, dc in next 2 sts, hdc in next st, sc in next st] 5 times, ch 2, skip 2 sts, sc in next st, hdc in next st, dc in next 2 sts; turn = 58 sts

Row 7: (WS) Ch 3, skip first st, dc in next st, hdc in next st, sc in next st, [ch 2, skip ch-2 sp, sc in next st, hdc in next st, dc in next 2 sts, tr in next 2 sts, dc in next 2 sts, hdc in next st, sc in next st] 5 times, ch 2, skip ch-2 sp, sc in next st, hdc in next st, dc in next 2 sts; change to **MC** and turn = 58 sts

Row 8: (RS) With **MC**, ch 1, sc in first st, sc in next 3 sts, *[FDC in next sc two rows below] 2 times, skip ch-2 sp, sc in next 10 sts**, repeat 4 more times from * to **, [FDC in next sc two rows below] 2 times, skip ch-2 sp, sc in next 4 sts; turn = 70 sts

Row 9: (WS) Ch 1, sc in first st, sc in next 69 sts; change to **CC1** and turn = 70 sts

Rows 10-12: Repeat Rows 2-4

Rows 13-60: Repeat Rows 5-12 in established pattern until the blanket is visually square, ending after Row 12. Break off **CC1**.

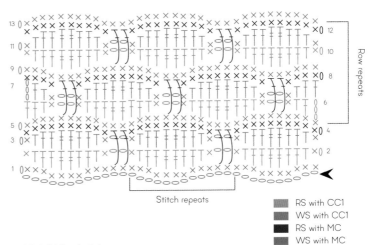

Stitch repeats

RS with CC1
WS with CC1
RS with MC
WS with MC

Row repeats

Edge: With **MC**, ch 1, *sc in next 2 sts, picot, repeat from * around, placing 3 sc in each corner for increasing; join

Fasten off and weave in the ends. Wet block the blanket (see General Techniques: Blocking).

HEAD

Make 1. Work in spiral rounds with a 3.75mm (F) hook and 1 strand of **MC**.

To beg: Ch 3, sl st in third ch from hook to form a ring (or start with a magic ring)

Rnd 1: Ch 1 (doesn't count as a st), 6 sc in ring; don't join now and throughout = 6 sts

Rnd 2: 2 sc in first st of previous rnd, 2 sc in next 4 sts, sc in next st = 11 sts

Rnd 3: 2 sc in each st around = 22 sts

Rnds 4-5: Sc in each st around = 22 sts

Rnd 6: [Sc in next st, 2 sc in next st] 11 times = 33 sts

Rnds 7-8: Sc in each st around = 33 sts

Rnd 9: [Sc in next 2 sts, 2 sc in next st] 11 times = 44 sts

Rnds 10-12: Sc in each st around = 44 sts

Rnd 13: [Sc in next 3 sts, 2 sc in next st] 11 times = 55 sts

Rnds 14-18: Sc in each st around = 55 sts

Rnd 19: [Sc in next 3 sts, sc2tog] 11 times = 44 sts

Rnd 20: Sc in each st around = 44 sts

Rnd 21: [Sc in next 2 sts, sc2tog] 11 times = 33 sts

Rnd 22: Sc in each st around = 33 sts

Rnd 23: [Sc in next st, sc2tog] 11 times = 22 sts

Sl st in next st and fasten off, leaving a long tail for sewing. Stuff the head.

Use a stitch marker to mark the beginning of each round as you go.

MUZZLE

Make 1. Work in spiral rounds with a 3.75mm (F) hook and 1 strand of **MC**.

To beg: Ch 5

Rnd 1: Sc in second ch from hook (the skipped ch doesn't count as a st), sc in next 2 chs, 3 sc in last ch, continue working across the bottom of the foundation ch, sc in next 2 chs, 2 sc in last ch; don't join now and throughout = 10 sts

Rnd 2: 2 sc in first st of previous rnd, sc in next 2 sts, 2 sc in next 3 sts, sc in next 2 sts, 2 sc in next 2 sts = 16 sts

Rnd 3: Sc in next st, 2 sc in next st, sc in next 2 sts, [sc in next st, 2 sc in next st] 3 times, sc in next 2 sts, [sc in next st, 2 sc in next st] 2 times = 22 sts

Rnd 4: 2 sc in next st, sc in next 4 sts, [2 sc in next st, sc in next 2 sts] 3 times, sc in next 2 sts, [2 sc in next st, sc in next 2 sts] 2 times = 28 sts

Rnds 5-6: Sc in each st around = 28 sts

Sl st in next st and fasten off, leaving a long tail for sewing.

> **Use a chopstick or a knitting needle for stuffing the horns.**

HORNS

Make 2. Work in spiral rounds with a 3.75mm (F) hook and 1 strand of yarn, changing colors (**MC** and **CC1**) as indicated in the pattern.

To beg: With **CC1**, ch 3, sl st in third ch from hook to form a ring (or start with a magic ring)

Rnd 1: Ch 1 (doesn't count as a st), 6 sc in ring, don't join now and throughout = 6 sts

Rnd 2: 2 sc in first st of previous rnd, sc in next st, [2 sc in next st, sc in next st] 2 times = 9 sts

Rnds 3-4: Sc in each st around = 9 sts

Rnd 5: [Sc in next st, sc2tog] 3 times, change to **MC**, break off **CC1** = 6 sts

Rnd 6: With **MC**, sl st in next st, ch 1, sc in same st as sl st, sc in next 5 sts = 6 sts

Rnds 7-9: Sc in first st of previous rnd, sc in next 5 sts = 6 sts

Sl st in next st, fasten off, leaving a long tail for sewing. Stuff the horns.

EARS

Make 2 front and 2 back pieces. Work in rows with a 3.75mm (F) hook and 1 strand of **MC**.

To beg: Ch 6

Row 1: (RS) Sc in second ch from hook, sc in next ch, hdc in next 2 chs, 5 dc in last ch, continue working across the bottom of the foundation ch, hdc in next 2 chs, sc in next 2 chs = 13 sts

Fasten off after finishing each front piece, but don't break off yarn after finishing each back piece.

Place the front and the back pieces together with WS facing each other. Work the next row through both pieces of fabric at the same time using **MC** from the back piece.

Joining row: (RS) Ch 1, sc in next 6 sts, 3 sc in next st, sc in next 6 sts = 15 sts

Fasten off, leaving a long tail for sewing. Hide all the other ends inside of the ear using a chopstick or a knitting needle.

ARMS

Make 2. Work in the round with a 3.75mm (F) hook and 1 strand of yarn, changing colors (**CC2** and **MC**) as indicated in the pattern. Stuff the arms as you go.

To beg: With **CC2**, ch 3, sl st in third ch from hook to form a ring (or start with a magic ring)

Rnd 1: Ch 1 (doesn't count as a st now and throughout), 6 sc in ring; join = 6 sts

Rnd 2: Ch 1, 2 sc in same st as join, 2 sc in next 5 sts; join = 12 sts

Rnd 3: Ch 1, 2 sc in same st as join, 2 sc in next 11 sts; join = 24 sts

Rnd 4: Ch 1, bpsc in same st as join, bpsc in next 23 sts; join = 24 sts

Rnd 5: Ch 1, sc in same st as join, sc in next st, sc2tog, [sc in next 2 sts, sc2tog] 5 times; join = 18 sts

Rnd 6: Ch 1, sc in same st as join, sc in next 17 sts; join = 18 sts

Rnd 7: Ch 1, sc in same st as join, sc2tog, [sc in next st, sc2tog] 5 times; join = 12 sts

Rnd 8: Ch 1, sc in same st as join, sc in next 11 sts; change to **MC**, break **CC2** = 12 sts

Rnd 9: With **MC**, ch 1, sc in same st as join, sc in next 11 sts; don't join now and throughout = 12 sts

Rnds 10-21: Sc in first st of previous rnd, sc in next 11 sts = 12 sts

Sl st in next st, fasten off, leaving a long tail for sewing. Holding the edge flat, whipstitch the opening and don't break off **MC**.

ASSEMBLING SECURITY BLANKET

Place the muzzle onto the head 2-3 rounds above the neck edge. Using the long **MC** tail from the muzzle, whipstitch around the edge leaving a small opening for stuffing. Stuff the muzzle and complete sewing (1).

Place the horns on the top of the head, one round apart from the center top and whipstitch around using the long **MC** tail from the horns. Place the ears on each side, right up against the horns and whipstitch around using the long **MC** tail from the ears (2).

Thread the needle with **CC1**. Chain stitch the smile, straight stitch the nostrils (3) and chain stitch the sleepy eyes (4).

Position the head in the center of the blanket and whipstitch around the neck edge using the long **MC** tail from the head.

Place the arms right up against the neck, facing both hooves in the same direction as the face. Whipstitch the arms around entire edge using the **MC** tail from the arms (5).

Prepare 3 groups of **MC** for the tail with 4 strands in each group, approximately 10in (25cm) long. Using a crochet hook, pull each bundle through the stitches on the back of the blanket and fold them in the middle. Braid the tail, then tie and trim the ends (6).

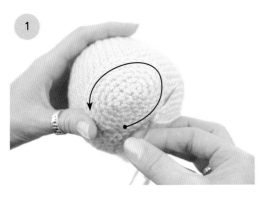

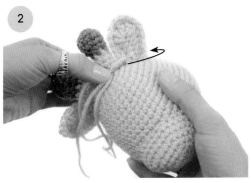

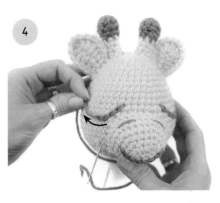

SASSY THE KITTY CAT

Rug, Pillow, and Place Mat

Bring your granny square skills to the next level with this cute and fun kitty collection. Granny squares are never out of fashion because they are just so versatile! You can use a variety of colored yarns to create interesting patterns or simplify the design by just using one or two shades.

Sassy was inspired by a traditional granny square motif that was adapted into a heart shape. I love the bold contrast between black cat and pastel colors in the heart as they create a beautiful modern appearance. However, you may chose to soften the look by using lighter colors for your kitty and hand stitch sleepy eyes.

KITTY RUG

SKILL LEVEL

FINISHED SIZE
48in x 40in (122cm x 101.6cm)

HOOKS
5.5mm (I), 9mm (M/N)

YARN WEIGHT
4

NUMBER OF STRANDS
1, 2, and 3

GAUGE WITH 3 STRANDS AND 9MM (M/N) HOOK
9 dc x 4.5 rows = 4in x 4in (10cm x 10cm)

STITCH SUMMARY
Ch, sl st, sc, sc2tog, rsc, hdc, dc, dc2tog, tr, picot, PC, beg PC, crest, cluster, shell, arch, join

SKILLS
Working in rows and in the round, working across the bottom of the foundation chain, changing colors, blocking, sewing

LEFT-HANDED CROCHET
See Crochet Techniques: Left-Handed Crochet

YARN

Abbreviation	Color	Amount
MC	Black or Gray	1039-1148yd (950-1050m)
CC1	Any leftover yarn in a variety of colors or a solid color yarn	1203-1312yd (1100-1200m)
CC2	Pink	93-109yd (85-100m)
CC3	Black	Small amount
CC4	White	Small amount
CC5	Blue or Green	Small amount
CC6	Burgundy (optional)	93-109yd (85-100m)

HEART

Make 1. Begin by working in the round with a 9mm (M/N) hook and 3 strands of **CC1**. Change colors in any round or use a solid color yarn for the entire heart.

STEP 1 - SET-UP

To beg: Ch 33

Set-up row: (RS) 3 dc in sixth ch from hook (5 skipped chs count as first dc plus ch 2), [skip 2 chs, 3 dc in next ch] 8 times, skip 2 chs, dc in last ch = 9 clusters and 2 dc

Don't turn. Continue to work **Step 2** around the set-up row on RS.

STEP 2 - HEART

Rnd 1: (Ch 3, 2 dc) in same end sp (counts as beg cluster now and throughout), [ch 3, 3 dc in same end sp] 2 times, continue working across the bottom of the foundation ch [skip cluster, 3 dc in next ch-2 sp between clusters] 8 times, 3 dc in next ch-5 sp, [ch 3, 3 dc in same end sp] 2 times, continue working across the top of the set-up row [skip cluster, 3 dc in next sp between clusters] 3 times, skip cluster, dc next 3 sts of the cluster, [skip cluster, 3 dc in next sp between clusters] 3 times; sl st in top of beg ch-3 = 20 clusters and 3 dc

Use stitch markers as you go to mark the **bottom point** and **center top.**

HEART CHART

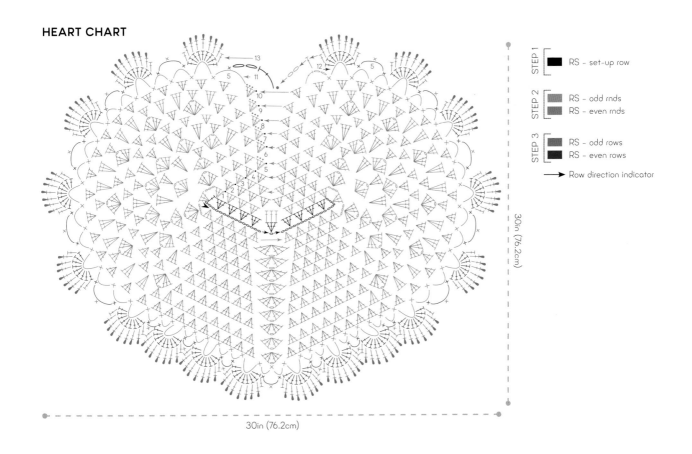

STEP 1
■ RS – set-up row

STEP 2
▨ RS – odd rnds
▨ RS – even rnds

STEP 3
▨ RS – odd rows
■ RS – even rows

→ Row direction indicator

30in (76.2cm)

30in (76.2cm)

Rnd 2: (Ch 3, 2 dc) in same sp between clusters, [skip cluster, (3 dc, ch 1, 3 dc) in next arch] 2 times, [skip cluster, 3 dc in next sp between clusters] 4 times, skip cluster, (3 dc, ch 1, 3 dc) in next sp between clusters (**bottom point**), [skip cluster, 3 dc in next sp between clusters] 4 times, [skip cluster, (3 dc, ch 1, 3 dc) in next arch] 2 times, [skip cluster, 3 dc in next sp between clusters] 4 times, skip 3 dc (**center top**), [3 dc in next sp between clusters, skip cluster] 3 times; sl st in top of beg ch-3 = 26 clusters

Rnd 3: (Ch 3, 2 dc) in same sp between clusters, skip cluster, 3 dc in next sp between clusters, [skip cluster, (3 dc, ch 1, 3 dc) in next sp between clusters] 3 times, [skip cluster, 3 dc in next sp between clusters] 5 times, skip cluster, (3 dc, ch 1, 3 dc) in next sp between clusters (**bottom point**), [skip cluster, 3 dc in next sp between clusters] 5 times, [skip cluster, (3 dc, ch 1, 3 dc) in next sp between clusters] 3 times, [skip cluster, 3 dc in next sp between clusters] 4 times, skip 2 clusters (**center top**), [3 dc in next sp between clusters, skip cluster] 2 times; sl st in top of beg ch-3 = 32 clusters

Rnd 4: (Ch 3, 2 dc) in same sp between clusters, [skip cluster, 3 dc in next sp between clusters] 13 times, skip cluster, (3 dc, ch 1, 3 dc) in next sp between clusters (**bottom point**), [skip cluster, 3 dc in next sp between clusters] 15 times, skip 2 clusters (**center top**), 3 dc in next sp between clusters; sl st in top of beg ch-3 = 32 clusters

Rnd 5: (Ch 3, 2 dc) in same sp between clusters, [skip cluster, 3 dc in next sp between clusters] 2 times, [skip cluster, (3 dc, ch 1, 3 dc) in next sp between clusters] 6 times, [skip cluster, 3 dc in next sp between clusters] 6 times, skip cluster, (3 dc, ch 1, 3 dc) in next sp between clusters (**bottom point**), [skip cluster, 3 dc in next sp between clusters] 6 times, [skip cluster, (3 dc, ch 1, 3 dc) in next sp between clusters] 6 times, [skip cluster, 3 dc in next sp between clusters] 3 times, skip 2 clusters (**center top**); sl st in top of beg ch-3 = 44 clusters

Rnds 6-7: Sl st in next 2 dc, sl st in sp between clusters, (ch 3, 2 dc) in same sp, [skip cluster, 3 dc in next sp between clusters] 20 times, skip cluster, (3 dc, ch 1, 3 dc) in next sp between clusters (**bottom point**), [skip cluster, 3 dc in next sp between clusters] 21 times, skip 2 clusters (**center top**); sl st in top of beg ch-3 = 44 clusters

Rnd 8: Sl st in next 2 dc, sl st in sp between clusters, (ch 3, 2 dc) in same sp, skip cluster, 3 dc in next sp between clusters, *skip cluster, 3 dc in next sp between clusters, skip cluster, (3 dc, ch 1, 3 dc) in next sp between clusters**, repeat 5 more times from * to **, [skip cluster, 3 dc in next sp between clusters] 7 times, skip cluster, (3 dc, ch 1, 3 dc) in next sp between clusters (**bottom point**), [skip cluster, 3 dc in next sp between clusters] 6 times, repeat 6 times from * to **, [skip cluster, 3 dc in next sp between clusters] 3 times, skip 2 clusters (**center top**); sl st in top of beg ch-3 = 56 clusters

Rnd 9: Sl st in next 2 dc, sl st in sp between clusters, (ch 3, 2 dc) in same sp, [skip cluster, 3 dc in next sp between clusters] 26 times, skip cluster, (3 dc, ch 1, 3 dc) in next sp between clusters (**bottom point**), [skip cluster, 3 dc in next sp between clusters] 27 times, skip 2 clusters (**center top**); sl st in top of beg ch-3 = 56 clusters

Rnd 10: Sl st in next 2 dc, sl st in sp between clusters, (ch 3, 2 dc) in same sp, [skip cluster, 3 dc in next sp between clusters] 26 times, skip cluster, (3 dc, ch 1, 3 dc) in next sp between clusters (**bottom point**), [skip cluster, 3 dc in next sp between clusters] 27 times, skip 2 clusters (**center top**); sl st in top of beg ch-3, sl st in next 2 dc; sl st in sp between clusters = 56 clusters

Don't break off yarn. Continue to work **Step 3** in rows, beginning on RS.

STEP 3 - EDGING

Row 11: (RS) [Ch 5, skip cluster, sc in next sp between clusters] 53 times, skip cluster, ch 2, dc in next sp between clusters (counts as last arch); turn = 54 arches

Row 12: (WS) Skip ch-2 sp, [9 dc in next arch, sc in next arch, ch 5, sc in next arch] 17 times, 9 dc in next arch, sc in next arch, skip next cluster of Rnd 10, ch 2, dc in next sp between clusters (counts as last arch); turn = 18 shells and 18 arches

Row 13: (RS) Skip ch-2 sp, [crest across next shell, sc in next arch] 17 times, crest across next shell, dc in last dc of Row 11, ch 2, skip next cluster of Rnd 10; sl st in sp between clusters (**center top**) = 18 crests

Fasten off and weave in the ends. Spray block the heart to enhance the finished look of the lace texture (see General Techniques: Blocking).

HEAD CHART

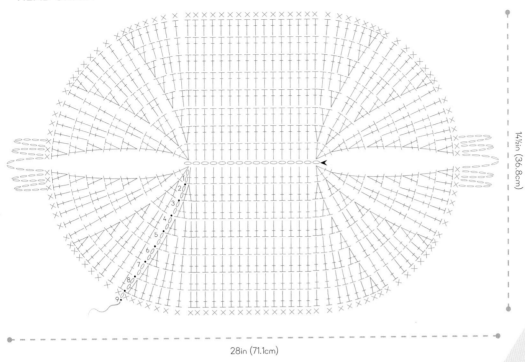

14½in (36.8cm)

28in (71.1cm)

HEAD

Make 1. Work in the round with a 9mm (M/N) hook and 3 strands of **MC**.

To beg: Ch 18

Rnd 1: Dc in third ch from hook (2 skipped chs don't count as a st), dc in next 14 chs, 6 dc in last ch, continue working across the bottom of the foundation ch, dc in next 14 chs, 5 dc in last ch; join = 40 sts

Rnd 2: Ch 2 (doesn't count as a st now and throughout), 2 dc in same st as join, dc in next 14 sts, 2 dc in next 6 sts, dc in next 14 sts, 2 dc in next 5 sts; join = 52 sts

Rnd 3: Ch 2, 2 dc in same st as join, dc in next 16 sts, [2 dc in next st, dc in next st] 2 times, 2 dc in next 2 sts, [dc in next st, 2 dc in next st] 2 times, dc in next 16 sts, [2 dc in next st, dc in next st] 2 times, 2 dc in next st, [2 dc in next st, dc in next st] 2 times; join = 64 sts

Rnd 4: Ch 2, 2 dc in same st as join, dc in next 18 sts, [2 dc in next st, dc in next 2 sts] 2 times, 2 dc in next 2 sts, [dc in next 2 sts, 2 dc in next st] 2 times, dc in next 18 sts, [2 dc in next st, dc in next 2 sts] 2 times, 2 dc in next st, [2 dc in next st, dc in next 2 sts] 2 times; join = 76 sts

Rnd 5: Ch 2, 2 dc in same st as join, dc in next 20 sts, [2 dc in next st, dc in next 3 sts] 2 times, 2 dc in next 2 sts, [dc in next 3 sts, 2 dc in next st] 2 times, dc in next 20 sts, [2 dc in next st, dc in next 3 sts] 2 times, 2 dc in next st, [2 dc in next st, dc in next 3 sts] 2 times; join = 88 sts

Rnd 6: Ch 2, 2 dc in same st as join, dc in next 22 sts, [2 dc in next st, dc in next 4 sts] 2 times, 2 dc in next 2 sts, [dc in next 4 sts, 2 dc in next st] 2 times, dc in next 22 sts, [2 dc in next st, dc in next 4 sts] 2 times, 2 dc in next st, [2 dc in next st, dc in next 4 sts] 2 times; join = 100 sts

Rnd 7: Ch 2, 2 dc in same st as join, dc in next 24 sts, [2 dc in next st, dc in next 5 sts] 2 times, 2 dc in next 2 sts, [dc in next 5 sts, 2 dc in next st] 2 times, dc in next 24 sts, [2 dc in next st, dc in next 5 sts] 2 times, 2 dc in next st, [2 dc in next st, dc in next 5 sts] 2 times; join = 112 sts

Rnd 8: Ch 2, 2 dc in same st as join, dc in next 26 sts, [2 dc in next st, dc in next 6 sts] 2 times, 2 dc in next 2 sts, [dc in next 6 sts, 2 dc in next st] 2 times, dc in next 26 sts, [2 dc in next st, dc in next 6 sts] 2 times, 2 dc in next st, [2 dc in next st, dc in next 6 sts] 2 times; join = 124 sts

Blocking will help to achieve a symmetrical appearance.

Rnd 9: Ch 1 (doesn't count as a st), sc in same st as join, sc in next 43 sts, [ch 8, sc in next st] 5 times, sc in next 57 sts, [ch 8, sc in next st] 5 times, sc in next 13 sts; join = 124 sts and 5 loops on each side of the head

Fasten off, leaving a long single strand of **MC** for sewing. Weave in the other ends. Block the head if shaping is necessary (see General Techniques: Blocking).

EARS

Make 2. Work in rows with a 9mm (M/N) hook and 3 strands of yarn, changing colors (**CC2** and **MC**) as indicated in the pattern.

To beg: With **CC2**, ch 2

Row 1: (WS) 3 sc in second ch from hook (the skipped ch doesn't count as a st); turn = 3 sts

Row 2: (RS) Ch 1 (doesn't count as a st now and throughout), 2 sc in first st, 3 sc in next st, 2 sc in last st; turn = 7 sts

Row 3: (WS) Ch 1, 2 sc in first st, sc in next 2 sts, 3 sc in next st, sc in next 2 sts, 2 sc in last st; turn = 11 sts

Row 4: (RS) Ch 1, 2 sc in first st, sc in next 4 sts, 3 sc in next st, sc in next 4 sts, 2 sc in last st; turn = 15 sts

Row 5: (WS) Ch 1, 2 sc in first st, sc in next 6 sts, 3 sc in next st, sc in next 6 sts, 2 sc in last st, change to **MC** and break off **CC2**; turn = 19 sts

Row 6: (RS) With **MC**, ch 1, 2 sc in first st, sc in next 8 sts, 3 sc in next st, sc in next 8 sts, 2 sc in last st; don't turn = 23 sts

Row 7: (RS) Ch 1, skip first st, rsc in next 21 sts; sl st in last st = 22 sts

Fasten off, leaving a long single strand of **MC** for sewing. Weave in the other ends.

NOSE

Make 1. Work in the round with a 5.5mm (I) hook and 1 strand of **CC2**.

To beg: Ch 6

Rnd 1: Sc in second ch from hook (the skipped ch doesn't count as a st), sc in next 3 chs, 3 sc in last ch, continue working across the bottom of the foundation ch, sc in next 3 chs, 2 sc in last ch; join = 12 sts

Rnd 2: Ch 1 (doesn't count as a st), 2 sc in same st as join, sc in next 3 sts, 2 sc in next 3 sts, skip st, (hdc, dc, hdc) in next st, skip st, 2 sc in next 2 sts; join = 18 sts

Fasten off, leaving a long tail for sewing.

EYES

Make 2. Each eye includes a basic eye, an iris, and an outer eye.

BASIC EYES

Make 2. Follow the instructions for the basic eyes (see Common Shapes: Basic Eyes). Work with a 5.5mm (I) hook using 1 strand of **CC3** for the pupils and 1 strand of **CC4** for the highlights.

IRISES

Make 2. Work in the round with a 5.5mm (I) hook and 1 strand of **CC5**.

To beg: Ch 3, sl st in third ch from hook to form a ring (or start with a magic ring)

Rnd 1: Ch 2 (doesn't count as a st), 12 dc in ring; join = 12 sts

Rnd 2: Ch 1 (doesn't count as a st now and throughout), 2 sc in same st as join, 2 sc in next 3 sts, skip st, (hdc, dc, tr) in next st, (tr, dc, hdc) in next st, skip st, 2 sc in next 4 sts; join = 22 sts

Rnd 3: Ch 1, sc in same st as join, sc in next 9 sts, 2 sc in next 2 sts, sc in next 10 sts; join = 24 sts

Fasten off, leaving a long tail for sewing.

EAR CHART

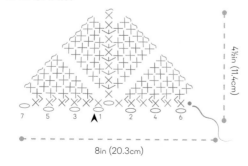

4½in (11.4cm)

7 5 3 1 2 4 6

8in (20.3cm)

NOSE CHART

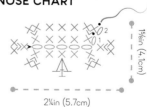

1⅝in (4.1cm)

2¼in (5.7cm)

OUTER EYES

Make 2. Work in the round with a 5.5mm (I) hook and 1 strand of **CC4**.

To beg: Ch 3, sl st in third ch from hook to form a ring (or start with a magic ring)

Rnd 1: Ch 2 (doesn't count as a st now and throughout), 12 dc in ring; join = 12 sts

Rnd 2: Ch 2, 2 dc in same st as join, 2 dc in next 11 sts; join = 24 sts

Rnd 3: Ch 1 (doesn't count as a st now and throughout), sc in same st as join, 2 sc in next st, [sc in next st, 2 sc in next st] 4 times, skip st, (hdc, dc, tr) in next st, (tr, dc, hdc) in next st, skip st, [sc in next st, 2 sc in next st] 5 times; join = 36 sts

Rnd 4: Ch 1, sc in same st as join, sc in next 16 sts, 2 sc in next 2 sts, sc in next 17 sts; join = 38 sts

Fasten off, leaving a long tail for sewing.

ASSEMBLING EYES

Place the basic eye on top of the iris and backstitch around using the long **CC3** tail from the pupil. Then place the iris on top of the outer eye and backstitch around using the long **CC5** tail from the iris (1). Finish the second eye in the same manner.

IRIS CHART

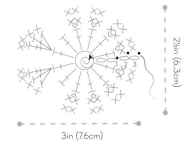

2½in (6.3cm)

3in (7.6cm)

OUTER EYE CHART

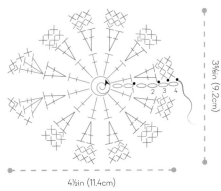

3⅝in (9.2cm)

4½in (11.4cm)

Line up all pieces as close to the pointy edges as possible.

PAWS

Make 4. Work in the round with a 9mm (M/N) hook and 3 strands of **MC**.

To beg: Ch 7

Rnd 1: Dc in third ch from hook (2 skipped chs don't count as a st), dc in next 3 chs, 6 dc in last ch, continue working across the bottom of the foundation ch, dc in next 3 chs, 5 dc in last ch; join = 18 sts

Rnd 2: Ch 2 (doesn't count as a st now and throughout), 2 dc in same st as join, dc in next 3 sts, 2 dc in next 6 sts, dc in next 3 sts, 2 dc in next 5 sts; join = 30 sts

Rnd 3: Ch 2, dc in same st as join, 2 dc in next st, dc in next 3 sts, [dc in next st, 2 dc in next st] 6 times, dc in next 3 sts, [dc in next st, 2 dc in next st] 5 times; join = 42 sts

Rnd 4: Ch 1 (doesn't count as a st), sc in same st as join, sc in next st, 2 sc in next st, sc in next 5 sts, 2 sc in next st, [sc in next 2 sts, 2 sc in next st] 2 times, *sc in next st, skip st, 6 dc in next st, skip st**, [sc in next st, skip 2 sts, 6 dc in next st, skip 2 sts] 2 times, repeat from * to **, sc in next 3 sts, 2 sc in next st, sc in next 2 sts, 2 sc in next st; join = 32 sc and 4 shells

Fasten off and weave in the ends.

Make 2 paws with pads and 2 paws without pads.

PAW PADS

Make 2 sets. Each set includes 4 toe pads and 1 palm pad. Work in the round with a 9mm (M/N) hook and 2 strands of **CC2**.

TOE PADS

To beg: Ch 3, sl st in third ch from hook to form a ring (or start with a magic ring)

Rnd 1: Ch 1 (doesn't count as a st), 6 sc in ring; join = 6 sts

Fasten off, leaving a long single strand of **CC2** for sewing. Weave in the other ends.

PALM PADS

To beg: Ch 7

Rnd 1: Dc in third ch from hook (2 skipped chs don't count as a st), dc in next 3 chs, 6 dc in last ch, continuing working across the bottom of the foundation ch, dc in next 3 chs, 5 dc in next ch; join = 18 sts

Rnd 2: Ch 1 (doesn't count as a st), 2 sc in same st as join, sc in next 3 sts, 2 sc in next 5 sts, skip 2 sts, 6 dc in next st, skip 2 sts, 2 sc in next 4 sts; join = 23 sc and 1 shell

Fasten off, leaving a long single strand of **CC2** for sewing. Weave in the other ends.

ASSEMBLING PAWS

With RS facing, place the first set of paw pads on top of the first paw and backstitch around the edge using the long tail from each piece (2). Finish the second paw in the same manner. The remaining 2 paws don't need paw pads.

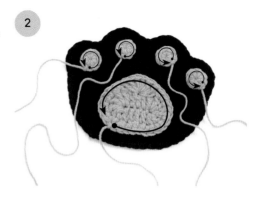

2

PAW CHART

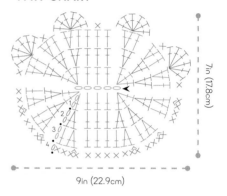

7in (17.8cm)

9in (22.9cm)

PAW PAD CHART

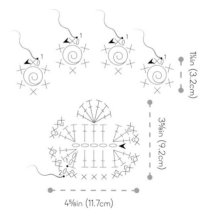

1¼in (3.2cm)

3⅝in (9.2cm)

4⅝in (11.7cm)

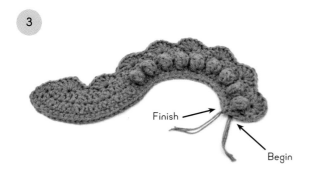

TAIL CHART

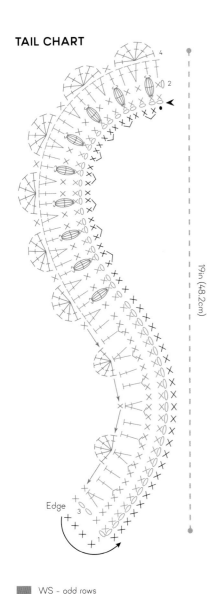

19in (48.2cm)

Edge

WS - odd rows
RS - even rows
RS - edging
→ Row direction

TAIL

Make 1. Work in rows with a 9mm (M/N) hook and 3 strands of **MC**.

To beg: Ch 52

Row 1: (WS) Sc in second ch from hook (the skipped ch doesn't count as a st), sc in next 50 chs; turn = 51 sts

Row 2: (RS) Ch 1 (doesn't count as a st now and throughout), sc in first st, [PC in next st, sc in next 2 sts] 9 times, [sc2tog, sc in next st] 7 times, sc in next 2 sts; turn = 9 PC and 35 sc

Row 3: (WS) Ch 2 (counts as first dc), skip first st, [dc2tog, dc in next 2 sts] 4 times, [2 dc in next st, dc in next 2 sts] 9 times; turn = 49 sts

Row 4: (RS) [Skip 2 sts, 6 dc in next st, skip 2 sts, sc in next st] 8 times, sc in last st = 8 shells and 9 sc

Don't break off yarn, but rotate your work and continue to work edging.

Edge: (RS) 4 sc evenly across the side sts of the tail, continue working across the bottom of the foundation ch, sc in next 27 sts, [sc2tog, sc in next st] 7 times, sc2tog; sl st in last st = 43 sts

Fasten off and weave in the ends (3).

BOW (OPTIONAL)

Make 1. Follow the instructions for the big bow (see Common Shapes: Big Bow). Use a 9mm (M/N) hook with 3 strands of **CC6**.

ASSEMBLING RUG

With RS facing, cover the bottom part of the head with the top edge of the heart (4).

Place 2 paws without pads on each side of the heart below the head, covering the scalloped edge. Place the remaining 2 paws at the bottom of the heart, covering the scalloped edge. All paws should be extending beyond the heart edge (4).

Place a portion of the tail under the scalloped edge of the heart (4).

Using the corresponding colors of yarn, backstitch across the overlapped edges of all pieces on RS (5-7).

Flip the rug to WS and whipstitch across the overlapped edges using the corresponding colors of yarn (8).

Place the eyes, nose and ears onto the head to create your chosen facial expression. Backstitch around the eyes using the long **CC4** tail from the outer eyes (9). Backstitch around the nose using the long **CC2** tail from the nose, then chain stitch a few stitches down from the center of the nose (10).

Using the long **MC** tail from the ears, whipstitch across the edges on RS and WS (11).

Position the bow (if using) and backstitch around the center of the bow using **CC6** (12). Keep the side edges of the bow unattached or whipstitch the corners if you would like to keep them in place.

If desired, make a removable non-slip lining (see General Techniques: Non-Slip Lining).

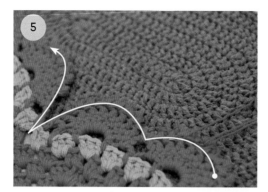

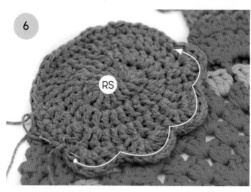

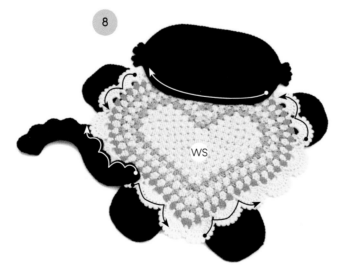

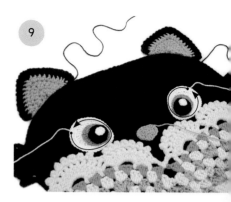

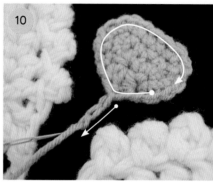

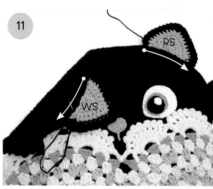

KITTY PILLOW

SKILL LEVEL

FINISHED SIZE
25in x 15½in (63.5cm x 39.4cm) including edging

HOOKS
5.5mm (I), 9mm (M/N)

YARN WEIGHT
4

NUMBER OF STRANDS
1 and 3

GAUGE WITH 1 STRAND AND 5.5MM (I) HOOK
14 sc x 16 rows = 4in x 4in (10cm x 10cm)

STITCH SUMMARY
Ch, sl st, sc, sc3tog, rsc, hdc, dc, PC, beg PC, join

SKILLS
Working in rows and in the round, working across the bottom of the foundation chain, sewing

LEFT-HANDED CROCHET
Fully compatible

YARN

Abbreviation	Color	Amount
MC	Black or Gray	547-569yd (500-520m)

Other contrasting colors are the same as for the Kitty Rug except CC1 (small amount of each).

HEAD PILLOW BASE

Make 1 front and 1 back with a 5.5mm (I) hook using 1 strand of MC. Follow the instructions for the oval pillow base (see Common Shapes: Oval Pillow Base). Fasten off after finishing the back piece, but don't break off yarn after finishing the front piece.

Fold the front piece in half horizontally and mark 6 stitches on each side for whiskers by placing a marker in first and sixth stitches. Holding the front and the back pieces together with WS facing each other, work the joining round through both pieces of fabric at the same time using the working yarn from the front piece. Remove markers as you go.

Rnd 26: Ch 1 (doesn't count as a st), sc in same st as previous sl st, sc in each st towards the next marker, *sc in st with marker, [ch 20, sc in next st] 5 times (ending in st with next marker)**, sc in each st towards the next marker, stuff the pillow (1), repeat from * to **, sc in each st towards the beg st; join = 196 sts and 5 loops on each side

Fasten off and weave in the ends.

EYES

Make 2 for kitty with opened eyes. Follow the instructions for the eyes from the Kitty Rug (see Kitty Rug: Eyes). Work with a 5.5mm (I) hook using 1 strand of CC3 for the pupils, 1 strand of CC4 for the highlights, 1 strand of CC5 for the irises, and 1 strand of CC4 for the outer eyes.

NOSE

Make 1. Follow the instructions for the nose from the Kitty Rug (see Kitty Rug: Nose). Work with a 5.5mm (I) hook and 1 strand of CC2.

EARS

Make 2. Follow the instructions for the ears from the Kitty Rug (see Kitty Rug: Ears). Work with a 9mm (M/N) hook and 3 strands of yarn, changing colors (CC2 and MC) as indicated in the pattern.

BOW (OPTIONAL)

Make 1. Working with CC6, follow the instructions for the big bow (see Common Shapes: Big Bow) or small bow (see Common Shapes: Small Bow).

ASSEMBLING PILLOW

Place the nose below the center of the pillow base and backstitch around using the long CC2 tail from the nose, then chain stitch a few stitches down from the center of the nose (2).

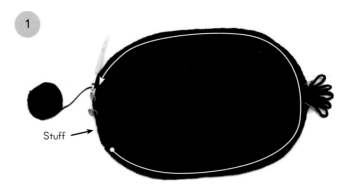

1

Stuff →

Place the eyes on each side of the nose and backstitch around using the long **CC4** tail from the eyes (2) or chain stitch sleepy eyes using **CC3** (3).

Place the ears on each side of the head, 3-4 rounds below the joining round. Use clips or stitch markers to hold the ears in place while sewing. Don't use straight basting pins as they can easily get lost in the pillow.

Using the long MC tail from the ears, whipstitch twice around the entire edge (4 and 5).

Place the bow onto the head and backstitch around the center using the long **CC6** tail from the bow (6).

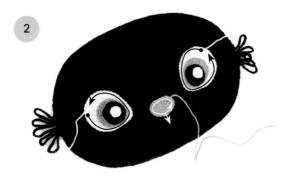

Simply chain stitch eyes for the sleepy kitty.

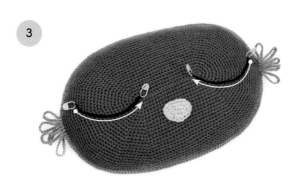

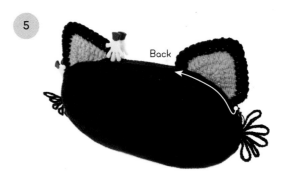

KITTY PLACE MAT

SKILL LEVEL

FINISHED SIZE

Place mat: 15½in x 10in (39.4cm x 25.4cm)

Coaster: 5¼in x 4¼in (13.3cm x 10.8cm)

HOOKS

3.75mm (F), 5mm (H)

YARN WEIGHT

4

NUMBER OF STRANDS

1

GAUGE WITH 1 STRAND AND 5MM (H) HOOK

15 dc x 8 rows = 4in x 4in (10cm x 10cm)

STITCH SUMMARY

Ch, sl st, sc, rsc, hdc, dc, join

SKILLS

Working in rows and in the round, working across the bottom of the foundation chain, sewing

LEFT-HANDED CROCHET

Fully compatible

YARN

Abbreviation	Color	Amount
MC	Black or Gray	148-180yd (135-165m)

Other contrasting colors are the same as for the Kitty Rug except **CC1** (small amount of each).

PLACE MAT

HEAD

Make 1. Follow the instructions for the head from the Kitty Rug (see Kitty Rug: Head). Work with a 5mm (H) hook and 1 strand of **MC**.

EYES

Make 2 for kitty with opened eyes. Follow the instructions for the eyes from the Kitty Rug (see Kitty Rug: Eyes). Work with a 3.75mm (F) hook using 1 strand of **CC3** for the pupils, 1 strand of **CC4** for the highlights, 1 strand of **CC5** for the irises, and 1 strand of **CC4** for the outer eyes.

NOSE

Make 1. Follow the instructions for the nose from the Kitty Rug (see Kitty Rug: Nose). Work with a 3.75mm (F) hook and 1 strand of **CC2**.

EARS

Make 2. Follow the instructions for the ears from the Kitty Rug (see Kitty Rug: Ears). Work with a 5mm (H) hook and 1 strand of yarn, changing colors (**CC3** and **MC**) as indicated in the pattern.

ASSEMBLING PLACE MAT

Place the eyes, nose, and ears onto the head to create a facial expression. Backstitch the eyes using the long **CC4** tail from the eyes (1) or chain stitch sleepy eyes using **CC3** (2).

Backstitch the nose using the long **CC2** tail from the nose, and chain stitch a few stitches down from the center of the nose (1). Whipstitch the ears around entire edge using the **MC** tail from the ears.

PAW COASTERS

Make 2. Follow the instructions for the paws from the Kitty Rug (see Kitty Rug: Paws). Work with a 5mm (H) hook and 1 strand of **MC**.

Block your finished pieces if shaping is necessary.

ROCK 'N' ROLL PANDA

Rug, Pillow, and Toy Bag

Pandas are the cutest bears in the world, and they
never hibernate, which means they rock all year
round! They love rolling in the grass and chewing on
bamboo sticks. What a fun way to spend a day.

This pattern collection was created for the love of pandas
inspired by our eldest daughter Amanda. Just like pandas,
she's cute and cuddly, but when agitated–watch out!!

You can make a playful panda with a star patch, or
just use oval patches for a classic panda look.

PANDA RUG

SKILL LEVEL

 ○ ○

FINISHED SIZE
42in x 32in (106.7cm x 81.3cm)

HOOK
9mm (M/N)

YARN WEIGHT
4

NUMBER OF STRANDS
3

GAUGE WITH 3 STRANDS AND 9MM (M/N) HOOK
9 dc x 4.5 rows = 4in x 4in (10cm x 10cm)

STITCH SUMMARY
Ch, sl st, sc, rsc, hdc, dc, tr, dc2tog, PC, shell, join

SKILLS
Working in rows and in the round, raw edge finishing, working across the bottom of the foundation chain, sewing

LEFT-HANDED CROCHET
Fully compatible

YARN

Abbreviation	Color	Amount
MC	White	1011-1202yd (925-1100m)
CC1	Black	612-656yd (560-600m)
CC2	Lush Green	459-546yd (420-500m)
CC3	Red (optional)	93-109yd (85-100m)

HEAD

Make 1. Work in the round with a 9mm (M/N) hook and 3 strands of **MC**.

To beg: Ch 3, sl st in third ch from hook to form a ring (or start with a magic ring)

Rnd 1: Ch 2 (doesn't count as a st now and throughout), 12 dc in ring; join = 12 sts

Rnd 2: Ch 2, 2 dc in same st as join, 2 dc in next 11 sts; join = 24 sts

Rnd 3: Ch 2, dc in same st as join, 2 dc in next st, [dc in next st, 2 dc in next st] 11 times; join = 36 sts

Rnd 4: Ch 2, 2 dc in same st as join, dc in next 2 sts, [2 dc in next st, dc in next 2 sts] 11 times; join = 48 sts

Rnd 5: Ch 2, dc in same st as join, dc in next 2 sts, 2 dc in next st, [dc in next 3 sts, 2 dc in next st] 11 times; join = 60 sts

Rnd 6: Ch 2, 2 dc in same st as join, dc in next 4 sts, [2 dc in next st, dc in next 4 sts] 11 times; join = 72 sts

Rnd 7: Ch 2, dc in same st as join, dc in next 4 sts, 2 dc in next st, [dc in next 5 sts, 2 dc in next st] 11 times; join = 84 sts

Rnd 8: Ch 2, 2 dc in same st as join, dc in next 6 sts, [2 dc in next st, dc in next 6 sts] 11 times; join = 96 sts

Rnd 9: Ch 2, dc in same st as join, dc in next 6 sts, 2 dc in next st, [dc in next 7 sts, 2 dc in next st] 11 times; join = 108 sts

Rnd 10: Ch 2, 2 dc in same st as join, dc in next 8 sts, [2 dc in next st, dc in next 8 sts] 11 times; join = 120 sts

HEAD CHART

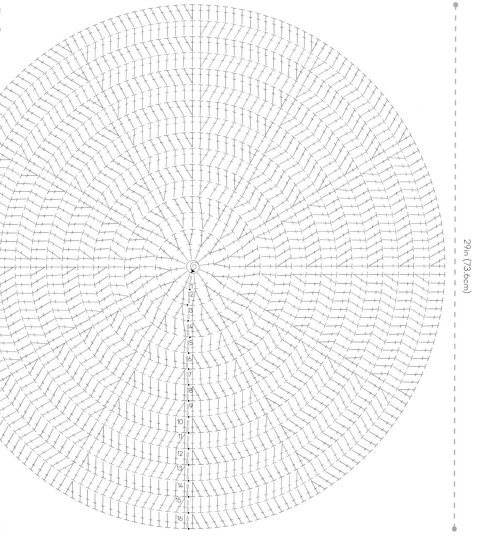

29in (73.6cm)

Rnd 11: Ch 2, dc in same st as join, dc in next 8 sts, 2 dc in next st, [dc in next 9 sts, 2 dc in next st] 11 times; join = 132 sts

Rnd 12: Ch 2, 2 dc in same st as join, dc in next 10 sts, [2 dc in next st, dc in next 10 sts] 11 times; join = 144 sts

Rnd 13: Ch 2, dc in same st as join, dc in next 10 sts, 2 dc in next st, [dc in next 11 sts, 2 dc in next st] 11 times; join = 156 sts

Rnd 14: Ch 2, 2 dc in same st as join, dc in next 12 sts, [2 dc in next st, dc in next 12 sts] 11 times; join = 168 sts

Rnd 15: Ch 2, dc in same st as join, dc in next 12 sts, 2 dc in next st, [dc in next 13 sts, 2 dc in next st] 11 times; join = 180 sts

Rnd 16: Ch 2, 2 dc in same st as join, dc in next 14 sts, [2 dc in next st, dc in next 14 sts] 11 times; join = 192 sts

Fasten off and weave in the ends.

EAR CHART

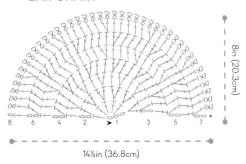

8in (20.3cm)

14½in (36.8cm)

NOSE CHART

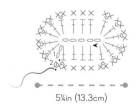

5¼in (13.3cm)

OVAL PATCH CHART

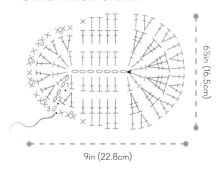

6½in (16.5cm)

9in (22.8cm)

EARS

Make 2. Work in rows with a 9mm (M/N) hook and 3 strands of **CC1**.

To beg: Ch 3

Row 1: (RS) 5 dc in third ch from hook (2 skipped chs count as first dc); turn = 6 sts

Row 2: (WS) Ch 2 (counts as first dc now and throughout), dc in first st, 2 dc in next 5 sts; turn = 12 sts

Row 3: (RS) Ch 2, dc in first st, dc in next st, [2 dc in next st, dc in next st] 5 times; turn = 18 sts

Row 4: (WS) Ch 2, dc in first st, dc in next 2 sts, [2 dc in next st, dc in next 2 sts] 5 times; turn = 24 sts

Row 5: (RS) Ch 2, dc in first st, dc in next 3 sts, [2 dc in next st, dc in next 3 sts] 5 times; turn = 30 sts

Row 6: (WS) Ch 2, dc in first st, dc in next 4 sts, [2 dc in next st, dc in next 4 sts] 5 times; turn = 36 sts

Row 7: (RS) Ch 2, dc in first st, dc in next 5 sts, [2 dc in next st, dc in next 5 sts] 5 times; don't turn = 42 sts

Row 8: (RS) Ch 1 (doesn't count as a st), skip first st, rsc in next 40 sts, sl st in last st = 41 sts

Fasten off and weave in the ends.

NOSE

Make 1. Work in the round with a 9mm (M/N) hook and 3 strands of **CC1**.

To beg: Ch 7

Rnd 1: Dc in third ch from hook (2 skipped chs don't count as a st), dc in next 3 chs, 6 dc in last ch, continue working across the bottom of the foundation ch, dc in next 3 chs, 5 dc in last ch; join = 18 sts

Rnd 2: Ch 1 (doesn't count as a st), 2 sc in same st as join, sc in next 3 sts, 2 sc in next 6 sts, sc in next 3 sts, 2 sc in next 5 sts; join = 30 sts

Fasten off, leaving a long single strand of **CC1** for sewing. Weave in the other ends.

EYE PATCHES

Make 1 oval patch and 1 star patch or 2 oval patches for a classic panda look. Work in the round with a 9mm (M/N) hook and 3 strands of **CC1**.

OVAL PATCH

To beg: Ch 9

Rnd 1: Dc in third ch from hook (2 skipped chs don't count as a st), dc in next 5 chs, 6 dc in last ch, continue working across the bottom of the foundation ch, dc in next 5 chs, 5 dc in last ch; join = 22 sts

Rnd 2: Ch 2 (doesn't count as a st), 2 dc in same st as join, dc in next 5 sts, 2 tr in next 2 sts, 3 tr in next 2 sts, 2 tr in next 2 sts, dc in next 5 sts, 2 dc in next 5 sts; join = 36 sts

Rnd 3: Ch 1 (doesn't count as a st), sc in same st as join, 2 sc in next st, sc in next st, hdc in next 2 sts, dc in next 3 sts, [2 dc in next st, dc in next st] 3 times, [dc in next st, 2 dc in next st] 3 times, dc in next 3 sts, hdc in next 2 sts, sc in next st, [sc in next st, 2 sc in next st] 5 times; join = 48 sts

Fasten off, leaving a long single strand of **CC1** for sewing. Weave in the other ends.

STAR PATCH CHART

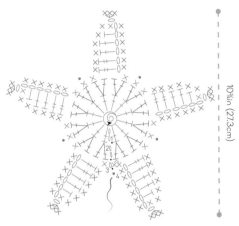

10¾in (27.3cm)

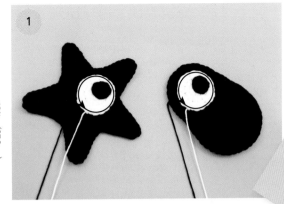

1

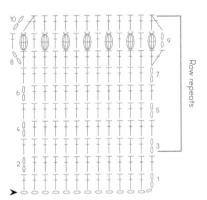

Make 2 matching oval patches for a classic panda look.

STAR PATCH

To beg: Ch 3, sl st in third ch from hook to form a ring (or start with a magic ring)

Rnd 1: Ch 2 (doesn't count as a st now and throughout), 12 dc in ring; join = 12 sts

Rnd 2: Ch 2, 2 dc in same st as join, 2 dc in next 11 sts; join = 24 sts

Rnd 3: Ch 1 (doesn't count as a st), 2 sc in same st as join, ch 7, sc in second ch from hook, hdc in next ch, dc in next 2 chs, tr in next 2 chs (first point made), *skip 2 sts of previous rnd, sc in next 3 sts, ch 7, sc in second ch from hook, hdc in next ch, dc in next 2 chs, tr in next 2 chs (next point made)**, repeat 3 more times from * to **, skip 2 sts of previous rnd, sc in next st; join = 5 points and 15 sc

Rnd 4: Skip st with join, *skip next st, sc across next 6 foundation sts of the point, 3 sc in last ch of the point, sc in next 6 sts of the point, skip next st, sl st in next st**, repeat 4 more times from * to ** = 80 sts

Fasten off, leaving a long single strand of **CC1** for sewing. Weave in the other ends.

EYES

Make 2 outer eyes with a 9mm (M/N) hook and 3 strands of **MC**, following the instructions for pupils (see Common Shapes: Basic Eyes). Make 2 pupils with a 9mm (M/N) hook and 3 strands of **CC1**, following the instructions for highlights, then assemble the eyes (see Common Shapes: Basic Eyes) (1).

BAMBOO

Make 1. Work in rows with a 9mm (M/N) hook and 3 strands of **CC2**.

To beg: Ch 15

Row 1: (RS) Dc in fourth ch from hook (3 skipped chs count as first dc), dc in next 11 chs; turn = 13 sts

Rows 2-7: Ch 2 (counts as first dc now and throughout), skip first st, dc in next 12 sts; turn = 13 sts

Row 8: (WS) Ch 2, dc in first st, dc in next 11 sts, 2 dc in last st; turn = 15 sts

Row 9: (RS) Ch 2, skip first st, [PC in next st, dc in next st] 7 times; turn = 15 sts

BAMBOO CHART

Row 10: (WS) Ch 2, skip first st, dc2tog, dc in next 10 sts, dc2tog; turn = 13 sts

Rows 11-34: Repeat Rows 3-10 in established pattern, ending on WS

Rows 35-41: Ch 2, skip first st, dc in next 12 sts; turn = 13 sts

Edge: (RS) Ch 1, sc evenly around entire edge, placing 3 sc in each corner for increasing; join

Fasten off and weave in ends.

PAWS

Make 2. Follow the instructions for the paws in the Kitty Rug (see Kitty Rug: Paws). Work with a 9mm (M/N) hook and 3 strands of **CC1**.

BOW (OPTIONAL)

Make 1. Follow the instructions for the big bow using **CC3** (see Common Shapes: Big Bow).

ASSEMBLING RUG

With RS facing, position the nose 4 rounds below the center of the head. Position the oval patch 4 rounds away from the center of the head. Position the star patch 5 rounds away from the center of the head. Place the bamboo to cover 5-7 bottom rounds of the head (2).

Using the corresponding colors of yarn, backstitch around the eyes, around the nose and across the overlapped edge of the bamboo.

With RS facing, place the ears slightly under the head edge, positioning them symmetrically on each side of the head with approximately 38 stitches between the ears (3).

Backstitch across the overlapped edge of the head using **MC**.

Position the paws diagonally on each side of the head, covering the edges of the head and the bamboo (3).

Backstitch across the overlapped edges of the paws using **CC1** (3).

Flip the rug to WS and whipstitch across the overlapped edges using the corresponding colors of yarn (4).

If using, place the bow onto the head and backstitch around the center with **CC3** (5).

Keep the side edges of the bow unattached or whipstitch the corners if you would like to keep them in place.

If desired, make a removable non-slip lining (see General Techniques: Non-Slip Lining).

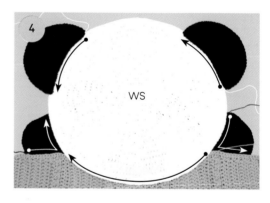

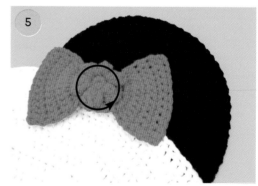

PANDA PILLOW

SKILL LEVEL

FINISHED SIZE
17in x 14½in (43.2cm x 36.8cm)

HOOKS
4mm (G), 5.5mm (I), 9mm (M/N)

YARN WEIGHT
4

NUMBER OF STRANDS
1 and 3

GAUGE WITH 1 STRAND AND 5.5MM (I) HOOK
14 sc x 16 rows = 4in x 4in (10cm x 10cm)

STITCH SUMMARY
Ch, sl st, sc, rsc, hdc, dc, tr, join

SKILLS
Working in rows and in the round, working across the bottom of the foundation chain, sewing

LEFT-HANDED CROCHET
Fully compatible

YARN

Abbreviation	Color	Amount
MC	White	120-164yd (110-150m)
CC1	Black	109-120yd (100-110m)
CC2	Red (optional)	93-109yd (85-100m)
CC3	Variegated Red	120-164yd (110-150m)

HEAD PILLOW BASE

Make 1 front using 1 strand of **MC** and 1 back with a 5.5mm (I) hook using 1 strand of **CC3**. Follow the instructions for the round pillow base (see Common Shapes: Round Pillow Base). Fasten off after finishing the back piece, but don't break off yarn after finishing the front piece.

Holding the front and the back pieces together with WS facing each other, work the joining round through both pieces of fabric at the same time, using the working yarn from the front piece.

Rnd 26: Ch 1 (doesn't count as a st), sc in same st as previous sl st, sc in next 140 sts, stuff the pillow, sc in next 15 sts; join = 156 sts

Fasten off and weave in the ends.

EARS

Make 2. Follow the instructions for the ears in the Panda Rug from the beginning to Row 3 (see Panda Rug: Ears). Use a 9mm (M/N) hook and 3 strands of **CC1**. Continue to work the last row as follows:

Row 4: (RS) Ch 1 (doesn't count as a st), skip first st, rsc in next 16 sts, sl st in last st = 17 sts

Fasten off, leaving a long tail for sewing.

NOSE

Make 1. Follow the instructions for the nose in the Panda Rug, omitting the last round (see Panda Rug: Nose). Work with a 4mm (G) hook and 1 strand of **CC1**.

EYE PATCHES

Make 1 oval patch and 1 star patch, or 2 oval patches for a classic panda look. Follow the instructions for the eye patches in the Panda Rug (see Panda Rug: Eye Patches). Work with a 4mm (G) hook and 1 strand of **CC1**.

EYES

Make 2 outer eyes with a 4mm (G) hook and 1 strand of **MC**, following the instructions for pupils (see Common Shapes: Basic Eyes). Make 2 pupils with a 4mm (G) hook and 1 strand of **CC1**, following the instructions for highlights, then assemble the eyes (see Common Shapes: Basic Eyes). Place the eyes on top of the eye patches and backstitch around using **MC**.

BOW (OPTIONAL)

Make 1. Follow the instructions for the big bow using **CC2** (see Common Shapes: Big Bow).

ASSEMBLING PILLOW

Position the nose 6 rounds below the center on the front side of the pillow base. Position the oval patch 6 rounds away from the center. Position the star patch 7 rounds away from the center (1).

Backstitch around each piece using **CC1**.

Place the ears on each side of the head, 3-4 rounds below the joining round. Use clips or stitch markers to hold the ears in place while sewing. Using **CC1**, whipstitch the ears twice around entire edge, removing clips as you sew (2 and 3).

If using, place the bow onto the head and backstitch around the center using **CC2** (4).

Avoid using pins as they may get lost in the pillow.

PANDA TOY BAG

SKILL LEVEL

FINISHED SIZE
18½in x 35in (47cm x 88.9cm)

HOOKS
3.75mm (F), 5.5mm (I), 9mm (M/N)

YARN WEIGHT
4

NUMBER OF STRANDS
1, 2, and 3

**GAUGE WITH 2 STRANDS
AND 9MM (M/N) HOOK**
10 dc x 5 rows = 4in x 4in (10cm x 10cm)

STITCH SUMMARY
Ch, sl st, sc, rsc, hdc, dc, tr, join

SKILLS
Working in rows and in the
round, working across the
bottom of the foundation chain,
changing colors, sewing

LEFT-HANDED CROCHET
Fully compatible

YARN

Abbreviation	Color	Amount
MC	White	93-109yd (85-100m)
CC1	Black	93-109yd (85-100m)
CC2	Lush Green	93-109yd (85-100m)
CC3	Red (optional)	Small amount
CC4	Variegated Red	1312-1531yd (1200-1400m)

TOY BAG

Make 1. Work in the round with a 9mm (M/N) hook and 2 strands of **CC4**.

To beg: Ch 45

Rnd 1: Dc in third ch from hook (2 skipped chs don't count as a st), dc in next 42 chs, 3 dc in last ch, continue working across the bottom of the foundation ch, dc in next 42 chs, 2 dc in last ch; join = 90 sts

Rnds 2-38: Ch 2 (doesn't count as a st), dc in same st as join, dc in next 89 sts; join = 90 sts

Break off **CC4**, join **CC2** and continue to work the edge:

Edge: Ch 1 (doesn't count as a st), sc in same st as join, sc in next 5 sts, *ch 10, sl st in second ch from hook, sc in next ch, hdc in next ch, dc in next 3 chs, hdc in next ch, sc in next 2 chs (leaf made)**, [sc in next 6 sts of previous rnd, repeat from * to ** for next leaf] 14 times; join = 15 leaves and 90 sc

Fasten off and weave in the ends.

DRAWSTRING

Make 1. Work with a 9mm (M/N) hook and 3 strands of **CC2**.

To beg: Ch 150

Fasten off and trim the ends. Using a crochet hook, pull the drawstring around the post of the center stitch 4 rounds below the edge and tie a knot to secure the drawstring. Thread each end of the drawstring through the stitches of the same round (1).

HEAD

Make 1. Follow the instructions for the head in the Panda Rug pattern from the beginning to Rnd 9 (see Panda Rug: Head). Use a 5.5mm (I) hook and 1 strand of **MC**. Continue to work the last round as follows:

Rnd 10: Ch 1 (doesn't count as a st), sc in same st as join, sc in next 107 sts; join = 108 sts

Fasten off, leaving a long tail for sewing.

EARS

Make 2. Follow the instructions for the ears in the Panda Rug from the beginning to Row 5 (see Panda Rug: Ears). Use a 5.5mm (I) hook and 1 strand of **CC1**. Continue to work the last row as follows:

Row 6: (RS) Ch 1 (doesn't count as a st), skip first st, rsc in next 28 sts, sl st in last st = 29 sts

Fasten off, leaving a long tail for sewing.

NOSE

Make 1. Follow the nose instructions in the Panda Rug, omitting the last round (see Panda Rug: Nose). Work with a 3.75mm (F) hook and 1 strand of **CC1**.

EYE PATCHES

Make 1 oval patch and 1 star patch, or 2 oval patches for a classic panda look. Work with a 3.75mm (F) hook and 1 strand of **CC1**.

OVAL PATCH

Follow the oval patch instructions in the Panda Rug, omitting the last round (see Panda Rug: Eye Patches).

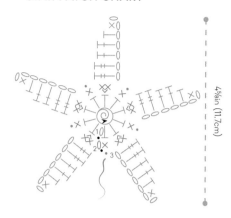

4⅝in (11.7cm)

STAR PATCH

To beg: Ch 3, sl st in third ch from hook to form a ring (or start with a magic ring)

Rnd 1: Ch 1 (doesn't count as a st now and throughout), 10 hdc in ring; join = 10 sts

Rnd 2: Ch 1, sc in same st as join, 2 sc in next st, [sc in next st, 2 sc in next st] 4 times; join = 15 sts

Rnd 3: Ch 7, sc in second ch from hook, hdc in next ch, dc in next 2 chs, tr in next 2 chs (first point made), skip st with join, skip next 2 sts, sl st in next st, *ch 7, sc in second ch from hook, hdc in next ch, dc in next 2 chs, tr in next 2 chs (next point made), skip 2 sts, sl st in next st**, repeat 3 more times from * to ** = 5 points

Fasten off, leaving a long tail for sewing.

EYES

Make 2 outer eyes with a 3.75mm (F) hook and 1 strand of **MC**, following the instructions for pupils (see Common Shapes: Basic Eyes). Make 2 pupils with a 3.75mm (F) hook and 1 strand of **CC1**, following the instructions for highlights, then assemble the eyes (see Common Shapes: Basic Eyes). Place the eyes on top of the eye patches and backstitch around using **MC**.

BOW (OPTIONAL)

Make 1. Follow the instructions for the big bow using **CC3** (see Common Shapes: Big Bow).

ASSEMBLING TOY BAG

With RS facing, position the nose and the eyes 2 rounds away from the center of the head and backstitch around each piece with **CC1** (2).

Place the ears slightly under the head edge, positioning them symmetrically on each side of the head with approximately 18 stitches between the ears (2). Backstitch across the overlapped edge of the head using **MC**.

Position the head in the middle of the bag. Backstitch around the head edge using the **MC** and backstitch around the outer edges of the ears using **CC1** (3).

If using, place the bow onto the head and backstitch around the center using **CC3** (4).

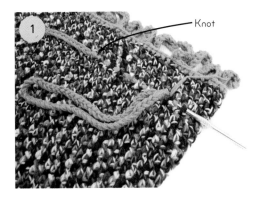

Knot

CHIP THE MONKEY

Rug, Pillow, and Toy Bag

This chapter is all about monkey business. If you enjoy crocheting for your little monkeys, here are a few ideas to keep them monkeying around. At the end of a long day in the jungle, cleaning up is a lot easier if you have a cheerful toy bag to help motivate your troop, who can look forward to a snuggly reading time with a cute monkey pillow on a matching reading rug when the job is done.

There is no better time to teach crafts to the next generation; as you know, monkey see - monkey do! You might even enjoy crocheting together ...

MONKEY RUG

SKILL LEVEL

FINISHED SIZE
36in x 35in (91.4cm x 88.9cm)

HOOK
Hook 9mm (M/N)

YARN WEIGHT
4

NUMBER OF STRANDS
3

**GAUGE WITH 3 STRANDS
AND 9MM (M/N) HOOK**
9 dc x 4.5 rows = 4in x 4in (10cm x 10cm)

STITCH SUMMARY
Ch, sl st, sc, sc2tog, fpsc, rsc,
hdc, dc, dc2tog, slipknot, join

SKILLS
Working in rows and in the round,
raw edge finishing, working across
the bottom of the foundation
chain, changing colors, sewing

LEFT-HANDED CROCHET
See Crochet Techniques:
Left-Handed Crochet

YARN

Abbreviation	Color	Amount
MC	Beige	710-820yd (650-750m)
CC1	Coffee	360-437yd (330-400m)
CC2	Yellow	710-820yd (650-750m)
CC3	Warm Brown	Small amount
CC4	Any color (optional)	93-109yd (85-100m)

HEAD

Make 1. Work in rows with a 9mm (M/N) hook and 3 strands of **CC1**.

To beg: Ch 8

Row 1: (WS) Dc in fourth ch from hook (3 skipped chs count as dc), dc in next 3 chs, 6 dc in last ch, continue working across the bottom of the foundation ch, dc in next 5 chs; turn = 16 sts

Row 2: (RS) Ch 2 (counts as first dc now and throughout), skip first st, dc in next 4 sts, 2 dc in next 6 sts, dc in next 5 sts; turn = 22 sts

Row 3: (WS) Ch 2, skip first st, dc in next 4 sts, [2 dc in next st, dc in next st] 6 times, dc in next 5 sts; turn = 28 sts

Row 4: (RS) Ch 2, skip first st, dc in next 4 sts, [2 dc in next st, dc in next 2 sts] 6 times, dc in next 5 sts; turn = 34 sts

Row 5: (WS) Ch 2, skip first st, dc in next 4 sts, [2 dc in next st, dc in next 3 sts] 6 times, dc in next 5 sts; turn = 40 sts

Row 6: (RS) Ch 2, skip first st, dc in next 4 sts, [2 dc in next st, dc in next 4 sts] 6 times, dc in next 5 sts; turn = 46 sts

Row 7: (WS) Ch 2, skip first st, dc in next 4 sts, [2 dc in next st, dc in next 5 sts] 6 times, dc in next 5 sts; turn = 52 sts

Row 8: (RS) Ch 2, skip first st, dc in next 4 sts, [2 dc in next st, dc in next 6 sts] 6 times, dc in next 5 sts; turn = 58 sts

Row 9: (WS) Ch 2, skip first st, dc in next 4 sts, [2 dc in next st, dc in next 7 sts] 6 times, dc in next 5 sts; turn = 64 sts

HEAD CHART

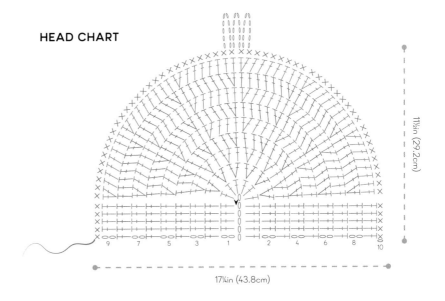

11½in (29.2cm)

17¼in (43.8cm)

Row 10: (RS) Ch 1 (doesn't count as a st), sc in first st, sc in next 30 sts, [ch 10, sc in next st] 3 times, sc in next 30 sts = 64 sc and 3 ch-10 loops

Fasten off, leaving a long single strand of **CC1** for sewing. Weave in the other ends.

EARS

Make 2. Work in rows with a 9mm (M/N) hook and 3 strands of yarn, changing colors (**MC** and **CC1**) as indicated in the pattern.

To beg: With **MC**, ch 3

Row 1: (WS) 5 dc in third ch from hook (2 skipped chs count as dc); turn = 6 sts

Row 2: (RS) Ch 2 (counts as first dc now and throughout), dc in first st, 2 dc in next 5 sts; turn = 12 sts

Row 3: (WS) Ch 2, dc in first st, dc in next st, [2 dc in next st, dc in next st] 5 times, change to **CC1** and break off **MC**; turn = 18 sts

EAR CHART

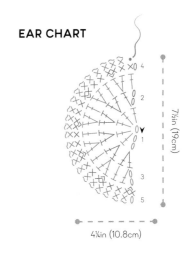

7½in (19cm)

4¼in (10.8cm)

Row 4: (RS) With **CC1**, ch 1 (doesn't count as a st now and throughout), sc in first st, sc in next st, 2 sc in next st, [sc in next 2 sts, 2 sc in next st] 5 times; don't turn = 24 sts

Row 5: (RS) Ch 1, skip first st, rsc in next 22 sts, sl st in last st = 23 sts

Fasten off, leaving a long single strand of **CC1** for sewing. Weave in the other ends.

MUZZLE

Make 1. Work in the round with a 9mm (M/N) hook and 3 strands of **MC**.

To beg: Ch 32

Rnd 1: Dc in third ch from hook (2 skipped chs don't count as a st), dc in next 28 chs, 6 dc in last ch, continue working across the bottom of the foundation ch, dc in next 28 chs, 5 dc in last ch; join = 68 sts

Rnd 2: Ch 2 (doesn't count as a st now and throughout), 2 dc in same st as join, dc in next 28 sts, 2 dc in next 6 sts, dc in next 28 sts, 2 dc in next 5 sts; join = 80 sts

Rnd 3: Ch 2, dc in same st as join, 2 dc in next st, dc in next 28 sts, [dc in next st, 2 dc in next st] 6 times, dc in next 28 sts, [dc in next st, 2 dc in next st] 5 times; join = 92 sts

Rnd 4: Ch 2, 2 dc in same st as join, dc in next 30 sts, [2 dc in next st, dc in next 2 sts] 6 times, dc in next 28 sts, [2 dc in next st, dc in next 2 sts] 5 times; join = 104 sts

Rnd 5: Ch 2, dc in same st as join, dc in next 2 sts, 2 dc in next st, dc in next 28 sts, [dc in next 3 sts, 2 dc in next st] 6 times, dc in next 28 sts, [dc in next 3 sts, 2 dc in next st] 5 times; join = 116 sts

Rnd 6: Ch 2, 2 dc in same st as join, dc in next 32 sts, [2 dc in next st, dc in next 4 sts] 6 times, dc in next 28 sts, [2 dc in next st, dc in next 4 sts] 5 times; join = 128 sts

Fasten off and weave in the ends.

SMILE

With RS of the muzzle facing, mark the bottom half of Rnd 2 for the smile (40 stitches).

Work around the marked stitches with a 9mm (M/N) hook and 3 strands of **CC1** as follows:

Make a slipknot and keep the loop on the hook, insert the hook from front to back to front through the first marked st, yo and pull up a loop, yo and pull through 2 loops on the hook (first fpsc made). Work fpsc around the post of next 39 sts (1).

Fasten off and weave in the ends on WS.

FACE

Make 1 left and 1 right. Work in rows with a 9mm (M/N) hook and 3 strands of **MC**.

MUZZLE CHART

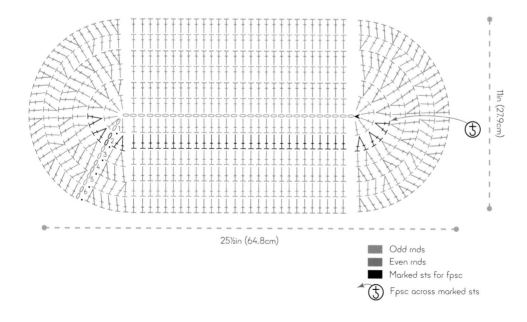

25½in (64.8cm)

11in (27.9cm)

Odd rnds
Even rnds
Marked sts for fpsc
Fpsc across marked sts

LEFT AND RIGHT

To beg: Ch 6

Row 1: (RS) Dc in fourth ch from hook (3 skipped chs count as dc), dc in next ch, 6 dc in last ch, continue working across the bottom of the foundation ch, dc in next 3 chs; turn = 12 sts

Row 2: (WS) Ch 2 (counts as first dc now and throughout), skip first st, dc in next 2 sts, 2 dc in next 6 sts, dc in next 3 sts; turn = 18 sts

Row 3: (RS) Ch 2, skip first st, dc in next 2 sts, [2 dc in next st, dc in next st] 6 times, dc in next 3 sts = 24 sts

Fasten off, leaving a long single strand of **MC** for sewing. Weave in the other ends.

SMILEY EYES

Finish the left and right pieces in the same manner. With RS facing, skip 3 sts on each side of Row 2 and mark the middle 12 sts for the eye. Work around the marked stitches with a 9mm (M/N) hook and 3 strands of **CC1** as follows:

Make a slipknot and keep the loop on the hook, insert the hook from front to back to front through the first marked st, yo and pull up a loop, yo and pull through 2 loops on the hook (first fpsc made). Work fpsc around the post of next 11 sts (2).

Fasten off and weave in the ends on WS.

ASSEMBLING FACE

Place the left and the right pieces side by side with the flat edges facing down. Using the long **MC** tail between the pieces, whipstitch across 5 sts (3).

Fasten off and weave in the end. Keep the other long tail at the face edge for future assembling.

FACE CHART

Left   Right

5in (12.7cm)

11¾in (29.8cm)

Odd rows
Even rows
Marked sts for fpsc
Fpsc across marked sts
Seam

HANDS

Make 2. Work in rows with a 9mm (M/N) hook and 3 strands of **MC**.

To beg: Ch 13

Row 1: (RS) 2 sc in second ch from hook (the skipped ch doesn't count as a st now and throughout), sc in next 10 chs, 2 sc in last ch; turn = 14 sts

Row 2: (WS) Ch 1 (doesn't count as a st now and throughout), 2 sc in first st, sc in next 13 sts; turn = 15 sts

Row 3: (RS) Ch 1, don't skip first st, sc2tog, sc in next 12 sts, 2 sc in last st; turn = 15 sts

Row 4: (WS) Ch 1, 2 sc in first st, sc in next 8 sts, ch 7; turn = 10 sts and 7 chs

Row 5: (RS) 2 sc in second ch from hook, sc in next 5 chs, sc in next 10 sts; turn = 17 sts

Row 6: (WS) Ch 1, sc in first st, sc in next 16 sts; turn = 17 sts

Row 7: (RS) Ch 1, don't skip first st, sc2tog, sc in next 15 sts; turn = 16 sts

Row 8: (WS) Ch 1, sc in first st, sc in next 9 sts, ch 7; turn = 10 sts and 7 chs

Rows 9-11: Repeat Rows 5-7

Row 12: (WS) Ch 1, don't skip first st, sc2tog, sc in next 8 sts, ch 7; turn = 9 sts and 7 chs

Row 13: (RS) 2 sc in second ch from hook, sc in next 5 chs, sc in next 7 sts, sc2tog; turn = 15 sts

Row 14: (WS) Ch 1, don't skip first st, sc2tog, sc in next 13 sts; turn = 14 sts

Row 15: (RS) Ch 1, don't skip first st, sc2tog, sc in next 10 sts, sc2tog = 12 sts

Fasten off and weave in the ends.

BANANA

Make 1. Work in rows with a 9mm (M/N) hook and 3 strands of yarn, changing colors (**CC3** and **CC2**) as indicated in the pattern.

To beg: With **CC3**, ch 5

Row 1: (WS) Sc in second ch from hook (the skipped ch doesn't count as a st), sc in next 3 chs; turn = 4 sts

Rows 2-5: Ch 1 (doesn't count as a st now and throughout), sc in first st, sc in next 3 sts; turn = 4 sts

Row 6: (RS) Ch 1, sc in first st, sc in next 3 sts, change to **CC2** and drop **CC3** (don't break off yarn); turn = 4 sts

Row 7: (WS) With **CC2**, ch 2 (counts as first dc now and throughout), dc in first st, dc in next 2 sts, 2 dc in last st; turn = 6 sts

Row 8: (RS) Ch 2, dc in first st, dc in next 4 sts, 2 dc in last st; turn = 8 sts

Row 9: (WS) Ch 2, dc in first st, dc in next 6 sts, 2 dc in last st; turn = 10 sts

Row 10: (RS) Ch 2, skip first st, dc in next 3 sts, hdc in next 3 sts, sc in next 3 sts; turn = 10 sts

Row 11: (WS) Ch 2, dc in first st, dc in next 8 sts, 2 dc in last st; turn = 12 sts

Row 12: (RS) Ch 2, skip first st, dc in next 3 sts, hdc in next 4 sts, sc in next 4 sts; turn = 12 sts

Row 13: (WS) Ch 2, dc in first st, dc in next 10 sts, 2 dc in last st; turn = 14 sts

Row 14: (RS) Ch 2, skip first st, dc in next 4 sts, hdc in next 5 sts, sc in next 4 sts; turn = 14 sts

Row 15: (WS) Ch 2, dc in first st, dc in next 12 sts, 2 dc in last st; turn = 16 sts

Row 16: (RS) Ch 2, skip first st, dc in next 5 sts, hdc in next 5 sts, sc in next 5 sts; turn = 16 sts

Row 17: (WS) Ch 2, dc in first st, dc in next 14 sts, 2 dc in last st; turn = 18 sts

HAND CHART

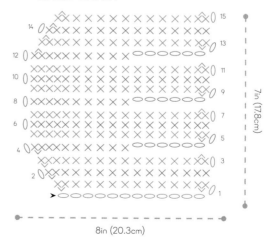

7in (17.8cm)

8in (20.3cm)

Row 18: (RS) Ch 2, skip first st, dc in next 5 sts, hdc in next 6 sts, sc in next 6 sts; turn = 18 sts

Row 19: (WS) Ch 2, skip first st, dc in next 17 sts; turn = 18 sts

Row 20: (RS) Ch 2, skip first st, dc in next 5 sts, hdc in next 6 sts, sc in next 6 sts; turn = 18 sts

Rows 21-46: Repeat Rows 19-20 in established pattern, ending on RS

Row 47: (WS) Ch 2, skip first st, dc2tog, dc in next 13 sts, dc2tog; turn = 16 sts

Row 48: (RS) Ch 2, skip first st, dc in next 5 sts, hdc in next 5 sts, sc in next 5 sts; turn = 16 sts

Row 49: (WS) Ch 2, skip first st, dc2tog, dc in next 11 sts, dc2tog; turn = 14 sts

Row 50: (RS) Ch 2, skip first st, dc in next 4 sts, hdc in next 5 sts, sc in next 4 sts; turn = 14 sts

Row 51: (WS) Ch 2, skip first st, dc2tog, dc in next 9 sts, dc2tog; turn = 12 sts

Row 52: (RS) Ch 2, skip first st, dc in next 3 sts, hdc in next 4 sts, sc in next 4 sts; turn = 12 sts

Row 53: (WS) Ch 2, skip first st, dc2tog, dc in next 7 sts, dc2tog; turn = 10 sts

Row 54: (RS) Ch 2, skip first st, dc in next 3 sts, hdc in next 3 sts, sc in next 3 sts; turn = 10 sts

Row 55: (WS) Ch 2, skip first st, dc2tog, dc in next 5 sts, dc2tog; turn = 8 sts

Row 56: (RS) Ch 2, skip first st, dc2tog, dc in next 3 sts, dc2tog; turn = 6 sts

Row 57: (WS) Ch 2, skip first st, dc2tog, dc in next st, dc2tog = 4 sts

Fasten off and weave in the ends.

EDGING

With RS facing, pick up **CC3** at the edge of Row 6 and work the edging as follows:

With **CC3**, ch 1 (doesn't count as a st), sc evenly around the edge of the stem, placing 3 sc in corners for increasing. Change to **CC2** and break off **CC3**, sc around the remaining edge of the banana, join (4). Fasten off and weave in the ends.

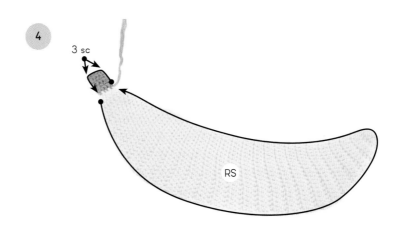

BANANA CHART

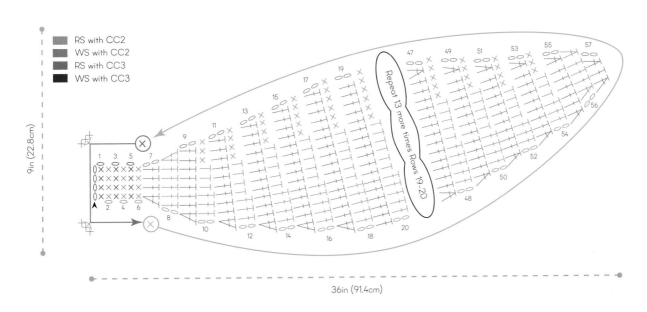

RS with CC2
WS with CC2
RS with CC3
WS with CC3

9in (22.8cm)

36in (91.4cm)

ASSEMBLING RUG

With RS facing, assemble all pieces as follows (5):

Place the muzzle to cover the bottom edge of the head and backstitch across the overlapped edge with **MC**. Place the face right up against the muzzle, whipstitch across the bottom edge and backstitch around the remaining edge of the face with **MC**. Place the ears on each side of the head slightly above the muzzle and whipstitch across the edge with **CC1**. Place the banana to cover the bottom edge of the muzzle and backstitch across the overlapped edge with **CC2**.

Flip the rug to WS. Using the corresponding colors of yarn, whipstitch across the overlapped edges of the muzzle and the banana, whipstitch across the edges of the ears (6).

Finish the nose as follows:

Place the first marker 3 rounds below the joined center of the face, place the second and third markers 2 rows above the first marker in sixth stitch to the right and to the left (7).

Thread the needle with 2 strands of **CC3** and chain stitch the v-shaped nose from the right marker towards the next 2 markers (7), remove the markers.

Place the hands on each side of the banana, overlapping the fingers onto the banana.

Thread the needle with a single strand of **MC** and backstitch around the edge of the fingers (8).

If desired, make a removable non-slip lining (see General Techniques: Non-Slip Lining).

5

RS

6

WS

Make a bow using **CC4** to finish the monkey (see Common Shapes: Big Bow).

7

8

MONKEY PILLOW

SKILL LEVEL

FINISHED SIZE
17½in (44.5cm) diameter

HOOKS
3.75mm (F), 5.5mm (I)

YARN WEIGHT
4

NUMBER OF STRANDS
1

GAUGE WITH 1 STRAND AND 5.5MM (I) HOOK
14 sc x 16 rows = 4in x 4in (10cm x 10cm)

STITCH SUMMARY
Ch, sl st, sc, rsc, dc, picot, crest, arch, shell, join

SKILLS
Working in rows and in the round, working across the bottom of the foundation chain, changing colors, sewing

LEFT-HANDED CROCHET
Fully compatible

YARN

Abbreviation	Color	Amount
MC	Beige	93-109yd (85-100m)
CC1	Coffee	93-109yd (85-100m)
CC2	Yellow	Small amount
CC4	Lush Green	328-383yd (300-350m)
CC5	Red	Small amount

HEAD PILLOW BASE

BACK

Make 1. Work with a 5.5mm (I) hook and 1 strand of **CC4**. Follow the instructions for the round pillow (see Common Shapes: Round Pillow Base). Fasten off after finishing Rnd 25.

FRONT

Make 1. Work with a 5.5mm (I) hook and 1 strand of **CC1**. Follow the instructions for the round pillow base (see Common Shapes: Round Pillow Base). Change to **CC4** after Rnd 17, then continue working to Rnd 25 and don't break off yarn.

EDGING

Holding the front and the back pieces together with WS facing each other, work Rnd 26 through both pieces of fabric at the same time using the working yarn from the front piece.

Rnd 26: Ch 1 (doesn't count as a st now and throughout), sc in same st as previous sl st, sc in next 140 sts, stuff the pillow, sc in next 15 sts; join = 156 sts

Rnd 27: Ch 1, sc in same st as join, ch 5, skip st, [sc in next st, ch 5, skip st] 76 times, sc in next st, ch 2, skip st, dc in beg st (counts as last arch) = 78 arches

Rnd 28: Ch 1, sc in same sp, 9 dc in next arch, sc in next arch, [ch 5, sc in next arch, 9 dc in next arch, sc in next arch] 25 times, ch 2, dc in beg st (counts as last arch) = 26 shells and 26 arches

Rnd 29: Ch 1, sc in same sp, crest across next shell, [sc in next arch, crest across next shell] 25 times; join = 26 crests

Fasten off and weave in the ends.

MUZZLE

Make 1. Work in spiral rounds with a 5.5mm (I) hook and 1 strand of **MC**.

To beg: Ch 21

Rnd 1: Sc in second ch from hook (the skipped ch doesn't count as a st), sc in next 18 chs, 3 sc in last ch, continue working across the bottom of the foundation ch, sc in next 18 chs, 2 sc in last ch; don't join now and throughout = 42 sts

Rnd 2: 2 sc in first st of previous rnd, sc in next 18 sts, 2 sc in next 3 sts, sc in next 18 sts, 2 sc in next 2 sts = 48 sts

Rnd 3: Sc in next st, 2 sc in next st, sc in next 18 sts, [sc in next st, 2 sc in next st] 3 times, sc in next 18 sts, [sc in next st, 2 sc in next st] 2 times = 54 sts

Rnd 4: Sc in next 2 sts, 2 sc in next st, sc in next 18 sts, [sc in next 2 sts, 2 sc in next st] 3 times, sc in next 18 sts, [sc in next 2 sts, 2 sc in next st] 2 times = 60 sts

Rnd 5: Sc in next 3 sts, 2 sc in next st, sc in next 18 sts, [sc in next 3 sts, 2 sc in next st] 3 times, sc in next 18 sts, [sc in next 3 sts, 2 sc in next st] 2 times = 66 sts

Rnd 6: Sc in next 4 sts, 2 sc in next st, sc in next 18 sts, [sc in next 4 sts, 2 sc in next st] 3 times, sc in next 18 sts, [sc in next 4 sts, 2 sc in next st] 2 times = 72 sts

Rnd 7: Sc in next 5 sts, 2 sc in next st, sc in next 18 sts, [sc in next 5 sts, 2 sc in next st] 3 times, sc in next 18 sts, [sc in next 5 sts, 2 sc in next st] 2 times = 78 sts

Rnds 8-10: Sc in each st around = 78 sts

Sl st in next st and fasten off, leaving a long tail for sewing.

Use a stitch marker to mark the beginning of each round as you go.

FACE

Make 1 left and 1 right. Work in rows with a 5.5mm (I) hook and 1 strand of **MC**.

LEFT AND RIGHT

To beg: Ch 6

Row 1: (RS) Sc in second ch from hook (the skipped ch doesn't count as a st), sc in next 3 chs, 3 sc in last ch, continue working across the bottom of the foundation ch, sc in next 4 chs; turn = 11 sts

Row 2: (WS) Ch 1 (doesn't count as a st now and throughout), sc in first st, sc in next 3 sts, 2 sc in next 3 sts, sc in next 4 sts; turn = 14 sts

Row 3: (RS) Ch 1, sc in first st, sc in next 3 sts, [2 sc in next st, sc in next st] 3 times, sc in next 4 sts; turn = 17 sts

Row 4: (WS) Ch 1, sc in first st, sc in next 3 sts, [2 sc in next st, sc in next 2 sts] 3 times, sc in next 4 sts; turn = 20 sts

Row 5: (RS) Ch 1, sc in first st, sc in next 3 sts, [2 sc in next st, sc in next 3 sts] 3 times, sc in next 4 sts; turn = 23 sts

Fasten off, leaving a long tail for sewing. Weave in the end from the beg.

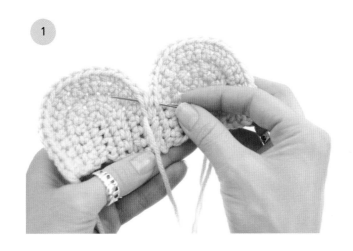

ASSEMBLING FACE

Place the left and the right pieces side by side with the flat edges facing down. Using the long **MC** tail between the pieces, whipstitch across 6 sts (1), fasten off and weave in the end. Keep the other long tail at the face edge for future assembly.

EARS

Make 2. Work in rows with a 5.5mm (I) hook and 1 strand of yarn, changing colors (**MC** and **CC1**) as indicated in the pattern.

To beg: With **MC**, ch 2

Row 1: (RS) 3 sc in second ch from hook (the skipped ch doesn't count as a st); turn = 3 sts

Row 2: (WS) Ch 1 (doesn't count as a st now and throughout), 2 sc in first st, 2 sc in next 2 sts; turn = 6 sts

Row 3: (RS) Ch 1, 2 sc in first st, sc in next st, [2 sc in next st, sc in next st] 2 times; turn = 9 sts

Row 4: (WS) Ch 1, 2 sc in first st, sc in next 2 sts, [2 sc in next st, sc in next 2 sts] 2 times, change to **CC1** and break off **MC**; turn = 12 sts

Row 5: (RS) With **CC1**, ch 1, 2 sc in first st, sc in next 3 sts, [2 sc in next st, sc in next 3 sts] 2 times; don't turn = 15 sts

Row 6: (RS) Ch 1, skip first st, rsc in next 13 sts, sl st in next st = 14 sts

Fasten off, leaving a long tail for sewing. Weave in the other ends.

PILLOW BASE EDGING CHART

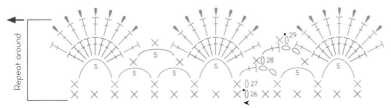

FACE CHART

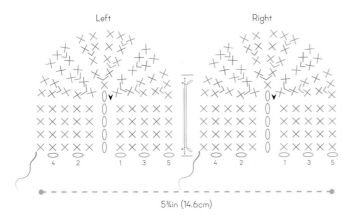

Left   Right

5¾in (14.6cm)

EAR CHART

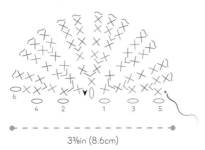

3⅜in (8.6cm)

ASSEMBLING PILLOW

Place the muzzle approximately 6 rounds below the center of the head, covering the color change between Rnds 17 and 18. Using the long **MC** tail, whipstitch around the muzzle, leaving an opening at the end for stuffing. Stuff the muzzle and complete sewing (2).

Place the face above the muzzle with its straight edge right up against the muzzle. Using the long **MC** tail, whipstitch across the bottom edge and backstitch around the remaining edge of the face (3).

Using a single strand of **CC1**, chain stitch the eyes 2 rows below the face edge and chain stitch the v-shaped nose (4).

Using a single strand of **CC5**, chain stitch the smile (5).

Place the ears on each side of the head slightly above the muzzle. Whipstitch each ear across the straight edge on RS and WS using the long **CC1** tail (6 and 7).

Cut 6 strands of **CC1** approximately 9in (23cm) long and fold the bundle in half. Using a crochet hook, pull the bundle through the stitches on the top of the head to create a loop (8), pull the loose ends through the loop and tighten up the tassel. Trim the ends to desired length.

If desired, make a small bow using 1 strand of **CC2** (see Common Shapes: Small Bow). Place the bow onto the head and backstitch around the center using the long tail from the bow (9).

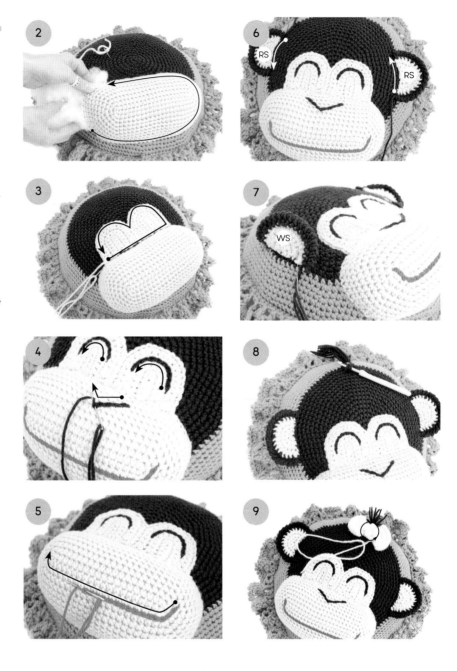

MONKEY TOY BAG

SKILL LEVEL

FINISHED SIZE
18½in x 30½in (47cm x 77.5cm)

HOOKS
3.75mm (F), 5.5mm (I), 9mm (M/N)

YARN WEIGHT
4

NUMBER OF STRANDS
1, 2, and 3

**GAUGE WITH 2 STRANDS
AND 9MM (M/N) HOOK**
10 dc x 5 rows = 4in x 4in (10cm x 10cm)

STITCH SUMMARY
Ch, sl st, sc, sc2tog, rsc, hdc, dc,
picot, crest, arch, shell, join

SKILLS
Working in rows and in the
round, working across the
bottom of the foundation chain,
changing colors, sewing

LEFT-HANDED CROCHET
Fully compatible

YARN

Abbreviation	Color	Amount
CC4	Lush Green	601-656yd (550-600m)
CC6	Carrot	546-601yd (500-550m)

All other colors and amounts are the
same as for the Monkey Pillow.

TOY BAG

Make 1. Work in the round with a 9mm (M/N) hook and 2 strands of yarn, changing colors (**CC6** and **CC4**) in every round until 3 rounds remain. Begin with **CC6**.

To beg: Ch 3, sl st in third ch from hook to form a ring (or start with a magic ring)

Rnd 1: Ch 2 (doesn't count as a st now and throughout), 12 dc in ring; join = 12 sts

Rnd 2: Ch 2, 2 dc in same st as join, 2 dc in next 11 sts; join = 24 sts

Rnd 3: Ch 2, dc in same st as join, 2 dc in next st, [dc in next st, 2 dc in next st] 11 times; join = 36 sts

Rnd 4: Ch 2, dc in same st as join, dc in next st, 2 dc in next st, [dc in next 2 sts, 2 dc in next st] 11 times; join = 48 sts

Rnd 5: Ch 2, dc in same st as join, dc in next 2 sts, 2 dc in next st, [dc in next 3 sts, 2 dc in next st] 11 times; join = 60 sts

Rnd 6: Ch 2, dc in same st as join, dc in next 3 sts, 2 dc in next st, [dc in next 4 sts, 2 dc in next st] 11 times; join = 72 sts

Rnd 7: Ch 2, dc in same st as join, dc in next 4 sts, 2 dc in next st, [dc in next 5 sts, 2 dc in next st] 11 times; join = 84 sts

Rnd 8: Ch 2, dc in same st as join, dc in next 12 sts, 2 dc in next st, [dc in next 13 sts, 2 dc in next st] 5 times; join = 90 sts

Rnds 9-35: Ch 2, dc in same st as join, dc in next 89 sts; join = 90 sts

Break off **CC6** and continue to work the remaining rounds with **CC4** as follows:

Rnd 36: Ch 1, sc in same st as join, ch 5, skip 2 sts, [sc in next st, ch 5, skip 2 sts] 28 times, sc in next st, ch 2, skip 2 sts, dc in beg st (counts as last arch) = 30 arches

Rnd 37: Ch 1, sc in same sp, 9 dc in next arch, sc in next arch, [ch 5, sc in next arch, 9 dc in next arch, sc in next arch] 9 times, ch 2, dc in beg st (counts as last arch) = 10 shells and 10 arches

Rnd 38: Ch 1, sc in same sp, crest across next shell, [sc in next arch, crest across next shell] 9 times; join = 10 crests

Fasten off and weave in the ends.

DRAWSTRING

Make 1. Work with a 9mm (M/N) hook and 3 strands of **CC1**.

To beg: Ch 140

Fasten off and trim the ends.

BANANAS

Make 2. Work in the round with a 3.75mm (F) hook and 1 strand of yarn, changing colors (**CC1** and **CC2**) as indicated in the pattern.

To beg: With **CC1**, ch 3, sl st in third ch from hook to form a ring (or start with a magic ring)

Rnd 1: Ch 1 (doesn't count as a st now and throughout), 6 sc in ring; join = 6 sts

Rnd 2: Ch 1, sc in same st as join, 2 sc in next st, [sc in next st, 2 sc in next st] 2 times, change to **CC2** and break off **CC1**; join = 9 sts

Rnd 3: With **CC2**, ch 1, sc in same st as join, sc in next st, hdc in next 6 sts, sc in next st; join = 9 sts

Rnd 4: Ch 1, sc in same st as join, sc in next st, 2 hdc in next st, hdc in next 4 sts, 2 hdc in next st, 2 sc in next st; join = 12 sts

Rnds 5-12: Ch 1, sc in same st as join, sc in next st, hdc in next 8 sts, sc in next 2 sts; join = 12 sts

Rnd 13: Ch 1, sc in same st as join, sc in next st, sc2tog, [sc in next 2 sts, sc2tog] 2 times; join = 9 sts

Rnd 14: Ch 1, sc in same st as join, sc in next 8 sts; join and stuff the banana = 9 sts

Rnd 15: Ch 1, sc in same st as join, [sc2tog] 4 times; join = 5 sts

Fasten off, leaving a long tail for sewing.

BANANA CUPS

Make 2. Work in spiral rounds with a 3.75mm (F) hook and 1 strand of **CC4**.

To beg: Ch 5, sl st in fifth ch from hook to form a ring

Rnd 1: Ch 1 (doesn't count as a st), 10 sc in ring; don't join now and throughout = 10 sts

Rnds 2-4: Sc in first st of previous rnd, sc in next 9 sts = 10 sts

Sl st in next st, fasten off and weave in the ends.

MONKEY HEAD

Make 1. Work with a 5.5mm (I) hook and 1 strand of **CC1**. Follow the head instructions of the Monkey Rug from the beginning to Row 6 (see Monkey Rug: Head). Continue to work edging as follows:

Edge: (RS) Ch 1 (doesn't count as a st), sc in first st, sc in next 21 sts, [ch 10, sc in next st] 3 times, sc in next 21 sts = 46 sts and 3 ch-10 loops

Fasten off, leaving a long tail for sewing.

MONKEY MUZZLE, FACE AND EARS

Follow the instructions for the muzzle, face and ears from the Monkey Pillow (see Monkey Pillow: Muzzle, Monkey Pillow: Face and Monkey Pillow: Ears).

ASSEMBLING TOY BAG

Position the head and the muzzle in the middle of the bag. Backstitch around the head edge using the long **CC1** tail. Using the long **MC** tail, whipstitch around the muzzle, leaving an opening at the end for stuffing. Stuff the muzzle and complete sewing (1).

Place the face above the muzzle with its straight edge right up against the muzzle. Using the long **MC** tail,

whipstitch across the bottom edge and backstitch around the remaining edge of the face (2).

Place the ears on each side of the head slightly above the muzzle. Using the long **CC1** tail, whipstitch each ear across the straight edge and backstitch around the remaining edge (2).

Chain stitch the eyes, nose and smile (3), following the instructions for the Monkey Pillow (see Monkey Pillow: Assembling Pillow).

If desired, make a small bow (see Common Shapes: Small Bow) using 1 strand of **CC2**. Place the bow onto the head and backstitch around the center (4).

Using a crochet hook, thread the drawstring through the arches of the bag under the shells (5).

Insert the ends of the drawstrings through the cups into banana openings. Using the long **CC2** tail, whipstitch around each banana opening to secure. Slide the cups down to cover the seams (6).

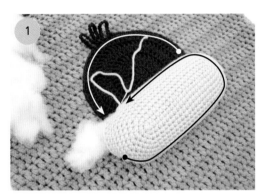

CRANKY THE CRAB

∿∿∿∿∿∿∿∿∿∿

Rug, Pillow, and Security Blanket

Like some children, crabs are independent and feisty. They like to do their own things and often get a bad reputation for being cranky. They just have their minds made up on what they want to do and don't like being interrupted.

When you think of the ocean and sandy beaches, I bet you think of our crusty friends, crabs. Most children find them fun and interesting, even though they are the best pinchers! Don't worry, Cranky the Crab has pincers made from yarn so they are soft and safe for kids to interact with. This adorable crab collection will lighten up your home or cottage with a fresh and crisp marine habitat.

CRAB RUG

FINISHED SIZE

42in x 30½in (106.7cm x 77.5cm)

HOOKS

3.75mm (F), 5mm (H),
5.5mm (I), 9mm (M/N)

YARN WEIGHT

4

NUMBER OF STRANDS

1 and 3

**GAUGE WITH 3 STRANDS
AND 9MM (M/N) HOOK**

9 dc x 4.5 rows = 4in x 4in (10cm x 10cm)

STITCH SUMMARY

Ch, sl st, sc, sc2tog, dc, join

SKILLS

Working in rows and in the round,
raw edge finishing, working across
the bottom of the foundation chain,
changing colors, blocking, sewing

LEFT-HANDED CROCHET

See Crochet Techniques:
Left-Handed Crochet

YARN

Abbreviation	Color	Amount
MC	Flamingo or Coral	1093-1421yd (1000-1300m)
CC1	Black	109-131yd (100-120m)
CC2	White	Small amount
CC3	Aquamarine	Small amount

BODY CHART

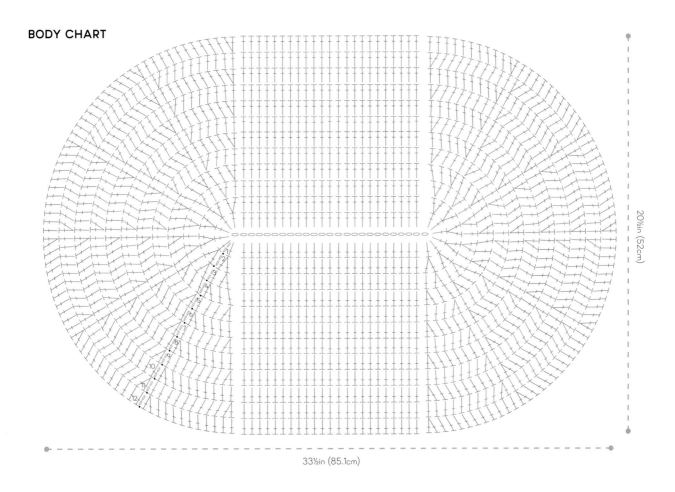

20½in (52cm)

33½in (85.1cm)

BODY

Make 1. Work in the round with a 9mm (M/N) hook and 3 strands of **MC**.

To beg: Ch 27

Rnd 1: Dc in third ch from hook (2 skipped chs don't count as a st), dc in next 23 chs, 6 dc in last ch, continue working across the bottom of the foundation ch, dc in next 23 chs, 5 dc in last ch; join = 58 sts

Rnd 2: Ch 2 (doesn't count as a st now and throughout), 2 dc in same st as join, dc in next 23 sts, 2 dc in next 6 sts, dc in next 23 sts, 2 dc in next 5 sts; join = 70 sts

Rnd 3: Ch 2, dc in same st as join, 2 dc in next st, dc in next 23 sts, [dc in next st, 2 dc in next st] 6 times, dc in next 23 sts, [dc in next st, 2 dc in next st] 5 times; join = 82 sts

Rnd 4: Ch 2, 2 dc in same st as join, dc in next 25 sts, [2 dc in next st, dc in next 2 sts] 6 times, dc in next 23 sts, [2 dc in next st, dc in next 2 sts] 5 times; join = 94 sts

Rnd 5: Ch 2, dc in same st as join, dc in next 2 sts, 2 dc in next st, dc in next 23 sts, [dc in next 3 sts, 2 dc in next st] 6 times, dc in next 23 sts, [dc in next 3 sts, 2 dc in next st] 5 times; join = 106 sts

Rnd 6: Ch 2, 2 dc in same st as join, dc in next 27 sts, [2 dc in next st, dc in next 4 sts] 6 times, dc in next 23 sts, [2 dc in next st, dc in next 4 sts] 5 times; join = 118 sts

Rnd 7: Ch 2, dc in same st as join, dc in next 4 sts, 2 dc in next st, dc in next 23 sts, [dc in next 5 sts, 2 dc in next st] 6 times, dc in next 23 sts, [dc in next 5 sts, 2 dc in next st] 5 times; join = 130 sts

Rnd 8: Ch 2, 2 dc in same st as join, dc in next 29 sts, [2 dc in next st, dc in next 6 sts] 6 times, dc in next 23 sts, [2 dc in next st, dc in next 6 sts] 5 times; join = 142 sts

Rnd 9: Ch 2, dc in same st as join, dc in next 6 sts, 2 dc in next st, dc in next 23 sts, [dc in next 7 sts, 2 dc in next st] 6 times, dc in next 23 sts, [dc in next 7 sts, 2 dc in next st] 5 times; join = 154 sts

Rnd 10: Ch 2, 2 dc in same st as join, dc in next 31 sts, [2 dc in next st, dc in next 8 sts] 6 times, dc in next 23 sts, [2 dc in next st, dc in next 8 sts] 5 times; join = 166 sts

Rnd 11: Ch 2, dc in same st as join, dc in next 8 sts, 2 dc in next st, dc in next 23 sts, [dc in next 9 sts, 2 dc in next st] 6 times, dc in next 23 sts, [dc in next 9 sts, 2 dc in next st] 5 times; join = 178 sts

Rnd 12: Ch 2, 2 dc in same st as join, dc in next 33 sts, [2 dc in next st, dc in next 10 sts] 6 times, dc in next 23 sts, [2 dc in next st, dc in next 10 sts] 5 times; join = 190 sts

Fasten off and weave in the ends.

> **Use stitch markers to indicate the start of spiral rounds.**

EYES

BASIC EYES

Make 2. Follow the instructions for the basic eyes (see Common Shapes: Basic Eyes). Use a 5mm (H) hook with 1 strand of **CC1** for the pupils and a 3.75mm (F) hook with 1 strand of **CC2** with for the highlights.

IRISES

Make 2. Work in spiral rounds with a 5mm (H) hook and 1 strand of **CC3**.

To beg: Ch 3, sl st in third ch from hook to form a ring (or start with a magic ring)

Rnd 1: Ch 1 (doesn't count as a st), 6 sc in ring; don't join now and throughout = 6 sts

Rnd 2: 2 sc in first st of previous rnd, 2 sc in next 5 sts = 12 sts

Rnd 3: 2 sc in each st around = 24 sts

Rnd 4: Sc in each st around = 24 sts

Sl st in next st, fasten off, leaving a long tail for sewing.

ASSEMBLING EYES

Place the basic eyes on top of the irises and backstitch around using **CC1**.

EYELIDS

Make 2. Work in rows from the top down, using a 5.5mm (I) hook and 1 strand of **MC**.

To beg: Ch 8

Row 1: (RS) 2 sc in second ch from hook (the skipped ch doesn't count as a st), sc in next 5 chs, 2 sc in last ch; turn = 9 sts

Row 2: (WS) Ch 1 (doesn't count as a st now and throughout), 2 sc in first st, sc in next 7 sts, 2 sc in last st; turn = 11 sts

Row 3: (RS) Ch 1, 2 sc in first st, sc in next 9 sts, 2 sc in last st; turn = 13 sts

Row 4: (WS) Ch 1, 2 sc in first st, sc in next 11 sts, 2 sc in last st; turn = 15 sts

Row 5: (RS) Ch 1, 2 sc in first st, sc in next 13 sts, 2 sc in last st; don't turn = 17 sts

Rotate the work in a clockwise direction (or in a counter-clockwise direction for left-handed crochet) and continue to work edging as follows:

Edge: (RS) Ch 1, sc evenly across the raw edges towards the beg of Row 5

Fasten off, leaving a long tail for sewing.

EYESTALKS

Make 2. Work in the round with a 9mm (M/N) hook and 3 strands of yarn, changing colors (**CC2** and **MC**) as indicated in the pattern.

To beg: With **CC2**, ch 3, sl st in third ch from hook to form a ring (or start with a magic ring)

Rnd 1: Ch 1 (doesn't count as a st now and throughout), 6 sc in ring; join = 6 sts

Rnd 2: Ch 1, 2 sc in same st as join, 2 sc in next 5 sts; join = 12 sts

Rnd 3: Ch 1, 2 sc in same st as join, 2 sc in next 11 sts, change to **MC** and break off **CC2**; join = 24 sts

Rnd 4: With **MC**, ch 1, sc in same st as join, sc in next 20 sts, ch 6, sc in second ch from hook, sc in next 4 chs, sc in next 2 sts of circle; turn, (WS) skip 2 sc just made, sc in next 5 sts; turn, (RS) ch 1, sc in first st, sc in next 4 sts, sc in last st of circle; join = 24 sts around circle and 3 rows of sideways sts

Fasten off and weave in the ends.

ASSEMBLING EYESTALKS

Position the eye along the bottom **CC2** edge of the eyestalk and backstitch around using **CC3** (1).

Place the curved edge of the eyelid along the top edge of the eyestalk, covering part of the eye. Whipstitch around the curved edge using **MC** (2). Finish the second eyestalk in the same manner.

LEGS

Make 6. Work in rows with a 9mm (M/N) hook and 3 strands of **MC**.

To beg: Ch 11

Row 1: (WS) Sc in second ch from hook (the skipped ch doesn't count as a st), sc in next 8 chs, 3 sc in last ch, continue working across the bottom of the foundation ch, sc in next 9 chs; turn = 21 sts

Row 2: (RS) Ch 1 (doesn't count as a st), sc in first st, sc in next 8 sts, 2 sc in next 3 sts, sc in next 9 sts = 24 sts

Fasten off, leaving a long single strand of **MC** for sewing. Weave in the other ends.

IRIS CHART

2½in (6.3cm)

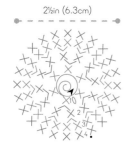

EYESTALK CHART

4¼in (10.8cm)

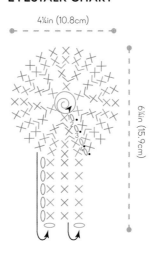

6¼in (15.9cm)

EYELID CHART

4¼in (10.8cm)

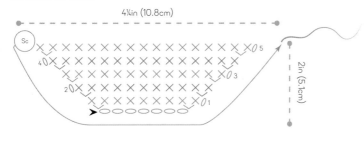

2in (5.1cm)

LEG CHART

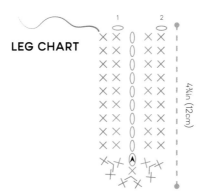

4¾in (12cm)

PINCERS

Make 1 left and 1 right pincer. Work in rows with a 9mm (M/N) hook and 3 strands of **MC**.

LEFT PINCER

To beg: Ch 12

Row 1: (RS) 2 dc in fourth ch from hook (3 skipped chs count as first dc), dc in next 7 chs, 6 dc in last ch, continue working across the bottom of the foundation ch, dc in next 7 chs, 3 dc in last ch; turn = 26 sts

Row 2: (WS) Ch 3 (counts as first dc now and throughout), 2 dc in first st, dc in next 9 sts, 2 dc in next 6 sts, dc in next 9 sts, 3 dc in last st; turn = 36 sts

Row 3: (RS) Ch 3, 2 dc in first st, dc in next 11 sts, [2 dc in next st, dc in next st] 6 times, dc in next 11 sts, 3 dc in last st; turn = 46 sts

Row 4: (WS) Ch 3, 2 dc in first st, dc in next 13 sts, [2 dc in next st, dc in next 2 sts] 6 times, dc in next 13 sts, 3 dc in last st; turn = 56 sts

Row 5: (RS) Ch 1 (doesn't count as a st), sc in first st, sc in next 26 sts; work arm – ch 21, sc in second ch from hook, sc in next 19 chs, sc in next 2 sts of pincer; turn, (WS) skip 2 sc just made, [sc in next 2 sts of arm, sc2tog] 5 times; turn, (RS) ch 1, don't skip st, [sc2tog, sc in next st of arm] 5 times, sc in next st of pincer; continue to work across pincer, sc in next 26 sts; don't turn = 56 sts of pincer and 3 rows of arm

To finish, rotate the work in a clockwise direction (or in a counter-clockwise direction for left-handed crochet), ch 1, sc evenly across the raw edges towards the beg of Row 5.

Fasten off and weave in the ends. Spray block if necessary (see General Techniques: Blocking).

RIGHT PINCER

Work from the beginning to Row 4, as for left pincer. Continue the next row as follows:

Row 5: (RS) Ch 1 (doesn't count as a st), sc in first st, sc in next 26 sts; work arm – ch 11 loosely, 2 sc in second ch from hook, sc in next ch, [2 sc in next ch, sc in next ch] 4 times, sc in next 2 sts of pincer; turn, (WS) skip 2 sc just made, [sc in next 2 sts of arm, 2 sc in next st] 5 times; turn, (RS) ch 1, sc in first st, sc in next 19 sts of arm, sc in next st of pincer; continue to work across pincer, sc in next 26 sts; don't turn = 56 sts of pincer and 3 rows of arm

Finish as for left pincer.

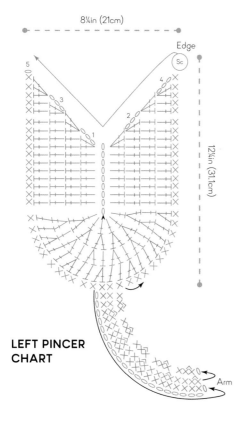

LEFT PINCER CHART

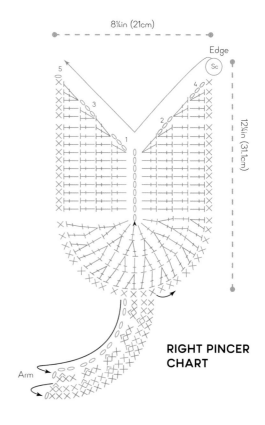

RIGHT PINCER CHART

BOW (OPTIONAL)

Make 1. Follow the instructions for the big bow using **CC1** (see Common Shapes: Big Bow).

ASSEMBLING RUG

Place the eyestalks tight up against the top edge of the body, leaving a space of 29 stitches in the middle between the eyestalks (3). Whipstitch across RS using **MC**, don't break off yarn.

Place 3 legs on each side of the body, leaving a space of 47 stitches in the middle of the bottom edge and a space of 2 stitches between the legs in each group (3). Whipstitch across RS using **MC**, don't break off yarn.

Place the pincers on each side of the body between the legs and the eyestalks (3).

Whipstitch the pincers across the corresponding edges of the body and the eyestalks using **MC** (4), don't break off yarn.

Flip the rug to WS and whipstitch across the same edges using **MC** tails from each piece (5).

Thread the needle with 2 strands of **CC1** and chain stitch a crooked smile approximately between the fourth and the sixth rounds below the body edge (6).

If using, position the bow below the crooked smile and backstitch around the center with a single strand of **CC1** (6). Keep the side edges of the bow unattached or whipstitch the corners to keep them in place.

If desired, make a removable non-slip lining (see General Techniques: Non-Slip Lining).

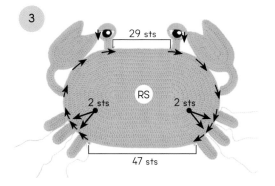

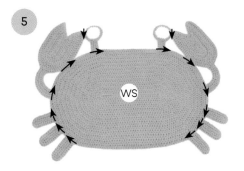

CRAB PILLOW

SKILL LEVEL

FINISHED SIZE
26in x 20in (66cm x 50.8cm)

HOOKS
3.75mm (F), 4mm (G), 5mm (H),
5.5mm (I), 6mm (J)

YARN WEIGHT
4

NUMBER OF STRANDS
1 and 2

**GAUGE WITH 1 STRAND
AND 5.5MM (I) HOOK**
14 sc x 16 rows = 4in x 4in (10cm x 10cm)

STITCH SUMMARY
Ch, sl st, sc, sc2tog, hdc, dc, join

SKILLS
Working in rows and in the round,
raw edge finishing, working across
the bottom of the foundation
chain, changing colors, sewing

LEFT-HANDED CROCHET
See Crochet Techniques:
Left-Handed Crochet

YARN

Abbreviation	Color	Amount
MC	Flamingo or Coral	874-929yd (800-850m)
CC4	Green (optional)	Small amount

All other contrasting colors are the same as
for the Crab Rug (small amount of each).

PILLOW BASE

Make 1 front and 1 back using 1 strand of **MC** with a 5.5mm (I) hook. Follow the instructions for the oval pillow base (see Common Shapes: Oval Pillow Base). Fasten off after finishing the back piece, but don't break off yarn after finishing the front piece.

Holding the front and the back pieces together with WS facing each other, work the joining round through both pieces of fabric at the same time, using the working yarn from the front piece.

Rnd 26: Ch 1 (doesn't count as a st), sc in same st as previous sl st, sc in next 180 sts, stuff the pillow, sc in next 15 sts; join = 196 sts

Fasten off and weave in the ends.

EYES

BASIC EYES

Make 2. Follow the instructions for the basic eyes (see Common Shapes: Basic Eyes). Work with a 4mm (G) hook and 1 strand of **CC1** for the pupils and 1 strand of **CC2** for the highlights.

IRISES

Make 2. Work in the round with a 5mm (H) hook and 1 strand of **CC3**.

To beg: Ch 3, sl st in third ch from hook to form a ring (or start with a magic ring)

Rnd 1: Ch 1 (doesn't count as a st now and throughout), 8 hdc in ring; join = 8 sts

Rnd 2: Ch 1, 2 hdc in same st as join, 2 hdc in next 7 sts; join = 16 sts

Rnd 3: Ch 1, sc in same st as join, sc in next 2 sts, 2 sc in next st, [sc in next 3 sts, 2 sc in next st] 3 times; join = 20 sts

Fasten off, leaving a long tail for sewing.

OUTER EYES

Make 2. Follow the instructions for the irises in the Crab Rug (see Crab Rug: Eyes), using a 5.5mm (I) hook and 1 strand of **CC2**.

ASSEMBLING EYES

Place the basic eyes on top of the irises and backstitch around using **CC1**. Place the irises on top of the outer eyes and backstitch around using **CC3**.

EYELIDS

Make 2. Work in spiral rounds with a 5.5mm (I) hook and 1 strand of **MC**.

To beg: Ch 3, sl st in third ch from hook to form a ring (or start with a magic ring)

Rnd 1: Ch 1 (doesn't count as a st), 6 sc in ring; don't join now and throughout = 6 sts

Rnd 2: 2 sc in first st of previous rnd, 2 sc in next 5 sts = 12 sts

Rnd 3: [Sc in next st, 2 sc in next st] 6 times = 18 sts

Rnd 4: [Sc in next 2 sts, 2 sc in next st] 6 times = 24 sts

Rnd 5: [Sc in next 3 sts, 2 sc in next st] 6 times = 30 sts

Rnd 6: [Sc in next 4 sts, 2 sc in next st] 6 times = 36 sts

Rnds 7-10: Sc in each st around = 36 sts

Sl st in next st, fasten off, leaving a long tail for sewing.

EYESTALKS

Make 2. Work in spiral rounds with a 5.5mm (I) hook and 1 strand of **MC**. Stuff as you go.

To beg: Ch 3, sl st in third ch from hook to form a ring (or start with a magic ring)

Rnds 1-5: Same as Rnds 1-5 of eyelids

Rnds 6-10: Sc in each st around = 30 sts

Rnd 11: [Sc in next 3 sts, sc2tog] = 24 sts

Rnd 12: [Sc in next 2 sts, sc2tog] = 18 sts

Rnd 13: [Sc in next st, sc2tog] = 12 sts

Rnds 14-19: Sc in each st around = 12 sts

Sl st in next st, fasten off, leaving a long tail for sewing.

Use stitch markers to indicate the start of spiral rounds.

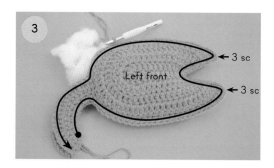

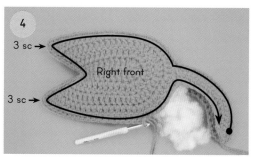

ASSEMBLING EYESTALKS

Position the eyes on the eyestalks and backstitch around using **CC2** (1).

Position the eyelids on top of the eyestalks, partially covering the eyes and backstitch around using **MC** (2).

PINCERS

Make 2. Work in rows with a 6mm (J) hook and 2 strands of **MC**.

FRONT AND BACK

Make 2 pieces following the left pincer instructions in the Crab Rug from the beginning to Row 5 (see Crab Rug: Left Pincer).

Fasten off and weave in the ends. Label the first piece as "Left front" and label the second piece as "Right back".

Make 2 pieces following the right pincer instructions in the Crab Rug from the beginning to Row 5 (see Crab Rug: Right Pincer).

Fasten off and weave in the ends. Label the first piece as "Left back" and label the second piece as "Right front".

ASSEMBLING LEFT PINCER

Place the left-front piece on top of the left-back piece with WS together. Join yarn at the bottom edge of the arm and work sc around the edge through the stitches of both pieces to join them, placing 3 sc in corners for increasing. Stuff lightly as you go (3).

Don't join the end opening of the arm. Fasten off, leaving a long single strand of **MC** for sewing, hiding all the other ends inside of the arm.

ASSEMBLING RIGHT PINCER

Place the right-front piece on top of the right-back piece with WS together. Join yarn at the bottom edge of the arm and work sc around the edge through the stitches of both pieces to join them, placing 3 sc in corners for increasing. Stuff lightly as you go (4).

Don't join the end opening of the arm. Fasten off, leaving a long single strand of **MC** for sewing, hiding all the other ends inside of the arm.

LEGS

Make 6. Work in spiral rounds with a 5.5mm (I) hook and 1 strand of **MC**. Stuff as you go.

To beg: Ch 3, sl st in third ch from hook to form a ring (or start with a magic ring)

Rnd 1: Ch 1 (doesn't count as a st), 6 sc in ring; don't join now and throughout = 6 sts

Rnd 2: 2 sc in first st of previous rnd, 2 sc in next 5 sts = 12 sts

Rnd 3: [Sc in next st, 2 sc in next st] 6 times = 18 sts

Rnds 4-13: Sc in each st around = 18 sts

Sl st in next st, fasten off, leaving a long tail for sewing.

BOW (OPTIONAL)

Make 1. Follow the instructions for the small bow using **CC4** (see Common Shapes: Small Bow).

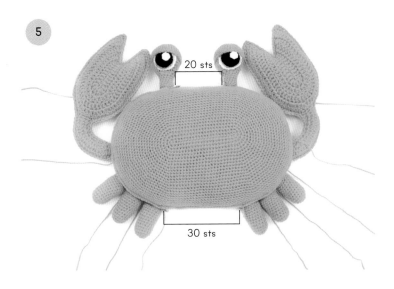

5

20 sts

30 sts

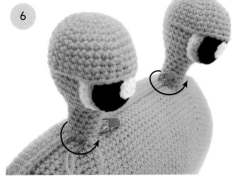

6

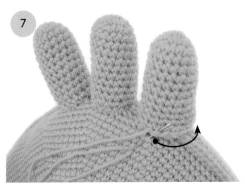

7

8

9

ASSEMBLING PILLOW

Place the eyestalks tight up against the top edge of the body (pillow base), leaving a space of 20 stitches in the middle between the eyestalks (5). Whipstitch twice around using **MC** (6).

Place 3 legs on each side of the body (pillow base), leaving a space of 30 stitches in the middle of the bottom edge and no spaces between the legs in each group (5). Whipstitch twice around using **MC** (7).

Place the pincers on each side of the body (pillow base) between the legs and the eyestalks (5). Whipstitch the pincers twice around the corresponding edges of the body and the eyestalks using **MC** (8).

Thread the needle with a single strand of **CC1** and chain stitch a crooked smile below the right eye (9).

If using, position the bow below the crooked smile and backstitch around the center using **CC4** (9).

CRAB SECURITY BLANKET

SKILL LEVEL

FINISHED SIZE
19½in x 19½in (49.5cm x 49.5cm)

HOOKS
3.75mm (F), 5mm (H), 6mm (J)

YARN WEIGHT
4

NUMBER OF STRANDS
1 and 2

**GAUGE WITH 1 STRAND
AND 5MM (H) HOOK**
15 dc x 8 rows = 4in x 4in (10cm x 10cm)

STITCH SUMMARY
Ch, sl st, sc, sc2tog, hdc,
dc, tr, picot, join

SKILLS
Working in rows and in the round,
raw edge finishing, changing
colors, blocking, sewing

LEFT-HANDED CROCHET
Fully compatible

YARN

Abbreviation	Color	Amount
CC3	Aquamarine	240-273yd (220-250m)
CC4	Variegated Blue	207-240yd (190-220m)

All other colors are the same as for the
Crab Rug (small amount of each).

BLANKET

Make 1. Work in rows with a 5mm (H) hook and 1 strand of yarn, changing colors (**CC3** and **CC4**) as indicated in the pattern.

To beg: With **CC4**, ch 71

Row 1: (WS) Sc in second ch from hook (the skipped ch doesn't count as a st), sc in next 69 chs; change to **CC3** and turn = 70 sts

Row 2: (RS) With **CC3**, ch 1 (doesn't count as a st now and throughout), sc in first st, hdc in next st, dc in next 2 sts, tr in next 2 sts, dc in next 2 sts, hdc in next 2 sts, [sc in next 2 sts, hdc in next 2 sts, dc in next 2 sts, tr in next 2 sts, dc in next 2 sts, hdc in next 2 sts] 4 times, sc in next 2 sts, hdc in next 2 sts, dc in next 2 sts, tr in next 2 sts, dc in next 2 sts, hdc in next st, sc in next st; turn = 70 sts

Row 3: (WS) Ch 1, sc in first st, hdc in next st, dc in next 2 sts, tr in next 2 sts, dc in next 2 sts, hdc in next 2 sts, sc in next 2 sts, [hdc in next 2 sts, dc in next 2 sts, tr in next 2 sts, dc in next 2 sts, hdc in next 2 sts, sc in next 2 sts] 4 times, hdc in next 2 sts, dc in next 2 sts, tr in next 2 sts, dc in next 2 sts, hdc in next st, sc in next st; change to **CC4** and turn = 70 sts

Row 4: (RS) With **CC4**, ch 1, sc in first st, sc in next 69 sts; turn = 70 sts

Row 5: (WS) Ch 1, sc in first st, sc in next 69 sts; change to **CC3** and turn = 70 sts

Row 6: (RS) With **CC3**, ch 3 (counts as first dc now and throughout), skip first st, dc in next st, hdc in next 2 sts, [sc in next 2 sts, hdc in next 2 sts, dc in next 2 sts, tr in next 2 sts, dc in next 2 sts, hdc in next 2 sts] 5 times, sc in next 2 sts, hdc in next 2 sts, dc in next 2 sts; turn = 70 sts

BLANKET CHART

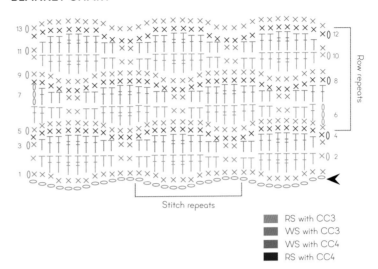

Stitch repeats

Row repeats

- RS with CC3
- WS with CC3
- WS with CC4
- RS with CC4

Row 7: (WS) Ch 3, skip first st, dc in next st, hdc in next 2 sts, sc in next 2 sts, [hdc in next 2 sts, dc in next 2 sts, tr in next 2 sts, dc in next 2 sts, hdc in next 2 sts, sc in next 2 sts] 5 times, hdc in next 2 sts, dc in next 2 sts; change to **CC4** and turn = 70 sts

Rows 8-9: Repeat Rows 4-5

Rows 10-12: Repeat Rows 2-4

Rows 13-60: Repeat Rows 5-12 in established pattern until the blanket is visually square, ending after Row 12. Break off **CC3**

Edge: With **CC4**, ch 1, *sc in next 2 sts, picot, repeat from * around, placing 3 sc in each corner for increasing; join

Fasten off and weave in the ends, wet block the blanket (see General Techniques: Blocking).

BODY WITH LEGS

Make 1. Work in spiral rounds with a 6mm (J) hook and 2 strands of **MC**.

To beg: Ch 3, sl st in third ch from hook to form a ring (or start with a magic ring)

Rnd 1: Ch 1 (doesn't count as a st), 6 sc in ring, don't join now and throughout = 6 sts

Rnd 2: 2 sc in first st of previous rnd, 2 sc in next 5 sts = 12 sts

Rnd 3: [Sc in next st, 2 sc in next st] 6 times = 18 sts

Rnd 4: [Sc in next 2 sts, 2 sc in next st] 6 times = 24 sts

Rnd 5: [Sc in next 3 sts, 2 sc in next st] 6 times = 30 sts

Rnds 6-8: Sc in each st around = 30 sts

Legs: Sl st in next st, [ch 7, sc in second ch from hook, sc in next 5 chs, sc in next 2 sts of body] 3 times, sc in next 6 sts, [ch 7, sc in second ch from hook, sc in next 5 chs, sc in next 2 sts of body] 2 times, ch 7, sc in second ch from hook, sc in next 5 chs, sl st in next st of body, leave the remaining stitches unworked and mark them as "Front" = 6 legs

Fasten off, leaving a long tail for sewing.

PINCERS

Make 2. Work in rows with a 6mm (J) hook and 2 strands of **MC**.

To beg: Ch 8

Row 1: (WS) Sc in second ch from hook (the skipped ch doesn't count as a st), sc in next 2 chs, 3 sc in next ch, sc in next 3 chs; turn = 9 sts

Row 2: (RS) Ch 1 (doesn't count as a st), 3 sc in first st, sc in next 3 sts, ch 9, dc in fourth ch from hook, dc in next 5 chs, skip next st of Row 1, sc in next 3 sts, 3 sc in next st = 18 sts

Fasten off and weave in the ends.

EYELIDS

Make 2. Work in spiral rounds with a 3.75mm (F) hook and 1 strand of **MC**.

To beg: Ch 3, sl st in third ch from hook to form a ring (or start with a magic ring)

Rnd 1: Ch 1 (doesn't count as a st), 6 sc in ring; don't join now and throughout = 6 sts

Rnd 2: Sc in first st of previous rnd, 2 sc in next st, [sc in next st, 2 sc in next st] 2 times = 9 sts

Rnd 3: [Sc in next 2 sts, 2 sc in next st] 3 times = 12 sts

Rnd 4: [Sc in next 3 sts, 2 sc in next st] 3 times = 15 sts

Rnd 5: [Sc in next 4 sts, 2 sc in next st] 3 times = 18 sts

Sl st in next st, fasten off, leaving a long tail for sewing.

EYESTALKS

Make 2. Work in spiral rounds with a 3.75mm (F) hook and 1 strand of yarn, changing colors (**CC2** and **MC**) as indicated in the pattern.

To beg: With **CC2**, ch 3, sl st in third ch from hook to form a ring (or start with a magic ring)

Rnd 1: Ch 1 (doesn't count as a st), 6 sc in ring, don't join now and throughout = 6 sts

Rnd 2: 2 sc in first st of previous rnd, sc in next st, [2 sc in next st, sc in next st] 2 times = 9 sts

Rnds 3-4: Sc in each st around = 9 sts

Rnd 5: [Sc in next st, sc2tog] 3 times, change to **MC**, break off **CC2** = 6 sts

Rnd 6: With **MC**, sl st in next st, ch 1, sc in same st as sl st, sc in next 5 sts = 6 sts

Rnds 7-8: Sc in first st of previous rnd, sc in next 5 sts = 6 sts

Sl st in next st, fasten off, leaving a long tail for sewing. Stuff eyestalks.

ASSEMBLING EYESTALKS

Thread the needle with a single strand of **CC1** and stitch a French knot on the front of each eyestalk (1 and 2). Finish off and weave the ends into the inside of the eyestalk.

Position the eyelids on the top of the eyestalks, covering the back side and backstitch around using **MC** (3).

Use a chopstick or a knitting needle for stuffing eyestalks.

PINCER CHART

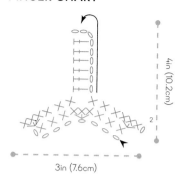

4in (10.2cm)

3in (7.6cm)

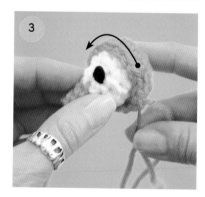

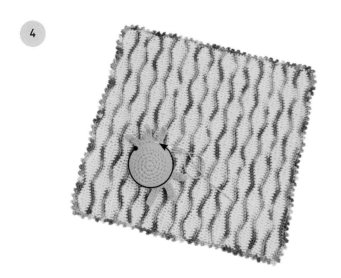

ASSEMBLING SECURITY BLANKET

With RS facing, position the body on the blanket as you like. Whipstitch around the edge of the body with **MC**, leaving an opening at the end for stuffing (4). Don't sew around the edges of the legs.

Stuff body and complete sewing (5).

Place the pincers right up against the front edge of the body and whipstitch across the corresponding edges using **MC** (6). Don't sew around the edges of the pincers.

Position the eyestalks on the top of the body, leaving 1 round space between them (7). Whipstitch each eyestalk around the edge using **MC**.

Thread the needle with a single strand of **CC1** and chain stitch a crooked smile below the right eye (8).

TOPS THE DINOSAUR

Rug, Pillow, and Book Bag

Welcome to the majestic world of dinosaurs! These mysterious creatures inhabited our planet a long time ago, but they are still the most attractive and noble animals loved by everyone. What happened to all of the dinosaurs? Any child would enjoy a bedtime story to discover the answers to all of their dinosaur questions!

Create a unique prehistoric bedroom by decorating it with this triceratops set. The matching rug, pillow, and book bag will fill bedtime with lasting memories.

DINOSAUR RUG

SKILL LEVEL

FINISHED SIZE
39in x 34½in (99cm x 87.6cm)

HOOKS
5.5mm (I), 9mm (M/N)

YARN WEIGHT
4

NUMBER OF STRANDS
1, 2, and 3

**GAUGE WITH 3 STRANDS
AND 9MM (M/N) HOOK**
9 dc x 4.5 rows = 4in x 4in (10cm x 10cm)

STITCH SUMMARY
Ch, sl st, sc, beg sc, hdc,
dc, dc3tog, picot, join

SKILLS
Working in rows and in the round,
working across the bottom of
the foundation chain, sewing

LEFT-HANDED CROCHET
Fully compatible

YARN

Abbreviation	Color	Amount
MC	Forest Green	1093-1312yd (1000-1200m)
CC1	Soft Taupe	218-273yd (200-250m)
CC2	Camo	218-273yd (200-250m)
CC3	Gold (optional)	93-109yd (85-100m)
CC4	Coffee	Small amount
CC5	Natural White	93-109yd (85-100m)

HEAD

Make 1. Work in the round with a 9mm (M/N) hook and 3 strands of **MC**.

NOTE: Ch-2 sps are not included in the total stitch count.

To beg: Ch 3, sl st in third ch from hook to form a ring (or start with a magic ring)

Rnd 1: Ch 2 (doesn't count as a st now and throughout), 12 dc in ring; join = 12 sts

Rnd 2: Ch 2, 2 dc in same st as join, 2 dc in next 11 sts; join = 24 sts

Rnd 3: Ch 2, dc in same st as join, 2 dc in next st, [dc in next st, 2 dc in next st] 11 times; join = 36 sts

Rnd 4: Ch 2, 2 dc in same st as join, dc in next 2 sts, [2 dc in next st, dc in next 2 sts] 11 times; join = 48 sts

Rnd 5: Ch 2, dc in same st as join, dc in next 2 sts, 2 dc in next st, [dc in next 3 sts, 2 dc in next st] 11 times; join = 60 sts

Rnd 6: Ch 2, 2 dc in same st as join, dc in next 4 sts, [2 dc in next st, dc in next 4 sts] 11 times; join = 72 sts

Rnd 7: Ch 2, dc in same st as join, dc in next 4 sts, 2 dc in next st, [dc in next 5 sts, 2 dc in next st] 11 times; join = 84 sts

Rnd 8: Ch 2, 2 dc in same st as join, dc in next 6 sts, [2 dc in next st, dc in next 6 sts] 11 times; join = 96 sts

Rnd 9: Ch 2, dc in same st as join, dc in next 6 sts, 2 dc in next st, [dc in next 7 sts, 2 dc in next st] 11 times; join = 108 sts

Rnd 10: Ch 2, 2 dc in same st as join, dc in next 8 sts, [2 dc in next st, dc in next 8 sts] 11 times; join = 120 sts

Rnd 11: Ch 2, dc in same st as join, dc in next 8 sts, 2 dc in next st, [dc in next 9 sts, 2 dc in next st] 11 times; join = 132 sts

Rnd 12: Ch 2, 2 dc in same st as join, dc in next 15 sts, (2 dc, ch 2, 2 dc) in next st, [dc in next 10 sts, (2 dc, ch 2, 2 dc) in next st] 8 times, dc in next 5 sts, [2 dc in next st, dc in next 10 sts] 2 times; join = 162 sts

Rnd 13: Ch 2, dc in same st as join, dc in next 10 sts, 2 dc in next st, skip st, dc in next 6 sts, (2 dc, ch 2, 2 dc) in next ch-2 sp, dc in next 6 sts, [skip 2 sts, dc in next 6 sts, (2 dc, ch 2, 2 dc) in next ch-2 sp, dc in next 6 sts] 8 times, skip st, [dc in next 11 sts, 2 dc in next st] 2 times; join = 183 sts

Rnd 14: Ch 2, 2 dc in same st as join, dc in next 12 sts, skip st, dc in next 7 sts, (2 dc, ch 2, 2 dc) in next ch-2 sp, dc in next 7 sts, [skip 2 sts, dc in next 7 sts, (2 dc, ch 2, 2 dc) in next ch-2 sp, dc in next 7 sts] 8 times, skip st, [2 dc in next st, dc in next 12 sts] 2 times; join = 204 sts

Rnd 15: Ch 2, dc in same st as join, dc in next 12 sts, 2 dc in next st, skip st, dc in next 8 sts, (2 dc, ch 2, 2 dc) in next ch-2 sp, dc in next 8 sts, [skip 2 sts, dc in next 8 sts, (2 dc, ch 2, 2 dc) in next ch-2 sp, dc in next 8 sts] 8 times, skip st, [dc in next 13 sts, 2 dc in next st] 2 times; join = 225 sts

Rnd 16: Ch 2, 2 dc in same st as join, dc in next 14 sts, skip st, dc in next 9 sts, (2 dc, ch 2, 2 dc) in next ch-2 sp, dc in next 9 sts, [skip 2 sts, dc in next 9 sts, (2 dc, ch 2, 2 dc) in next ch-2 sp, dc in next 9 sts] 8 times, skip st, [2 dc in next st, dc in next 14 sts] 2 times; join = 246 sts

Rnd 17: Ch 2, dc in same st as join, dc in next 14 sts, 2 dc in next st, skip st, dc in next 10 sts, (2 dc, ch 2, 2 dc) in next ch-2 sp, dc in next 10 sts, [skip 2 sts, dc in next 10 sts, (2 dc, ch 2, 2 dc) in next ch-2 sp, dc in next 10 sts] 8 times, skip st, [dc in next 15 sts, 2 dc in next st] 2 times; join = 267 sts

Skip 29 sts and place **Marker A** in next ch-2 sp, fasten off and weave in the ends. Continue to work edging with a 9mm (M/N) hook and 3 strands of **CC2**.

Edge: (RS) Beg sc in sp with **Marker A** and remove the marker, (picot, sc) in same sp, sc in next 11 sts, [skip 2 sts, sc in next 11 sts, (2 sc, picot, sc) in next ch-2 sp, sc in next 11 sts] 7 times, skip 2 sts, sc in next 11 sts, (2 sc, picot) in next ch-2 sp = 201 sts and 9 picots

Fasten off and weave in the ends.

Spray block the head if necessary (see General Techniques: Blocking).

HEAD CHART

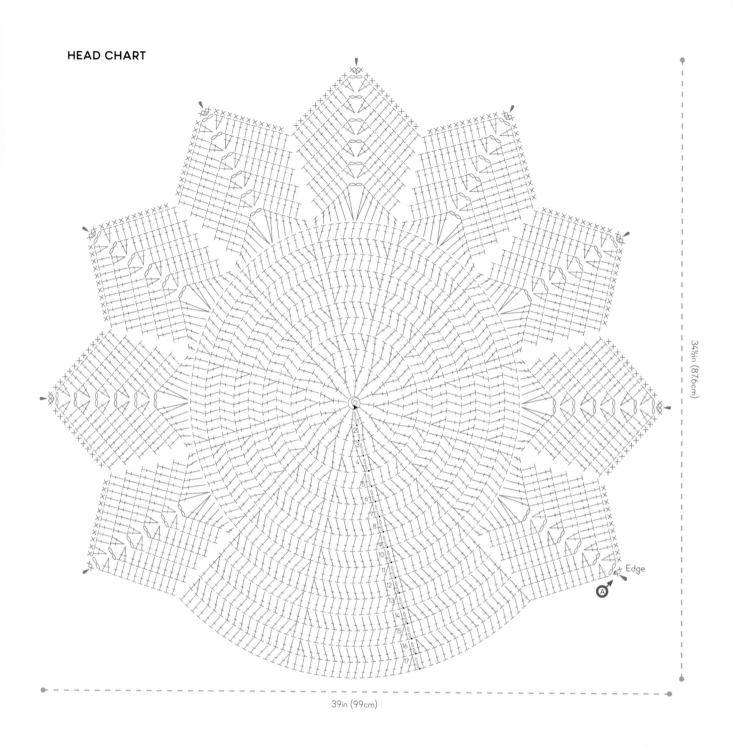

34½in (87.6cm)

Edge

A

39in (99cm)

HORN CHART

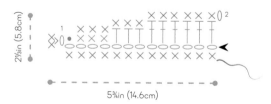

2¼in (5.8cm)

5¾in (14.6cm)

MUZZLE

Make 1. Work in the round with a 9mm (M/N) hook and 2 strands of **CC1**.

To beg: Ch 29

Rnd 1: Dc in third ch from hook (2 skipped chs don't count as a st), dc in next 25 chs, 6 dc in last ch, continue working across the bottom of the foundation ch, dc in next 25 chs, 5 dc in last ch; join = 62 sts

Rnd 2: Ch 2 (doesn't count as a st now and throughout), 2 dc in same st as join, dc in next 12 sts, 3 dc in next st (**bottom point**), dc in next 12 sts, 2 dc in next 6 sts, dc in next 11 sts, dc3tog (**center top**), dc in next 11 sts, 2 dc in next 5 sts; join = 74 sts

Rnd 3: Ch 2, 2 dc in same st as join, dc in next 14 sts, 3 dc in next st (**bottom point**), dc in next 13 sts, [dc in next st, 2 dc in next st] 6 times, dc in next 10 sts, dc3tog (**center top**), dc in next 10 sts, [2 dc in next st, dc in next st] 5 times; join = 86 sts

Rnd 4: Ch 2, dc in same st as join, dc in next st, 2 dc in next st, dc in next 14 sts, 3 dc in next st (**bottom point**), dc in next 14 sts, [2 dc in next st, dc in next 2 sts] 6 times, dc in next 9 sts, dc3tog (**center top**), dc in next 9 sts, [dc in next 2 sts, 2 dc in next st] 5 times; join = 98 sts

Rnd 5: Ch 2, 2 dc in same st as join, dc in next 18 sts, 3 dc in next st (**bottom point**), dc in next 15 sts, [dc in next 3 sts, 2 dc in next st] 6 times, dc in next 8 sts, dc3tog (**center top**), dc in next 8 sts, [2 dc in next st, dc in next 3 sts] 5 times; join = 110 sts

Fasten off, leaving a long tail for sewing.

MUZZLE CHART

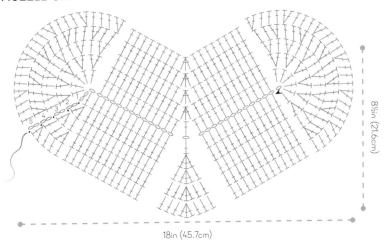

8½in (21.6cm)

18in (45.7cm)

HORNS

Make 3. Work in rows with a 9mm (M/N) hook and 2 strands of **CC5**.

To beg: Ch 14

Row 1: (WS) Sl st in second ch from hook (the skipped ch doesn't count as a st), sc in next 3 chs, hdc in next 3 chs, dc in next 6 chs; turn = 13 sts

Row 2: (RS) Ch 1 (doesn't count as a st), sc in next 13 sts, 2 sc in end ch, continue working across the bottom of the foundation ch, sc in next 13 sts = 28 sts

Fasten off, leaving a long single strand of **CC5** for sewing. Weave in the other ends.

EYES

Make 2. Follow the instructions for the basic eyes (see Common Shapes: Basic Eyes). Use 2 strands of **CC4** with a 9mm (M/N) hook for the pupils and 1 strand of **CC5** with a 5.5mm (I) hook for the highlights.

Use stitch markers to mark the **bottom point** and the **center top** of the muzzle.

BOW (OPTIONAL)

Make 1. Follow the instructions for the big bow using **CC3** (see Common Shapes: Big Bow).

ASSEMBLING RUG

With RS facing, place the muzzle onto the head so that the pointy edge of the muzzle is 1 round above the bottom edge of the head. Backstitch around the muzzle edge using the long **CC1** tail from the muzzle (1).

Place the first horn right up against the muzzle, centering it at the top edge. Using the long **CC5** tail from the horn, whipstitch across the bottom edge and backstitch around the remaining edge of the horn (1).

Position the other 2 horns on each side of the head with the top 3 spikes of the head between the horns (1). The tips of the horns should extend beyond the head edge by approximately 2in (5cm). Using **CC5**, whipstitch across the bottom edge and backstitch around the remaining edge of the horns, leaving the tips of the horns unstitched (2).

Place the eyes on each side above the muzzle and backstitch around using the long **CC4** tail from the eyes (3).

If using, place the bow onto the head, covering the bottom edge of the left horn (optional) and backstitch around the center of the bow using **CC3** (4). Keep the side edges of the bow unattached or whipstitch the corners to keep them in place.

If desired, make a removable non-slip lining (see General Techniques: Non-Slip Lining).

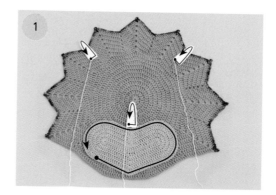

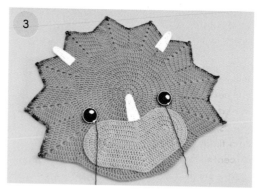

DINOSAUR PILLOW

SKILL LEVEL

FINISHED SIZE

17½in (44.5cm) diameter

HOOKS

3.75mm (F), 4mm (G), 5mm (H), 5.5mm (I)

YARN WEIGHT

4

NUMBER OF STRANDS

1

GAUGE WITH 1 STRAND AND 5.5MM (I) HOOK

14 sc x 16 rows = 4in x 4in (10cm x 10cm)

STITCH SUMMARY

Ch, sl st, sc, beg sc, sc3tog, hdc, dc, dc3tog, tr, picot, join

SKILLS

Working in rows and in the round, working across the bottom of the foundation chain, blocking, sewing

LEFT-HANDED CROCHET

Fully compatible

YARN

Abbreviation	Color	Amount
MC	Forest Green	93-109yd (85-100m)
CC2	Camo	185-251yd (170-230m)
CC3	Gold	273-328yd (250-300m)

All other contrasting colors are the same as for the Dinosaur Rug (small amount of each).

PILLOW BASE

Make 1 front and 1 back using 1 strand of **CC3** with a 5.5mm (I) hook. Follow the instructions for the round pillow base (see Common Shapes: Round Pillow Base). Fasten off after finishing each piece.

Holding the front and the back pieces together with WS facing each other, work Rnd 26 through both pieces of fabric at the same time using 1 strand of **CC2**.

Rnd 26: Beg sc in same st as previous sl st, sc in next 140 sts, stuff the pillow, sc in next 15 sts; join = 156 sts

Rnd 27: Ch 9, dc in third ch from hook, 2 dc in next 6 chs (first spiral made), skip st with join, skip next 2 sts of Rnd 26, sl st in next st, *ch 9, dc in third ch from hook, 2 dc in next 6 chs (next spiral made), skip 2 sts of Rnd 26, sl st in next st**, repeat around from * to ** (1) = 52 spirals

Fasten off and weave in the ends.

HEAD

Make 1. Work in the round with a 3.75mm (F) hook and 1 strand of **MC**.

NOTE: Ch-2 sps are not included in the total stitch count.

To beg: Ch 3, sl st in third ch from hook to form a ring (or start with a magic ring)

Rnd 1: Ch 2 (doesn't count as a st now and throughout), 12 dc in ring; join = 12 sts

Rnd 2: Ch 2, 2 dc in same st as join, 2 dc in next 11 sts; join = 24 sts

Rnd 3: Ch 2, dc in same st as join, 2 dc in next st, [dc in next st, 2 dc in next st] 11 times; join = 36 sts

HEAD CHART

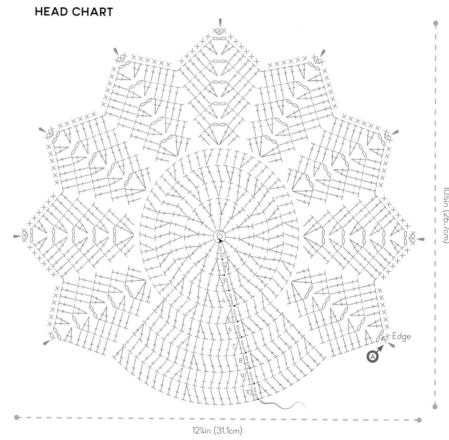

10½in (26.7cm)

12¼in (31.1cm)

Edge

Rnd 4: Ch 2, 2 dc in same st as join, dc in next 2 sts, [2 dc in next st, dc in next 2 sts] 11 times, join = 48 sts

Rnd 5: Ch 2, dc in same st as join, dc in next 2 sts, 2 dc in next st, [dc in next 3 sts, 2 dc in next st] 11 times; join = 60 sts

Rnd 6: Ch 2, 2 dc in same st as join, dc in next 4 sts, skip st, dc in next st, (2 dc, ch 2, 2 dc) in next st, dc in next st, [skip 2 sts, dc in next st, (2 dc, ch 2, 2 dc) in next st, dc in next st] 8 times, skip st, [2 dc in next st, dc in next 4 sts] 2 times; join = 72 sts

Rnd 7: Ch 2, dc in same st as join, dc in next 4 sts, 2 dc in next st, skip st, dc in next 2 sts, (2 dc, ch 2, 2 dc) in next ch-2 sp, dc in next 2 sts, [skip 2 sts, dc in next 2 sts, (2 dc, ch 2, 2 dc) in next ch-2 sp, dc in next 2 sts] 8 times, skip st, [dc in next 5 sts, 2 dc in next st] 2 times; join = 93 sts

Rnd 8: Ch 2, 2 dc in same st as join, dc in next 6 sts, skip st, dc in next 3 sts, (2 dc, ch 2, 2 dc) in next ch-2 sp, dc in next 3 sts, [skip 2 sts, dc in next 3 sts, (2 dc, ch 2, 2 dc) in next ch-2 sp, dc in next 3 sts] 8 times, skip st, [2 dc in next st, dc in next 6 sts] 2 times; join = 114 sts

Rnd 9: Ch 2, dc in same st as join, dc in next 6 sts, 2 dc in next st, skip st, dc in next 4 sts, (2 dc, ch 2, 2 dc) in next ch-2 sp, dc in next 4 sts, [skip 2 sts, dc in next 4 sts, (2 dc, ch 2, 2 dc) in next ch-2 sp, dc in next 4 sts] 8 times, skip st, [dc in next 7 sts, 2 dc in next st] 2 times; join = 135 sts

Rnd 10: Ch 2, 2 dc in same st as join, dc in next 8 sts, skip st, dc in next 5 sts, (2 dc, ch 2, 2 dc) in next ch-2 sp, dc in next 5 sts, [skip 2 sts, dc in next 5 sts, (2 dc, ch 2, 2 dc) in next ch-2 sp, dc in next 5 sts] 8 times, skip st, [2 dc in next st, dc in next 8 sts] 2 times; join = 156 sts

MUZZLE CHART

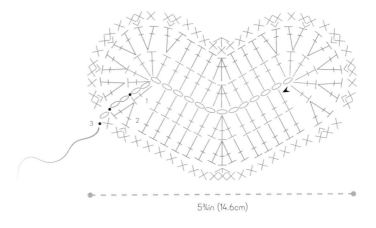

5¾in (14.6cm)

SHORT HORN CHART

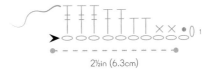

2½in (6.3cm)

Skip 17 sts and place **Marker A** in next ch-2 sp, fasten off, leaving a long **MC** tail for sewing. Continue to work edging with a 3.75mm (F) hook and 1 strand of **CC2** as follows:

Edge: (RS) Beg sc in sp with **Marker A** and remove the marker, (picot, sc) in same sp, sc in next 6 sts, [skip 2 sts, sc in next 6 sts, (2 sc, picot, sc) in next ch-2 sp, sc in next 6 sts] 7 times, skip 2 sts, sc in next 6 sts, (2 sc, picot) in next ch-2 sp = 121 sts and 9 picots

Fasten off and weave in the ends. Wet block the head (see General Techniques: Blocking).

MUZZLE

Make 1. Work in the round with a 5mm (H) hook and 1 strand of **CC1**.

To beg: Ch 15

Rnd 1: Dc in third ch from hook (2 skipped chs don't count as a st), dc in next 5 chs, 3 dc in next ch, dc in next 5 chs, 6 dc in last ch, continue working across the bottom of the foundation ch, dc in next 4 chs, dc3tog, dc in next 4 chs, 5 dc in last ch; join = 34 sts

Rnd 2 Ch 2 (doesn't count as a st), 2 dc in same st as join, dc in next 6 sts, 3 dc in next st, dc in next 6 sts, 2 dc in next 6 sts, dc in next 3 sts, dc3tog, dc in next 3 sts, 2 dc in next 5 sts; join = 46 sts

Rnd 3: Ch 1 (doesn't count as a st), sc in same st as join, 2 sc in next st, sc in next 7 sts, 3 sc in next st, sc in next 7 sts, [2 sc in next st, sc in next st] 6 times, sc in next 2 sts, sc3tog, sc in next 3 sts, 2 sc in next st, [sc in next st, 2 sc in next st] 4 times; join = 58 sts

Fasten off, leaving a long tail for sewing. Weave in the end from the beg.

SHORT HORN

Make 1. Work in rows with a 4mm (G) hook and 1 strand of **CC5**.

To beg: Ch 11

Row 1: (RS) Sl st in second ch from hook (the skipped ch doesn't count as a st), sc in next 2 chs, hdc in next 2 chs, dc in next 2 chs, tr in next 3 chs = 10 sts

Fasten off, leaving a long tail for sewing. Weave in the end from the beg.

LONG HORNS

Make 2. Follow the instructions for the horns in Dinosaur Rug (see Dinosaur Rug: Horns). Use a 4mm (G) hook and 1 strand of **CC5**.

EYES

Make 2. Follow the instructions for the basic eyes (see Common Shapes: Basic Eyes). Use a 4mm (G) hook with 1 strand of **CC4** for the pupils and 1 strand of **CC5** for the highlights.

ASSEMBLING PILLOW

Place the head onto the front of the pillow and backstitch around using the long **MC** tail from the head (2).

Position the muzzle so that the pointy edge of the muzzle is just above the bottom edge of the head. Backstitch around the edge of the muzzle using the long **CC1** tail from the muzzle (3).

Position the 2 long horns on each side of the head with the top 3 spikes of the head between the horns. The tips of the horns should extend beyond the edge of the head by approximately 1½in (3.8cm). Using the long **CC5** tail from the horns, whipstitch across the bottom edge and backstitch around the remaining edge of the horns (3).

Place the short horn right up against the muzzle, centering it at the top edge. Using the long **CC5** tail from the horn, whipstitch across the bottom edge and backstitch around the remaining edge of the horn (4).

Place the eyes on each side right up against the muzzle and backstitch around using the long **CC4** tail from the eyes (4).

If desired, make a small bow using 1 strand of **CC3** (see Common Shapes: Small Bow). Place the bow onto the head, covering the bottom edge of the left long horn and backstitch around the center of the bow using **CC3**.

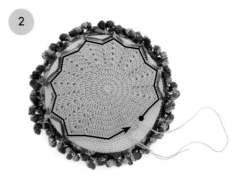

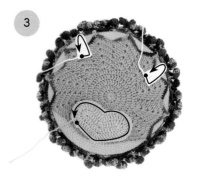

Make the pillow even more fun by adding a dinosaur head on the back as well.

DINOSAUR BOOK BAG

SKILL LEVEL

FINISHED SIZE
12¾in x 12¼in (32.4cm x 31.1cm)

HOOKS
3.75mm (F), 4mm (G), 5mm (H)

YARN WEIGHT
4

NUMBER OF STRANDS
1

GAUGE WITH 1 STRAND AND 5MM (H) HOOK
15 dc x 8 rows = 4in x 4in (10cm x 10cm)

STITCH SUMMARY
Ch, sl st, sc, beg sc, sc3tog, hdc, dc, dc3tog, tr, cluster, picot, join

SKILLS
Working in rows and in the round, working across the bottom of the foundation chain, changing colors, blocking, sewing

LEFT-HANDED CROCHET
Fully compatible

YARN

Abbreviation	Color	Amount
MC	Forest Green	93-109yd (85-100m)
CC3	Gold	93-109yd (85-100m)
CC4	Coffee	93-109yd (85-100m)
CC6	Pumpkin	93-109yd (85-100m)

All other contrasting colors are the same as for the Dinosaur Rug (small amount of each).

BOOK BAG

Make 1. Work in the round with a 5mm (H) hook and 1 strand of yarn, changing colors (**CC4**, **CC3** and **CC6**) in every round. Begin with **CC4**.

To beg: Ch 43

Rnd 1: Dc in third ch from hook (2 skipped chs don't count as a st), dc in next 39 chs, 3 dc in last ch, continue working across the bottom of the foundation ch, dc in next 39 chs, 2 dc in last ch; join = 84 sts

Rnd 2: (Ch 3, 2 dc) in same st as join (counts as beg cluster now and throughout), skip 2 sts, [3 dc in next st, skip 2 sts] 27 times, sl st in top of beg ch-3 = 28 clusters

Rnds 3-25: (Ch 3, 2 dc) in same sp between clusters, [skip cluster, 3 dc in next sp between clusters] 27 times, sl st in top of beg ch-3 = 28 clusters

Check the bag length, add or omit rounds if alterations are needed. Change to **CC2** and break off all other colors.

Rnds 26-27: With **CC2**, ch 1 (doesn't count as a st now and throughout), sc in same st as join, sc in next 83 sts; join = 84 sts

Fasten off and weave in the ends.

TIES

Holding the bag flat, mark 6 stitches on each side of the bag by placing a stitch marker in first and sixth stitches (1).

Work with a 5mm (H) hook and 1 strand of **CC2**.

To beg: (RS) Ch 60, sc across 6 marked sts on one side of the bag, ch 62, turn = 6 sts and 2 long ch-tails (2)

Row 1: (WS) Dc in third ch from hook (2 skipped chs count as first dc), 2 dc in next 6 chs, sc in next 53 chs, sc in next 6 sts, sc in next 53 chs, 2 dc in next 7 chs = 140 sts

Fasten off and weave in the ends. Finish the second tie in the same manner.

DINOSAUR

Make the head, muzzle, horns and eyes following the instructions in Dinosaur Pillow (see Dinosaur Pillow: Head, Dinosaur Pillow: Muzzle, Dinosaur Pillow: Horns and Dinosaur Pillow: Eyes).

ASSEMBLING BOOK BAG

Holding the bag flat, place the head onto the bag and backstitch around using the long **MC** tail from the head (3).

Sew all the other parts (4) in the same way as for Dinosaur Pillow (see Dinosaur Pillow: Assembling Pillow).

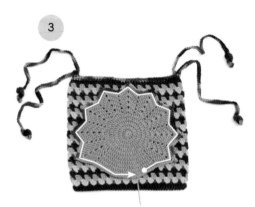

USEFUL INFORMATION

CROCHET TERMINOLOGY

The patterns featured in this section are written using abbreviations in American crochet terms. Please use the comparison chart below to convert the patterns to British terminology if needed.

Abbreviation	Symbol	American (US) Term	British (UK) Term
Ch	○	Chain	Chain
Sl st	•	Slip stitch	Slip stitch
Sc	×	Single crochet	Double crochet
Hdc	T	Half double crochet	Half treble crochet
Dc	₸	Double crochet	Treble crochet
Tr	₮	Treble crochet	Double treble crochet
		Skip	Miss
		Gauge	Tension

ABBREVIATIONS

This table explains all of the standard abbreviations and symbols used in this section.

Abbreviation	Symbol	Description in US Terms
Arch	⌒5	**Arch** is a group of 3 or more chains as indicated in the pattern; when working in arch, insert the hook under the arch (and not into a specific chain), unless otherwise stated
Beg		Begin(ning)

Abbreviation	Symbol	Description in US Terms
Beg dc	‡	**Beginning (standing) double crochet** – Make a slipknot and keep the loop on the hook, yo, insert the hook through the stitch and complete dc as normal
Beg PC	🮲	**Beginning popcorn stitch** – Ch 3 (counts as dc), 4 dc in same st, remove the hook from the loop and insert hook from front to back through the top of beg ch-3, replace the loop onto the hook (from the last dc) and pull it through
Beg sc	✗	**Beginning (standing) single crochet** – Make a slipknot and keep the loop on the hook, insert the hook through the stitch and complete sc as normal
Bpsc	♭	**Back post single crochet** – Insert the hook from back to front to back around the post of the stitch, yo and pull up a loop, yo and pull yarn through 2 loops on the hook
CC		Contrasting color (might be indicated by a number)
Ch(s)	ᴑ	**Chain(s)** – Yo and pull through the loop on the hook
Ch-		Indicates a number of chains or spaces previously made (example: ch-2 sp)
Cluster	⋎	**Cluster** – 3 dc in same space

Abbreviation	Symbol	Description in US Terms
Cm		Centimeter(s)
Crest		**Crest** is a combination of stitches worked across the shell – Dc in first st of the shell, [dc in next st, picot] 7 times, dc in last st = 9 dc and 7 picots
Dc		**Double crochet** – Yo, insert the hook in stitch, yo and pull up a loop, [yo and pull through 2 loops] 2 times
Dc2(3)tog		**Double crochet 2 (3) together (decrease)** – [Yo, insert the hook in next stitch, yo and pull up a loop, yo and pull through 2 loops] 2 (3) times, yo and pull through all loops on the hook (1 stitch made)
		2 (3) dc in same stitch or space
		Direction indicators
Fasten off		Cut working yarn, draw the end through the loop on the hook, and pull up tight
FDC		**Double crochet in front of work** – Yo, insert the hook under both loops of sc two rows below and complete dc as normal, leaving the two rows of ch-2 sps in the back unworked

Abbreviation	Symbol	Description in US Terms
Fpsc		**Front post single crochet** – Insert the hook from front to back to front around the post of the stitch, yo and pull up a loop, yo and pull yarn through 2 loops on the hook 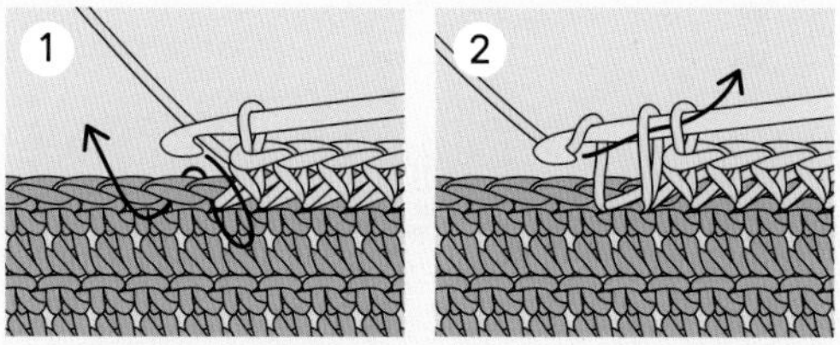
Hdc		**Half double crochet** – Yo, insert the hook in stitch, yo and pull up a loop, yo and pull through all loops on the hook 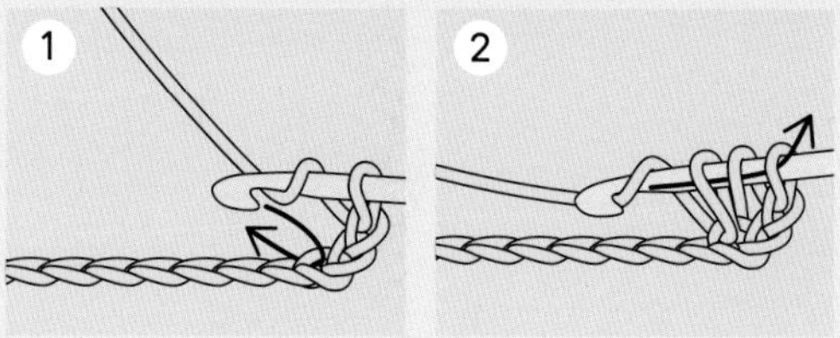
		2 hdc in same stitch or space
In		Inch(es)
Join		Sl st in top of the first stitch (not a ch)
M		Meter(s)
		Magic ring or ch-3 circle
Marker		Stitch marker (indicated by a letter)
MC		Main color
OS		**Open shell** – (2 dc, ch 1, 2 dc) in same space
OS over shell		Work OS in ch-1 sp (the center) of open shell below

Abbreviation	Symbol	Description in US Terms
PC		**Popcorn stitch** – 5 dc in stitch indicated in pattern, remove the hook from the loop and insert it from front to back through the top of the first dc, replace the loop onto the hook (from the last dc) and pull through
Picot		**Picot** – Ch 3, insert the hook from right to left under the front loop and bottom vertical bar of previously made stitch (the base of the stitch), yo and pull through all loops on the hook
Rnd(s)		**Round**(s) – Work in spiral or join the rounds, as indicated in the pattern
Row(s)		**Row**(s) – Turn after finishing each row, as indicated in the pattern
RS		Right side (front side of the item)
Rsc		**Reverse single crochet (crab stitch)** – Insert the hook in stitch to the right from front to back, yo and pull it through, yo and pull through all loops on the hook (see Crochet Techniques: Left-Handed Crochet for left-handed conversion)
Sc	×	**Single crochet** – Insert the hook in stitch, yo and pull up a loop, yo and pull through all loops on the hook

Abbreviation	Symbol	Description in US Terms
Sc2(3)tog	⋙ ⋙	**Single crochet 2 (3) together (decrease)** - [Insert the hook in next stitch, yo and pull up a loop] 2 (3) times, yo and pull through all loops on the hook (1 stitch made)
	⋙ ⋙	2 (3) sc in same stitch or space
		Seam
Shell		**Shell** - 6 or more stitches worked in same space
Slipknot		**Slipknot** - Twist the end of working yarn to form a loop, insert the hook through the loop, yo and draw working yarn through the loop, pull the end to tighten the knot and adjust the size of the loop on the hook
Sl st	•	**Slip stitch** - Insert the hook in stitch, yo and pull through the stitch and loop on the hook
Sp		**Space** is a gap created by one or more chains; it might also be a space between two stitches or groups of stitches. Insert the hook into a chain space or in a space between stitches (not a specific chain or stitch)
St(s)		**Stitch**(es)

Abbreviation	Symbol	Description in US Terms
Tr		**Treble crochet** – Yo twice, insert the hook in stitch, yo and pull up a loop, [yo and pull through 2 loops] 3 times
		2 tr in same stitch or space
WS		Wrong side (back side of the item)
Yd		Yard(s)
Yo		Yarn over hook
		Yarn tail left for sewing
[]		Work the instructions written within brackets as many times as indicated after brackets
()		Parentheses are used in explanations or to indicate a group of stitches
* or **		Asterisks are used as reference marks
=		Equal sign indicates the total stitch count at the end of the row/rnd

COMMON SHAPES

BASIC EYES

FINISHED SIZE
Varies depending
on pattern

HOOK
See pattern

YARN WEIGHT
4

NUMBER OF STRANDS
See pattern

GAUGE
Varies, depending
on pattern

STITCH SUMMARY
Ch, sl st, sc, join

SKILLS
Working in the round,
sewing

LEFT-HANDED CROCHET
Fully compatible

PUPILS

Make 2. Work in the round using
the suggested yarn and hook for the
specific pattern.

To beg: Ch 3, sl st in third ch from
hook to form a ring (or start with a
magic ring)

Rnd 1: Ch 1 (doesn't count as a st
now and throughout), 6 sc in ring; join
= 6 sts

Rnd 2: Ch 1, 2 sc in same st as join,
2 sc in next 5 sts; join = 12 sts

Rnd 3: Ch 1, sc in same st as join,
2 sc in next st, [sc in next st, 2 sc in
next st] 5 times; join = 18 sts

Fasten off, leaving a long single
strand of yarn for sewing. Weave in
the other ends.

HIGHLIGHTS

Make 2. Work in the round using
the suggested yarn and hook for the
specific pattern.

To beg: Ch 3, sl st in third ch from
hook to form a ring (or start with a
magic ring)

Rnd 1: Ch 1 (doesn't count as a st),
6 sc in ring; join = 6 sts

Fasten off, leaving a long single
strand of yarn for sewing. Weave in
the other ends.

ASSEMBLING EYES

Place the highlight on top of the
pupil and backstitch around using the
long tail from the highlight (1). Finish
the second eye in the same manner.

PUPIL CHART

HIGHLIGHT CHART

1

BOWS

FINISHED SIZE
Big bow: 6¼in x 10¼in
(15.9cm x 26cm)

Small bow: 2¾in x 4in
(7cm x 10.2cm)

HOOK
Big bow: 9mm (M/N)

Small bow: 3.75mm (F)

YARN WEIGHT
4

NUMBER OF STRANDS
1 and 3

GAUGE
Not important

STITCH SUMMARY
Ch, sl st, sc, sc3tog,
PC, beg PC, join

SKILLS
Working in rows and
in the round, sewing

LEFT-HANDED CROCHET
Fully compatible

BIG BOW

Make 1. Begin by working in the round with a 9mm (M/N) hook and 3 strands of yarn, using the recommended color for the specific pattern.

To beg: Ch 3, sl st in third ch from hook to form a ring (or start with a magic ring)

Rnd 1: Ch 1 (doesn't count as a st now and throughout), 6 sc in ring; join = 6 sts

Rnd 2: Beg PC in same st as join, ch 2, [PC in next st, ch 2] 5 times; join = 6 PC

Rnd 3: Ch 1, [3 sc in next ch-2 sp] 6 times; join = 18 sts

Work the bow sides in rows from now on:

Row 4: (RS) Ch 1, 3 sc in same st as join, [3 sc in next st] 3 times, *skip 5 sts, place **Marker A** in next st**; turn = 12 sts

Rows 5-10: Ch 1, sc in first st, sc in next 11 sts; turn = 12 sts

Fasten off and weave in the ends.

With RS facing you, join 3 strands of yarn in st with **Marker A** leaving a long single strand of yarn at the beginning for sewing. Repeat Rows 4 to 10 and finishing, omitting the instructions from * to **. Remove the marker. To assemble, see Assembling Bow.

SMALL BOW

Make 1. Begin by working in the round with a 3.75mm (F) hook and 1 strand of yarn, using the recommended color for the specific pattern.

To beg: Ch 3, sl st in third ch from hook to form a ring (or start with a magic ring)

Rnd 1: Ch 1 (doesn't count as a st now and throughout), 6 sc in ring; join = 6 sts

Rnd 2: Beg PC in same st as join, ch 2, [PC in next st, ch 2] 5 times; join = 6 PC

Rnd 3: Ch 1, [3 sc in next ch-2 sp] 6 times; join = 18 sts

Work the bow sides in rows from now on:

Row 4: (RS) Ch 1, 3 sc in same st as join, [3 sc in next st] 3 times, *skip 5 sts, place **Marker A** in next st**; turn = 12 sts

Rows 5–11: Ch 1, sc in first st, sc in next 11 sts; turn = 12 sts

Row 12: Ch 1, don't skip first st, [sc3tog] 4 times = 4 sts

Fasten off, leaving a long tail for sewing. Weave in the other ends.

With RS facing you, join yarn in st with **Marker A**. Repeat Rows 4 to 12 and finishing, omitting the instructions from * to **. Remove the marker. To assemble, see Assembling Bow.

ASSEMBLING BOW

Fold both gathered sides of the bow towards the center on WS and whipstitch across each edge to secure (2). Weave in the end after finishing the first edge, but leave a long tail for sewing after finishing second edge.

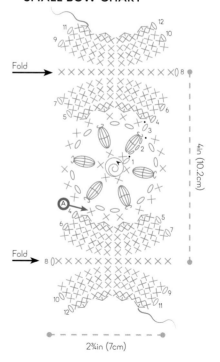

BIG BOW CHART

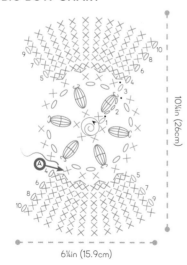

10¼in (26cm)

6¼in (15.9cm)

SMALL BOW CHART

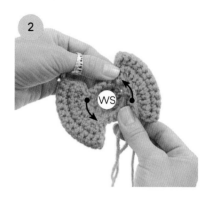

Fold

Fold

4in (10.2cm)

2¾in (7cm)

PILLOW BASES

FINISHED SIZE
Round pillow: 13in
(33cm) diameter
Oval pillow: 13in x 18½in
(33cm x 47cm)

HOOK
5.5mm (I)

YARN WEIGHT
4

NUMBER OF STRANDS
1

**GAUGE WITH 1 STRAND
AND 5.5MM (I) HOOK**
14 sc x 16 rows = 4in x 4in
(10cm x 10cm)

STITCH SUMMARY
Ch, sl st, sc

SKILLS
Working in spiral
rounds and working
across the bottom of
the foundation chain

LEFT-HANDED CROCHET
Fully compatible

ROUND PILLOW BASE

Make 1 front and 1 back. Work in spiral rounds with a 5.5mm (I) hook and 1 strand of yarn as recommended for the specific pattern. Use a stitch marker to mark the beginning of each round as you go.

To beg: Ch 3, sl st in third ch from hook to form a ring (or start with a magic ring)

Rnd 1: Ch 1 (doesn't count as a st), 6 sc in ring, don't join now and throughout = 6 sts

Rnd 2: 2 sc in first st of previous rnd, 2 sc in next 5 sts = 12 sts

Rnd 3: 2 sc in each st around = 24 sts

Rnd 4: Sc in each st around = 24 sts

Rnd 5: [Sc in next st, 2 sc in next st] 12 times = 36 sts

Rnd 6: Sc in each st around = 36 sts

Rnd 7: [Sc in next 2 sts, 2 sc in next st] 12 times = 48 sts

Rnd 8: Sc in each st around = 48 sts

Rnd 9: [Sc in next 3 sts, 2 sc in next st] 12 times = 60 sts

Rnd 10: Sc in each st around = 60 sts

Rnd 11: [Sc in next 4 sts, 2 sc in next st] 12 times = 72 sts

Rnd 12: Sc in each st around = 72 sts

Rnd 13: [Sc in next 5 sts, 2 sc in next st] 12 times = 84 sts

Rnd 14: Sc in each st around = 84 sts

Rnd 15: [Sc in next 6 sts, 2 sc in next st] 12 times = 96 sts

Rnd 16: Sc in each st around = 96 sts

Rnd 17: [Sc in next 7 sts, 2 sc in next st] 12 times = 108 sts

Rnd 18: Sc in each st around = 108 sts

Rnd 19: [Sc in next 8 sts, 2 sc in next st] 12 times = 120 sts

Rnd 20: Sc in each st around = 120 sts

Rnd 21: [Sc in next 9 sts, 2 sc in next st] 12 times = 132 sts

Rnd 22: Sc in each st around = 132 sts

Rnd 23: [Sc in next 10 sts, 2 sc in next st] 12 times = 144 sts

Rnd 24: Sc in each st around = 144 sts

Rnd 25: [Sc in next 11 sts, 2 sc in next st] 12 times = 156 sts

Sl st in next st. Fasten off if indicated in the pattern and check tips for assembling pillow (see Assembling Pillow).

ROUND PILLOW BASE CHART

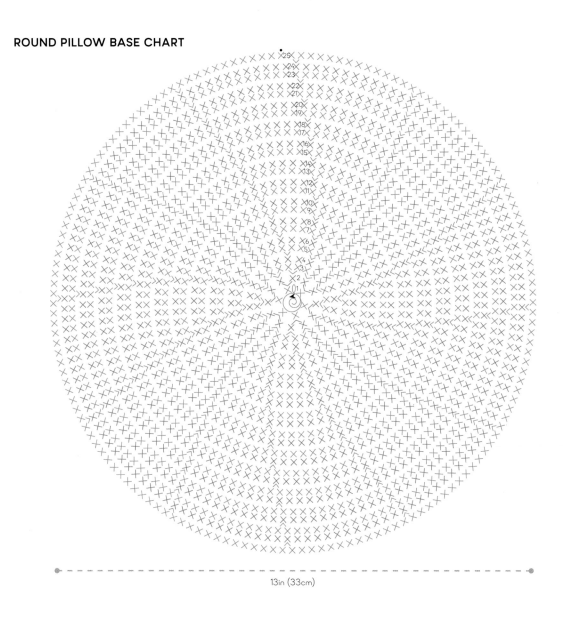

13in (33cm)

OVAL PILLOW BASE

Make 1 front and 1 back. Work in spiral rounds with a 5.5mm (I) hook and 1 strand of yarn as recommended for the specific pattern. Use a stitch marker to mark the beginning of each round as you go.

To beg: Ch 23

Rnd 1: Sc in second ch from hook (the skipped ch doesn't count as a st), sc in next 20 chs, 3 sc in last ch, continuing working across the bottom of the foundation ch, sc in next 20 chs, 2 sc in last ch; don't join now and throughout = 46 sts

Rnd 2: 2 sc in first st of previous rnd, sc in next 20 sts, 2 sc in next 3 sts, sc in next 20 sts, 2 sc in next 2 sts = 52 sts

Rnd 3: 2 sc in next 2 sts, sc in next 20 sts, 2 sc in next 6 sts, sc in next 20 sts, 2 sc in next 4 sts = 64 sts

Rnd 4: Sc in each st around = 64 sts

Rnd 5: [Sc in next st, 2 sc in next st] 2 times, sc in next 20 sts, [sc in next st, 2 sc in next st] 6 times, sc in next 20 sts, [sc in next st, 2 sc in next st] 4 times = 76 sts

Rnd 6: Sc in each st around = 76 sts

Rnd 7: [Sc in next 2 sts, 2 sc in next st] 2 times, sc in next 20 sts, [sc in next 2 sts, 2 sc in next st] 6 times, sc in next 20 sts, [sc in next 2 sts, 2 sc in next st] 4 times = 88 sts

Rnd 8: Sc in each st around = 88 sts

OVAL PILLOW BASE CHART

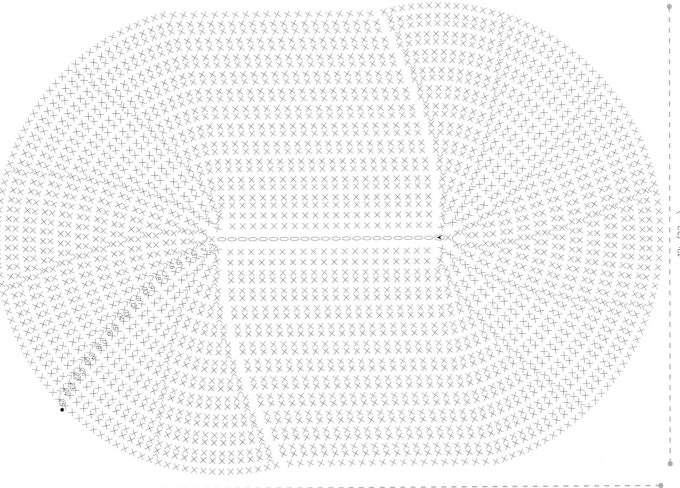

13in (33cm)

18½in (47cm)

Rnd 9: [Sc in next 3 sts, 2 sc in next st] 2 times, sc in next 20 sts, [sc in next 3 sts, 2 sc in next st] 6 times, sc in next 20 sts, [sc in next 3 sts, 2 sc in next st] 4 times = 100 sts

Rnd 10: Sc in each st around = 100 sts

Rnd 11: [Sc in next 4 sts, 2 sc in next st] 2 times, sc in next 20 sts, [sc in next 4 sts, 2 sc in next st] 6 times, sc in next 20 sts, [sc in next 4 sts, 2 sc in next st] 4 times = 112 sts

Rnd 12: Sc in each st around = 112 sts

Rnd 13: [Sc in next 5 sts, 2 sc in next st] 2 times, sc in next 20 sts, [sc in next 5 sts, 2 sc in next st] 6 times, sc in next 20 sts, [sc in next 5 sts, 2 sc in next st] 4 times = 124 sts

Rnd 14: Sc in each st around = 124 sts

Rnd 15: [Sc in next 6 sts, 2 sc in next st] 2 times, sc in next 20 sts, [sc in next 6 sts, 2 sc in next st] 6 times, sc in next 20 sts, [sc in next 6 sts, 2 sc in next st] 4 times = 136 sts

Rnd 16: Sc in each st around = 136 sts

Rnd 17: [Sc in next 7 sts, 2 sc in next st] 2 times, sc in next 20 sts, [sc in next 7 sts, 2 sc in next st] 6 times, sc in next 20 sts, [sc in next 7 sts, 2 sc in next st] 4 times = 148 sts

Rnd 18: Sc in each st around = 148 sts

Rnd 19: [Sc in next 8 sts, 2 sc in next st] 2 times, sc in next 20 sts, [sc in next 8 sts, 2 sc in next st] 6 times, sc in next 20 sts, [sc in next 8 sts, 2 sc in next st] 4 times = 160 sts

Rnd 20: Sc in each st around = 160 sts

Rnd 21: [Sc in next 9 sts, 2 sc in next st] 2 times, sc in next 20 sts, [sc in next 9 sts, 2 sc in next st] 6 times, sc in next 20 sts, [sc in next 9 sts, 2 sc in next st] 4 times = 172 sts

Rnd 22: Sc in each st around = 172 sts

Rnd 23: [Sc in next 10 sts, 2 sc in next st] 2 times, sc in next 20 sts, [sc in next 10 sts, 2 sc in next st] 6 times, sc in next 20 sts, [sc in next 10 sts, 2 sc in next st] 4 times = 184 sts

Rnd 24: Sc in each st around = 184 sts

Rnd 25: [Sc in next 11 sts, 2 sc in next st] 2 times, sc in next 20 sts, [sc in next 11 sts, 2 sc in next st] 6 times, sc in next 20 sts, [sc in next 11 sts, 2 sc in next st] 4 times = 196 sts

Sl st in next st. Fasten off if indicated in the pattern and check tips for assembling pillow (see Assembling Pillow).

ASSEMBLING PILLOW

Place the front and the back pieces together with WS facing each other. Work the edging as indicated for the specific pattern, inserting the hook through both pieces of fabric at the same time to join them as you go (3). Leave an opening at the end for stuffing.

Stuff the pillow firmly, but don't over-stuff to prevent filling from showing through the fabric stitches (4). Complete the remaining stitches of the edging. Fasten off and weave in the ends.

CROCHET TECHNIQUES

COLOR CHANGE

To change yarn colors, leave the last stitch unfinished with 2 loops on the hook of the currently used color. Drop working yarn, pick up the new color and pull it through the remaining 2 loops of the previously used color (1). The last st is completed with the new color on the hook (2).

To begin the next row (or round) after a color change, crochet the first st over the previous yarn color, holding it on WS of the project (3). Continue to work as usual, following the pattern (4). This method will ensure a neat finishing of the edges and secure color changes on WS of the work.

WEAVING IN YARN ENDS

Neat finishing is the key for professional-looking work. My favorite tools for weaving in the yarn ends are (5):

- **A** – Latch hook (mid or standard gauge)
- **B** – Darning needle with latch hook eye
- **C** – Tapestry needle

LATCH HOOK

The latch hook is my most favorite tool of all. Mid or standard gauge latch hooks can be found in transfer tools for knitting machines.

Start by inserting the latch hook into the work on WS approximately 1½in (3.8cm) away from the yarn tail. Push the hook through the stitches of the row towards the yarn tail, grab the end of the tail and pull it back through the stitches (6). Now insert and push the hook through the same stitches but in the opposite direction. Grab the yarn end, skipping the last stitch and pull it back through the stitches. Repeat weaving one more time for extra security if desired. Trim the remaining tail.

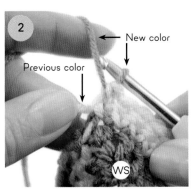

1
New color
Previous color
WS

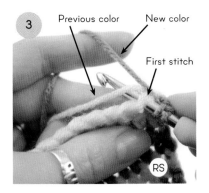

3
Previous color   New color
First stitch
RS

5
A B C

2
New color
Previous color
WS

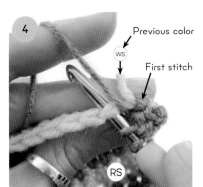

4
Previous color
WS
First stitch
RS

6

DARNING NEEDLE WITH LATCH HOOK EYE OR A TAPESTRY NEEDLE

A darning needle with a latch hook eye is perfect for multi-ply and bulky yarn projects. It makes threading extremely easy (7).

A basic tapestry needle is also great for weaving in any single strand of yarn.

Start by threading the yarn tail through the needle. With WS facing, insert the threaded needle into the work as close to the last stitch as possible and pull it through the stitches of the row, approximately 1½in (3.8cm) away from that point (8). Turn and run the needle through the same stitches in the opposite direction, skipping the first stitch after turning. Turn and repeat weaving one more time for extra security if desired. Trim the remaining tail.

RAW EDGE FINISHING

There are no rules on how many stitches to work in each edge stitch. Work evenly across the side stitches without over-tightening or buckling the edge. To avoid holes when working across the raw edge, insert the hook through the stitches instead of working under the stitches (9).

BOTTOM OF FOUNDATION CHAIN

By working into both sides of the foundation chain we create the beginning round (or row) of ovals and other shapes that are done in the round, as well as half ovals and other shapes that are done in rows. Complete all of the required stitches across the chain, rotate

the work in a clockwise direction (or in a counterclockwise direction for left-handed crochet) and crochet along the bottom loops of the foundation chain (10 and 11).

WORKING WITH 2-3 STRANDS

If the pattern calls for working with 2 or 3 strands of yarn held together, it can be done by pulling 1 strand of yarn from individual skeins to create a group of 2 or 3 yarn strands. However, sometimes the number of available skeins is not a multiple of the required number of strands, so here are some alternative options.

DIVIDING SKEINS

Wind 2 or 3 balls out of 1 skein of yarn. Use an electronic scale to check the weight of the balls for accuracy (12).

Not under the stitch

Through the stitch

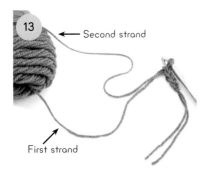

Second strand

First strand

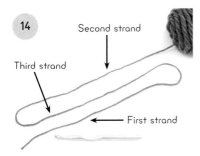

Second strand

Third strand

First strand

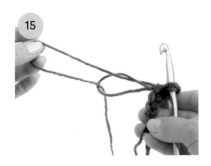

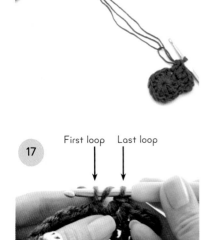

First loop   Last loop

2 STRANDS FROM 1 SKEIN

Pull the tail from the center of the skein and use the tail from the outside of the skein as the second strand. Hold these 2 ends together to crochet with 2 strands at once from a single skein of yarn (13).

3 STRANDS FROM 1 SKEIN

Fold the long yarn tail twice to triple it (14). Gather the ends and make a slipknot. Holding the 3 strands of yarn over your index finger, crochet to the end of the long loop. *Pull working yarn through the loop to create a new long loop (15 and 16). The longer the loop the better! Crochet to the end of the long loop and work the same from now on, repeating from*. This method was named "Long chain" for resembling the basic foundation chain commonly used in crochet projects.

FLAT CIRCLES

The formula for making flat crochet circles is very simple. Any double crochet circle begins with 12 stitches and increases by 12 in every round. Any single crochet circle begins with 6 stitches and increases by 6 in every round or increases by 12 in every other round. Always check the gauge and the total stitch count to ensure the correct result. Wet blocking can save the day if the finished circle doesn't lay perfectly flat (see General Techniques: Blocking).

If this isn't enough, it's possible to fix the gauge. If the circle ruffles, it means the stitches are too short or too wide. If the circle has a dome shape, it means the stitches are too tall or too narrow.

The height of the stitches can be adjusted by the length of the first loop that is pulled through the stitch to create a new stitch. The width of the stitches can be adjusted by the hook size or by the looseness/tightness of the last loop on the hook (17).

If your gauge is off, try to use a smaller or larger hook to obtain the gauge.

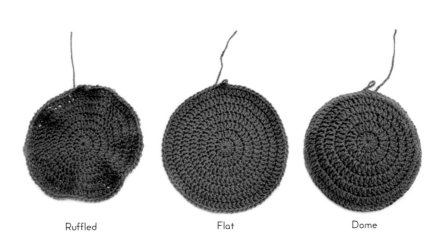

Ruffled   Flat   Dome

LEFT-HANDED CROCHET

Left-handed crocheters need not be discouraged by these patterns. Simply follow the same instructions, but work in the opposite direction. Work clockwise when crocheting in the round or from left to right when crocheting in rows. Here are a few minor notes for individual projects.

REVERSE SINGLE CROCHET

Work in the same manner as for right-handed crochet but insert the hook in the stitch to the left rather than in the stitch to the right.

GIRAFFE RUG & PILLOW

Head edge – Work sc from the left to the right corner and work rsc from the right to the left corner.

ELEPHANT RUG

Head – The trunk will be curved to the left instead of right (18).

Big circles for both ears – In Rnd 9 place **Marker A** in 14th st to the left (instead of right) and place **Marker B** in 14th st to the right (instead of left).

Small circles for both ears – After Row 6 place **Marker C** in 7th st to the left (instead of right). In Row 7 place **Marker D** in 7th st to the right (instead of left).

Assembling circles – Follow the right ear instructions for assembling the left ear circles and the left ear instructions for assembling the right ear circles. Remember, the left-handed ears and markers will be mirror images of the right-handed ears and markers (19).

Edging – Follow the right ear instructions for finishing the edge of the left ear and the left ear instructions for the edge of the right ear.

KITTY RUG

Tail – Place the tail under the left edge of the heart instead of the right edge as it will be curved in the opposite direction (20).

MONKEY RUG

Banana – Place the banana with the stem facing to the right instead of to the left as it will be curved in the opposite direction (21).

CRAB RUG

Pincers – Follow the right pincer instructions for making the left pincer and the left pincer instructions for making the right pincer.

CRAB PILLOW

Assembling pincers – Join the front and back pieces of both pincers by working sc around the edge from left to right (22).

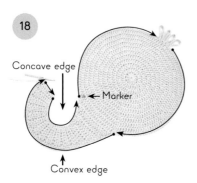

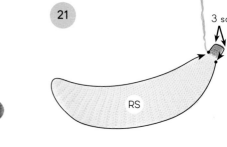

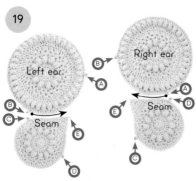

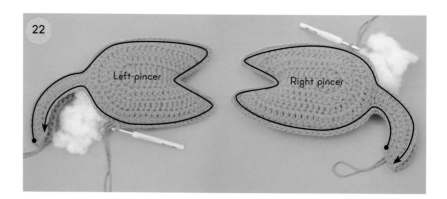

SEWING STITCHES

BACKSTITCH

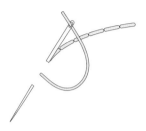

CHAIN STITCH

FRENCH KNOT

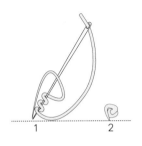

1   2

STRAIGHT STITCH

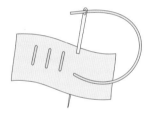

WHIPSTITCH

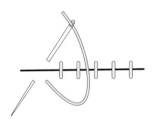

SEWING TIPS

Always use 1 strand of yarn and a tapestry needle for sewing (unless otherwise stated).

Take extra care to pull the needle along the top layer of the fabric (not all the way through) to prevent contrasting color yarn from showing on the back of the work (1).

1

GENERAL TECHNIQUES

BLOCKING

Blocking is an essential finishing technique that improves the look of the stitches as well as the overall appearance of finished items. Not every project needs to be blocked, however blocking is recommended for crochet lace or advanced shapes. If the gauge is slightly off, blocking will help to remove creases and adjust the shape of crochet pieces. Spray blocking works best for heavy projects like rugs, whereas wet blocking is commonly used for light or medium weight projects.

SPRAY BLOCKING

Lay the crochet project on a blocking board. Spray the front and back of the project with warm water until it's thoroughly wet (1), stretching and shaping it to the specified measurements (2). Rotate and flip the project periodically to ensure even drying.

WET BLOCKING

Soak the crochet project in warm water, then gently squeeze the excess moisture out. Lay a towel onto the blocking board and roll the project in the towel to absorb extra moisture (3). Remove the towel and spread out the project on the blocking board, shaping it to the specified measurements (4). Rotate and flip the project periodically to ensure even drying.

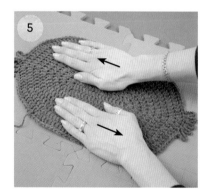

BLOCKING TIPS

Please keep in mind that the drying process might take 2-3 hours outdoors under open sun in the summer or up to several days indoors, depending on the temperature and the humidity level.

Symmetry is very important for some patterns. The kitty face with the whiskers on each side is a good example of a symmetrical pattern. If the crochet piece turned out asymmetrical due to the personal style of crocheting, just try wet blocking and shaping (5). Try it, it really works!

NON-SLIP LINING

This lining prevents rugs from slipping. Non-slip lining is not required, but is recommended for safety reasons if the rug is intended for children.

TOOLS AND MATERIALS

- Straight stitch sewing machine
- Non-adhesive shelf liner with grip or rug gripper pad
- Hook and loop tape (strip with hooks only) - 1in (2.5cm) wide
- Scissors
- All-purpose sewing thread

Lay out the liner on the back of the rug and cut a rectangle that doesn't expand beyond the rug edges. Cut 4 strips with hooks from the hook and loop tape, using the measurement from the shortest edge of the liner. Place the strips evenly spaced onto the liner (6). Sew each strip around the perimeter using a straight stitch on the sewing machine (7). Roll the finished liner with the hook strips facing out. Place the lining roll at the top edge of the rug and unroll it towards the bottom edge (8). Hand press the lining to help the hooks stick to the fabric.

Gently remove the liner before washing (9). Wash the rug and the liner individually, following the care instructions on the labels of the materials used.

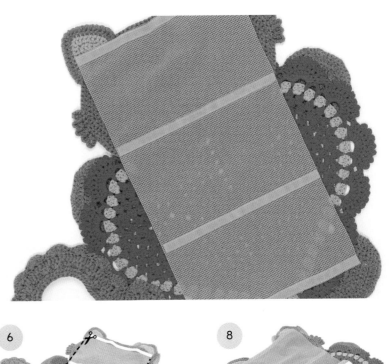

WALL DECORATION

If a crochet rug seems too beautiful to step on, why not make it into wall art? Just use the same pattern with thinner thread and a smaller size hook.

TOOLS AND MATERIALS

- Size 10 crochet thread – approximately 875yd (800m)
- 1.9mm (US size 5) steel hook
- Wall frame or poster frame, at least 3in (7.6cm) larger than the finished wall hanging on each side
- Matboard backing that fits in frame
- Matboard edging that fits in frame
- Chenille needle with sharp point
- Finger guard (thimble)
- Fabric stiffener or corn starch
- Blocking board
- Rust-proof straight pins
- Scotch tape or packing tape

Follow the pattern instructions, working with 1 strand of size 10 crochet thread and a 1.9mm (US size 5) steel hook to make a 14in x 10½in (35.5cm x 26.7cm) elephant wall hanging.

Soak the finished wall hanging in the fabric stiffener or in the corn starch mixture for 2-5 minutes (see Corn Starch Recipe).

Remove the wall hanging from the stiffener and squeeze the excess moisture out. Stretch and pin the wall hanging onto the blocking board (10), allow it to dry. It may take up to 24 hours to dry at room temperature or just a few hours in the sun.

Position the wall hanging in the middle of the matboard backing inside the matboard edging (11).

Make a few tubes out of packing tape with the sticky side facing out (12). Use these tubes to secure the wall hanging onto the matboard backing temporarily (13).

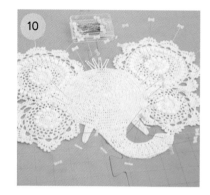

Thread the chenille needle with the crochet thread used for making the wall hanging. Attach the wall hanging to the matboard backing by basting (tacking) it around the edge (14). Make a few tiny stitches on RS between the long thread floats on WS. Remove the packing tape tubes as you go.

Tie all the ends on the back of the matboard to secure them. Insert the matboard backing with the attached wall hanging into the frame along with the matboard edging and seal the frame. Mount the frame onto the wall (15).

CORN STARCH RECIPE

Dissolve 2-3 tablespoons of corn starch in ½ cup (100ml-125ml) of cold water. Boil 3 cups (700ml) of water in a pot and slowly add the starch mixture to the boiling water, stirring it constantly for 40-60 seconds until the mixture looks clear. Remove the mixture from the heat at the boiling point and let it cool down to a temperature comfortable for hands.

ABOUT THE AUTHOR

Coming from a family of textile engineers, I was surrounded by fabrics and yarn from the time I was born. Thus working with yarn has always felt natural to me.

I learned to knit and crochet at a very young age by watching my mom, grandma, and great-grandma. Crocheting along with my grandma was the happiest time of my childhood. My dad has taught me the basics of machine knitting: he could patiently answer all of my childish questions.

Over the years I learned new techniques and I developed some of my own. My earlier designs include lace dresses, skirts, tops, and cardigans. Many of them were inspired by spectacular Irish crochet.

After the big transatlantic move to Canada in 2008, my design aesthetic has been transformed into a new style that I can describe as "fun creations inspired by animals".

Find Ira on Facebook: IraRott Designs

www.irarott.com

THANKS

I would like to say thank you to my wonderful husband Maurice for his endless support, to our children (Amanda, Andrew, Amy, Polina) for being so inspiring and to my parents (Serge and Elena) who are the reason why I crochet.

Also, huge thank you to all our creative team members for testing IraRott patterns. Special thanks for the additional help with this book to Carmen Carpenter, Cheryl McNichols, Courtney Knorr, Kimberly Rose, Penny Shilling, Polina MacGarvey, Ryan Nicole Hazeltine, Susan Baker, and Tammy Rollston. I could not have done it without you!

SUPPLIERS

Bernat Super Value Yarn

www.yarnspirations.com

Red Heart Super Saver Yarn

www.redheart.com

General Yarn

Canada: www.michaels.com

USA: www.joann.com

UK: www.sewandso.co.uk

Worldwide: www.loveknitting.com

Stuffing and Shelf Liner

Canada: www.walmart.ca

USA: www.walmart.com

Australia and New Zealand: www.spotlightstores.com

Worldwide: www.amazon.com

Snuggle & Play Crochet

CAROLINA GUZMAN BENITEZ

This is just the beginning of a wonderful story of friendship. These cute characters are destined to be carried around endlessly in the tight little hand of a small person you know. The fun and colorful crochet designs, from a dog and cat to a zebra, monkey, and reindeer, will become adorable characters that are sure to accompany your little one on their journey through childhood and to share their adventures along the way.

By using your imagination with colors, yarns, expressions, and accessories, and choosing from the different blanket patterns in the section, you can combine the patterns in dozens of ways to create your very own versions.

These patterns will last for years. You can use them for children from the earliest age, who love to carry a little blanket wherever they go, and for older children who will enjoy playing with the fun amigurumi toys. These toys and loveys also make perfect gifts. Everyone is sure to have a different favorite character!

MATERIALS AND EQUIPMENT

Most of the characters and loveys in this section are made out of worsted weight yarn using a 4mm (G) hook. Where a larger hook is required this will be specified in the pattern. If no hook size is specified, use your 4mm (G) hook. All blankets are made with a 5mm (H) hook. I recommend using a soft yarn, like merino.

Take care when attaching safety eyes, as you'll not be able to remove them once they have been secured in place. If you are making the toys for young children, I recommend embroidering the eyes instead.

You'll need the same equipment for most of the toys as listed below:

- 4mm (G) hook
- 5mm (H) hook
- Stitch markers
- Tapestry needle
- Polyester stuffing
- 12mm amigurumi safety eyes – two for each character
- Scissors

You can use up odd balls of yarn for the toys and feel free to use different colors to those specified in the patterns! Who says a zebra has to be black and white?

Stuff your toys with polyester fiberfill, which is inexpensive, washable and non-allergenic. Avoid over-stuffing, because the stitches will stretch and the stuffing will show through.

HOW TO USE THIS SECTION

WHAT IS A LOVEY?

A lovey is a small comfort blanket, designed to be carried around by a young child. This section contains five patterns for small blankets, or loveys, and patterns for 20 cute characters.

You can make the characters on their own, or you can use the patterns to make a lovey from each of the characters. To do this you'll need to crochet most of the character, without its body and legs - and its tail if it has one!

Then you'll make a blanket and, following the instructions in the pattern, attach the character to the blanket. By stitching the two together you can make an adorable comfort blanket or lovey that your little one will enjoy carrying around with them.

Either follow the patterns as we have suggested, which have paired up the blankets and the characters, or make any combination you wish. You can change the colors or swap the suggested blanket for another one in the section to create your own unique toys and loveys.

Use your imagination to make any number of toys that are completely unique to you!

SKILL LEVEL REQUIRED

The Granny Blanket is the easiest of the five blankets and suitable for new crocheters. The character patterns are all labeled as intermediate – they involve some counting and perhaps some skills that you might not have learnt before, such as surface slip stitch or using a magic ring.

We have explained these stitches at the end of my section of the book, so you can look up anything you are unfamiliar with.

HOW TO USE THE PATTERNS

Each pattern includes a table that tells you which body parts are required and where you'll find the pattern. Most of the heads and bodies are the same as Theo the Teddy Bear. For every part there is a chart to accompany the pattern, which you can refer to if you prefer working from a chart.

I recommend assembling the features on the head of the loveys before finishing off the head.

HOW TO READ A CHART

The charts in this section are drawn in different colors to make them easy to read. Start in the center of the chart where you see the little white arrow head. ◁
Follow each round counterclockwise, working your way out from the center. The symbols used in the charts are standard crochet symbols, and are listed at the end of the section. The chart should give you an idea of the shape of the piece you are making and can be used together with the written pattern.

GRanny
Blanket

Skill level
Easy

You will need
- Worsted weight yarn in chosen colors
- 5mm (H) hook
- Tapestry needle
- Scissors

Stitch summary
ch, dc, sl st

Finished size
Approximately 13in x 13in (33cm x 33cm)

PATTERN

Foundation ring: using 5mm (H) hook, make a magic ring.

Round 1: ch3 (counts as first dc), then working into the ring, work 2dc, ch2, (3dc, ch2) three times. Join with a sl st in the top of initial ch3.

Round 2: sl st in next 2 dc, sl st in next ch2 corner space, ch3 (counts as first dc), 2dc, ch2, 3dc in the same space, (ch1, 3dc, ch2, 3dc in next ch2 corner space) three times, ch1. Join with sl st in top of initial ch3.

Round 3: sl st in next 2 dc, sl st in next ch2 corner space, ch3 (counts as first dc), 2dc, ch2, 3dc in the same space, (ch1, 3dc in next ch space, ch1, 3dc, ch2, 3dc in next corner space) three times, ch1, 3dc in next ch space, ch1. Join with sl st in top of initial ch3.

Round 4: sl st in next 2 dc, sl st in next ch2 corner space, ch3 (counts as first dc), 2dc, ch2, 3dc in the same space, [(ch1, 3dc in next ch space) twice, ch1, 3dc, ch2, 3dc in next corner space] three times, ch1, (3dc in next ch space, ch1) twice. Join with sl st in top of initial ch3.

Round 5: sl st in next 2 dc, sl st in next ch2 corner space, ch3 (counts as first dc), 2dc, ch2, 3dc in the same space, [(ch1, 3dc in next ch space) three times, ch1, 3dc, ch2, 3dc in next corner space] three times, ch1, (3dc in next ch space, ch1) three times. Join with sl st in top of initial ch3.

Round 6: sl st in next 2 dc, sl st in next ch2 corner space, ch3 (counts as first dc), 2dc, ch2, 3dc in the same space, [(ch1, 3dc in next ch space) four times, ch1, 3dc, ch2, 3dc in next corner space] three times, ch1, (3dc in next ch space, ch1) four times. Join with sl st in top of initial ch3.

Round 7: sl st in next 2 dc, sl st in next ch2 corner space, ch3 (counts as first dc), 2dc, ch2, 3dc in the same space, [(ch1, 3dc in next ch space) five times, ch1, 3dc, ch2, 3dc in next corner space] three times, ch1, (3dc in next ch space, ch1) five times. Join with sl st in top of initial ch3.

Round 8: sl st in next 2 dc, sl st in next ch2 corner space, ch3 (counts as first dc), 2dc, ch2, 3dc in the same space, [(ch1, 3dc in next ch space) six times, ch1, 3dc, ch2, 3dc in next corner space] three times, ch1, (3dc in next ch space, ch1) six times. Join with sl st in top of initial ch3.

Round 9: sl st in next 2 dc, sl st in next ch2 corner space, ch3 (counts as first dc), 2dc, ch2, 3dc in the same space, [(ch1, 3dc in next ch space) seven times, ch1, 3dc, ch2, 3dc in next corner space] three times, ch1, (3dc in next ch space, ch1) seven times. Join with sl st in top of initial ch3.

Round 10: sl st in next 2 dc, sl st in next ch2 corner space, ch3 (counts as first dc), 2dc, ch2, 3dc in the same space, [(ch1, 3dc in next ch space) eight times, ch1, 3dc, ch2, 3dc in next corner space] three times, ch1, (3dc in next ch space, ch1) eight times. Join with sl st in top of initial ch3.

Round 11: sl st in next 2 dc, sl st in next ch2 corner space, ch3 (counts as first dc), 2dc, ch2, 3dc in the same space, [(ch1, 3dc in next ch space) nine times, ch1, 3dc, ch2, 3dc in next corner space] three times, ch1, (3dc in next ch space, ch1) nine times. Join with sl st in top of initial ch3.

Round 12: sl st in next 2 dc, sl st in next ch2 corner space, ch3 (counts as first dc), 2dc, ch2, 3dc in the same space, [(ch1, 3dc in next ch space) ten times, ch1, 3dc, ch2, 3dc in next corner space] three times, ch1, (3dc in next ch space, ch1) ten times. Join with sl st in top of initial ch3.

Round 13: sl st in next 2 dc, sl st in next ch2 corner space, ch3 (counts as first dc), 5dc, skip next st, sl st in next st, skip next st, [(3dc in next ch space, skip next st, sl st in next st, skip next st) eleven times, 6dc in next corner space, skip next st, sl st in next st, skip next st] three times, (3dc in next ch space, skip next st, sl st in next st, skip next st) ten times. Join with sl st in top of initial ch3.

Fasten off.

Note: If you'd like to make a color change in this blanket, you should do so in the first ch2 space.

GRANNY BLANKET
FIRST ROUNDS

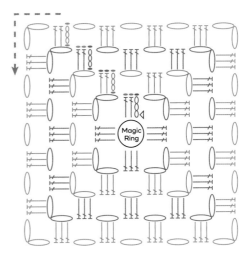

GRANNY BLANKET
LAST ROUND

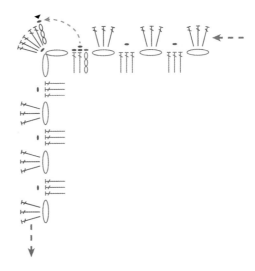

Peaks
Blanket

Skill level
Intermediate

You will need
- Worsted weight yarn in chosen colors
- 5mm (H) hook
- Stitch marker
- Tapestry needle
- Scissors

Stitch summary
ch, dc, sl st, reverse sc

Finished size
Approximately 16in x 16in (40cm x 40cm)

PATTERN

Foundation ring: using 5mm (H) hook, work a magic ring.

Round 1: ch3 (counts as first dc), work 9dc into the ring. Join with sl st in top of initial ch3. (10 sts)

Round 2: ch3 (counts as first dc), 1dc in the same st, 2dc in next 9 sts. Join with sl st in top of initial ch3. (20 sts)

Round 3: ch3 (counts as first dc), 2dc in the same st, skip next st, (3dc in next st, skip next st) nine times. Join with sl st in top of initial ch3. (30 sts)

Round 4: sl st in next 2 sts, sl st in next space, ch3 (counts as first dc), 1dc, ch2, 2dc in the same space. (Skip next 3 sts, then work 2dc, ch2, 2dc in next space) nine times. Join with sl st in top of initial ch3. (40 sts)

Round 5: sl st in next st, ch3 (counts as first dc), 2dc, ch2, 2dc in next ch2 space, 1dc in next st. (Skip next 2 sts, 1dc in next st, 2dc, ch2, 2dc in next ch2 space, 1dc in next st) nine times. Join with sl st in top of initial ch3. (60 sts)

Round 6: sl st in next st, ch3 (counts as first dc), 1dc in next st, 1dc, ch2, 1dc in next ch2 space, 1dc in next 2 sts. (Skip next 2 sts, 1dc in next 2 sts, 1dc, ch2, 1dc in next ch2 space, 1dc in next 2 sts) nine times. Join with sl st in top of initial ch3. (60 sts)

Round 7: sl st in next st, ch3 (counts as first dc), 1dc in next st, 2dc, ch2, 2dc in next ch2 space, 1dc in next 2 sts. (Skip next 2 sts, 1dc in next 2 sts, 2dc, ch2, 2dc in next ch2 space, 1dc in next 2 sts) nine times. Join with sl st in top of initial ch3. (80 sts)

Round 8: sl st in next st, ch3 (counts as first dc), 1dc in next 2 sts, 1dc in next ch2 space, 1dc in next 3 sts. (Skip next 2 sts, 1dc in next 3 sts, 1dc, ch2, 1dc in next ch2 space, 1dc in next 3 sts) nine times. Join with sl st in top of initial ch3. (80 sts)

Round 9: sl st in next st, ch3 (counts as first dc), 1dc in next 2 sts, 2dc, ch2, 2dc in next ch2 space, 1dc in next 3 sts. (Skip next 2 sts, 1dc in next 3 sts, 2dc, ch2, 2dc in next ch2 space, 1dc in next 3 sts) nine times. Join with sl st in top of initial ch3. (100 sts)

Round 10: sl st in next st, ch3 (counts as first dc), 1dc in next 3 sts, 1dc, ch2, 1dc in next ch2 space, 1dc in next 4 sts. (Skip next 2 sts, 1dc in next 4 sts, 1dc, ch2, 1dc in next ch2 space, 1dc in next 4 sts) nine times. Join with sl st in top of initial ch3. (100 sts)

Round 11: sl st in next st, ch3 (counts as first dc), 1dc in next 3 sts, 2dc, ch2, 2dc in next ch2 space, 1dc in next 4 sts. (Skip next 2 sts, 1dc in next 4 sts, 2dc, ch2, 2dc in next ch2 space, 1dc in next 4 sts) nine times. Join with sl st in top of initial ch3. (120 sts)

Round 12: sl st in next st, ch3 (counts as first dc), 1dc in next 4 sts, 1dc, ch2, 1dc in next ch2 space, 1dc in next 5 sts. (Skip next 2 sts, 1dc in next 5 sts, 1dc, ch2, 1dc in next ch2 space, 1dc in next 5 sts) nine times. Join with sl st in top of initial ch3. (120 sts)

Round 13: sl st in next st, ch3 (counts as first dc), 1dc in next 4 sts, 2dc, ch2, 2dc in next ch2 space, 1dc in next 5 sts. (Skip next 2 sts, 1dc in next 5 sts, 2dc, ch2, 2dc in next ch2 space, 1dc in next 5 sts) nine times. Join with sl st in top of initial ch3. (140 sts)

Round 14: sl st in next st, ch3 (counts as first dc), 1dc in next 5 sts, 2dc, ch2, 2dc in next ch2 space, 1dc in next 6 sts. (Skip next 2 sts, 1dc in next 6 sts, 2dc, ch2, 2dc in next ch2 space, 1dc in next 6 sts) nine times. Join with sl st in top of initial ch3. (160 sts)

Round 15: reverse sc in all sts and finish off.

PEAKS BLANKET
FIRST ROUNDS

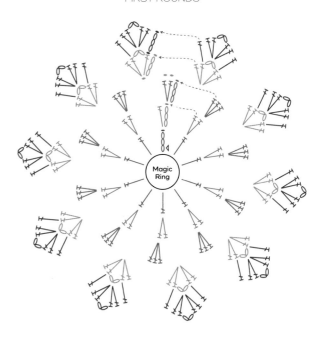

PEAKS BLANKET
ROUND VARIATIONS

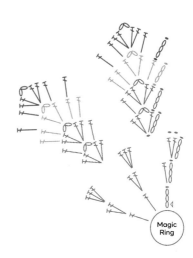

TexturE
Blanket

Skill level
Intermediate

You will need
- Worsted weight yarn in chosen colors
- 5mm (H) hook
- Stitch marker
- Tapestry needle
- Scissors

Stitch summary
ch, sc, dc, sl st

Finished size
Approximately 12in x 13in (30cm x 33cm)

PATTERN

Foundation row: using 5mm (H) hook, ch47.

Row 1: starting in sixth ch from hook, dc in next 2 sts, dc in fifth ch from hook, (skip next ch, dc in next 2 dc, dc in skipped ch) thirteen times, dc in next ch, ch3 and turn. (43 sts)

Rows 2-20: (skip next st, dc in next 2 sts, dc in skipped st) fourteen times, dc in top of turning ch, ch3 and turn. (43 sts)

Row 21: (skip next st, dc in next 2 sts, dc in skipped st) fourteen times, 1dc in top of turning ch. (43 sts)

Now you'll work down the left side of the blanket, inserting your hook in the spaces between stitches.

Round 22: (sc in next st, ch) twenty times, sc, ch2, sc in next corner space.

Now you'll work along the foundation chain of the blanket.

Round 22 (cont): ch, skip next st, sc in next st, (ch, skip next 2 ch, sc in next st) thirteen times, ch, skip next st, sc, ch2, sc in next corner space.

Now work up the right side of the blanket, inserting your hook in the spaces between stitches.

Round 22 (cont): ch, (sc in next st, ch) nineteen times, sc, ch2, sc in next corner space.

Now work along the top of the blanket, inserting your hook in the spaces between stitches.

Round 22 (cont): ch, skip next st, sc in next st, (ch, skip next 2 sts, sc in next st) thirteen times, ch, skip next st, sc, ch2 in corner space, sl st in first sc of this round.

Round 23: ch2, (sc in next ch space, ch) twenty times, (sc, ch2, sc) in next ch2 corner space, (ch, sc in next ch space) fifteen times, ch, (sc, ch2, sc) in next ch2 corner space, (ch, sc in next ch space) twenty times, ch, (sc, ch2, sc) in next ch2 corner space, (ch, sc in next ch space) fifteen times, ch, (sc, ch2, sc) in next ch2 corner space. Join with sl st in first ch2 space of this round.

Round 24: ch, sc in initial ch2, ch, (sc in next ch space, ch) twenty times, (sc, ch2, sc) in next ch2 corner space, (ch, sc in next ch space) sixteen times, ch, (sc, ch2, sc) in next ch2 corner space, (ch, sc in next ch space) twenty-one times, ch, (sc, ch2, sc) in next ch2 corner space, (ch, sc in next ch space) sixteen times, ch, (sc, ch2, sc) in next ch2 corner space, ch. Join with sl st in first sc of this round.

Round 25: (sc in next sc, 4hdc in next sc) ten times, sc in next sc, 7hdc in next ch2 corner space, skip next sc, (sc in next sc, 4hdc in next sc) eight times, sc in next sc, 7hdc in next ch2 corner space, skip next sc, (sc in next sc, 4hdc in next sc) ten times, sc in next sc, 7hdc in next ch2 corner space, skip next sc, (sc in next sc, 4hdc in next sc) eight times, sc in next sc, 7hdc in next ch2 corner space, sl st in first sc of this round.

TEXTURE BLANKET
FIRST ROUNDS

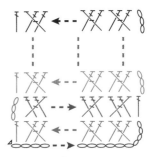

TEXTURE BLANKET
LAST ROUNDS

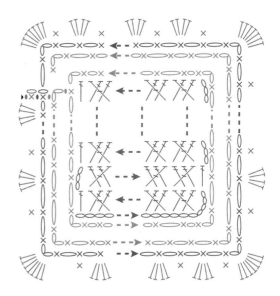

Round
Blanket

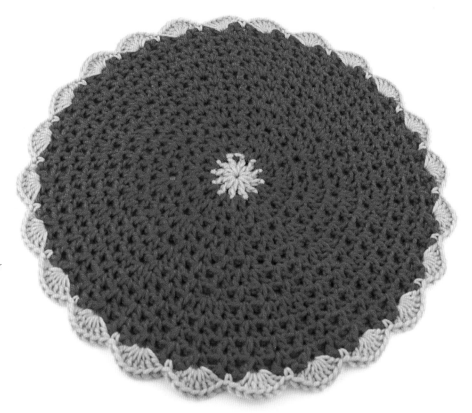

Skill level
Intermediate

You will need
- Worsted weight yarn in chosen colors
- 5mm (H) hook
- Tapestry needle
- Scissors

Stitch summary
ch, V-stitch, dc, sc, sl st

Finished size
Approximately 14in (35cm) diameter

PATTERN

Note: When you make the first V-stitch of each round you must replace the first dc with ch 3.

To make a V-stitch work 1dc, ch, 1dc into the same stitch.

Foundation ring: using 5mm (H) hook, make a magic ring.

Round 1: ch3 (counts as first dc), ch1, (dc, ch1) eleven times into the magic ring. Join with a sl st in top of initial ch3. (12 dc)

Round 2: sl st in next chain space, V-stitch in the same chain space. V-stitch in each chain space around. Join with a sl st in top of initial ch3. (24 dc)

Round 3: sl st in next chain space, V-stitch in the same chain space, V-stitch in space between next two dc, V-stitch in next chain space. (V-stitch in next chain space, V-stitch between next two dc, V-stitch in next chain space) five times. Join with a sl st in top of initial ch3. (36 dc)

Round 4: sl st in next chain space, V-stitch in the same chain space, V-stitch in each chain space around. Join with a sl st in top of initial ch3. (36 dc)

Round 5: sl st in next chain space, V-stitch in the same chain space, V-stitch between next two dc. (V-stitch in next 2 chain spaces, V-stitch between next two dc) eight times. V-stitch in next chain space. Join with a sl st in top of initial ch3. (54 dc)

Round 6: sl st in next chain space, V-stitch in the same chain space, V-stitch in each chain space around. Join with a sl st in top of initial ch3. (54 dc)

Round 7: sl st in next chain space , V-stitch in the same chain space, V-stitch in next chain space, V-stitch between next two dc, (V-stitch in next 3 chain spaces, V-stitch between next two dc) eight times, V-stitch in next chain space. Join with a sl st in top of initial ch3. (72 dc)

Round 8: sl st in next chain space, V-stitch in the same chain space, V-stitch in each chain space around. Join with a sl st in top of initial ch3. (72 dc)

Round 9: sl st in next chain space, V-stitch in the same chain space, V-stitch in next chain space, V-stitch between next two dc, (V-stitch in next 3 chain spaces, V-stitch between next two dc) eleven times, V-stitch in next chain space. Join with a sl st in top of initial ch3. (96 dc)

Rounds 10-12: sl st in next chain space, V-stitch in the same st, V-stitch in each chain space around. Join with a sl st in top of initial ch3. (96 dc)

Round 13: sl st in next chain space, ch3 (counts as first dc), 6dc in the same chain space, sc in next chain space. (7dc in next chain space, sc in next chain space) twenty-three times. Join with a sl st in top of initial ch3. (192 sts)

ROUND BLANKET

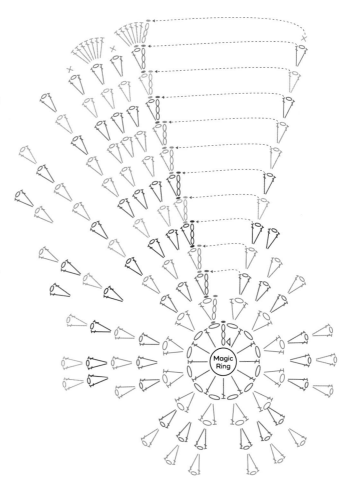

Block
Blanket

Skill level

Intermediate

You will need

- Worsted weight yarn in chosen colors
- 5mm (H) hook
- Tapestry needle
- Scissors

Stitch summary

ch, sc, dc, sl st

Finished size

Approximately 14½in x 14½in (37 x 37cm)

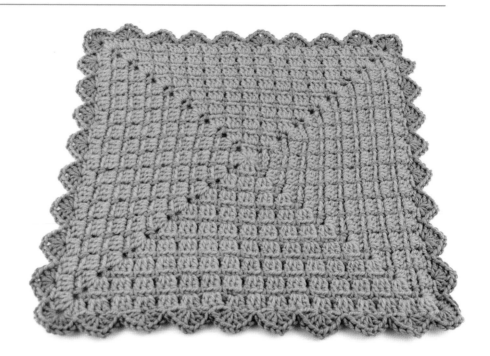

PATTERN

Foundation round: using a 5mm (H) hook, make a magic ring.

Round 1: ch3 (counts as first dc), 2dc, (ch2, 3dc) three times into the ring, ch2. Join with sl st in top of initial ch3. (12dc and four chain spaces)

Round 2: sl st in next 2 sts, sl st in corner space, ch1, sc, ch3, sc in the same space, (ch2, sc, ch3, sc in next corner space) three times, ch 2. Join with sl st in first sc of this round.

Round 3: sl st in next ch3 corner space, ch 3 (counts as first dc), 2dc, ch2, 3dc in the same space, (3dc in next ch2 space, 3dc, ch2, 3dc in next ch3 corner space) three times, 3 dc in next ch2 space. Join with sl st in top of initial chain.

Round 4: sl st in next 2 sts, sl st in next ch2 corner space, ch1, sc, ch3, sc in the same space. [(Ch 2, sc in next dc space) twice, ch2. (Sc, ch3, sc) in next ch2 corner space] three times. (Ch 2, sc in next dc space) twice, ch 2. Join with sl st in first sc of this round.

Round 5: sl st in next ch3 corner space, ch3 (counts as first dc), (2dc, ch2, 3dc) in the same space. [(3dc in next ch2 space) three times, 3dc, ch2, 3dc in next ch3 corner space] three times, (3dc in next ch2 space) three times. Join with sl st in top of initial chain.

Round 6: sl st in next 2 sts, sl st in next ch2 corner space, ch, sc, ch3, sc in the same space, [(ch2, sc in next dc space) four times, ch2, sc, ch3, sc in next ch2 corner space] three times, (ch2, sc in next dc space) four times, ch2. Join with sl st in first sc of this round.

Round 7: sl st in next ch3 corner space, ch3 (counts as first dc), 2dc, ch2, 3dc in the same space, [(3dc in next ch2 space) five times, 3dc, ch2, 3dc in next ch3 corner space] three times, (3dc in next ch2 space) five times. Join with sl st in top of initial chain.

Round 8: sl st in next 2 sts, sl st in next ch2 corner space, ch, sc, ch3, sc in the same ch2 space, [(ch2, sc in next dc space) six times, ch2, sc, ch3, sc in next ch2 corner space] three times, (ch2, sc in next dc space) six times, ch2. Join with sl st in first sc of this round.

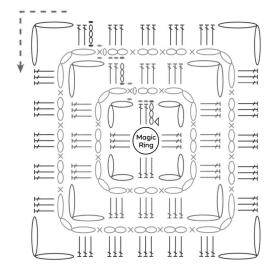

Round 9: sl st in next ch3 corner space, ch3 (counts as first dc), 2dc, ch2, 3dc in the same space, [(3dc in next ch2 space) seven times, 3dc, ch2, 3dc in next ch3 corner space] three times, (3dc in next ch2 space) seven times. Join with sl st in top of initial chain.

Round 10: sl st in next 2 sts, sl st in next ch2 corner space, ch, sc, ch3, sc in the same space, [(ch2, sc in next dc space) eight times, ch2, sc, ch3, sc in next ch2 corner space] three times, (ch2, sc in next dc space) eight times, ch2. Join with sl st in first sc of this round.

Round 11: sl st in next ch3 corner space, ch3 (counts as first dc), 2dc, ch2, 3dc in the same space, [(3dc in next ch2 space) nine times, 3dc, ch2, 3dc in next ch3 corner space] three times, (3dc in next ch2 space) nine times. Join with sl st in top of initial chain.

Round 12: sl st in next 2 sts, sl st in next ch2 corner space, ch, sc, ch3, sc in the same space, [(ch2, sc in next dc space) repeat ten times, ch2, sc, ch3, sc in next ch2 corner space] three times, (ch2, sc in next dc space) ten times, ch2. Join with sl st in first sc of this round.

Round 13: sl st in next ch3 corner space, ch3 (counts as first dc), 2dc, ch2, 3dc in the same space, [(3dc in next ch2 space) eleven times, 3dc, ch2, 3dc in next ch3 corner space] three times, (3dc in next ch2 space) eleven times. Join with sl st in top of initial chain.

Round 14: sl st in next 2 sts, sl st in next ch2 corner space, ch, sc, ch3, sc in the same space, [(ch2, sc in next dc space) twelve times, ch2, sc, ch3, sc in next ch2 corner space] three times, (ch2, sc in next dc space) twelve times, ch2. Join with sl st in first sc of this round.

Round 15: sl st in next ch3 corner space, ch3 (counts as first dc), 2dc, ch2, 3dc in the same space, [(3dc in next ch2 space) thirteen times, 3dc, ch2, 3dc in next ch3 corner space] three times, (3dc in next ch2 space) thirteen times. Join with sl st in top of initial chain.

Round 16: sl st in next 2 sts, sl st in next ch2 corner space, ch, sc, ch3, sc in the same space, [(ch2, sc in next dc space) fourteen times, ch2, sc, ch3, sc in next ch2 corner space] three times, (ch2, sc in next dc space) fourteen times, ch2. Join with sl st in first sc of this round.

Round 17: sl st in next ch3 corner space, ch3 (counts as first dc), 2dc, ch2, 3dc in the same space, [(3dc in next ch2 space) fifteen times, 3dc, ch2, 3dc in next ch3 corner space] three times, (3dc in next ch2 space) fifteen times. Join with sl st in top of initial chain.

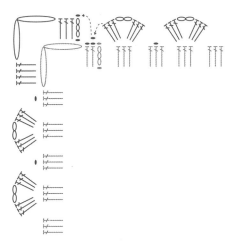

Round 18: sl st in next 2 sts, sl st in next ch2 corner space, ch3 (counts as first dc), 3dc, ch2, 4dc in the same space. [Skip next st, sl st in next st, (skip next 2 sts, 3dc, ch2, 3dc in next st, skip next 2 sts, sl st in next st) eight times, skip next st, 4dc, ch2, 4dc in next ch2 corner space] three times. Skip next st, sl st in next st, (skip next 2 sts, 3dc, ch2, 3dc in next st, skip next 2 sts, sl st in next st) eight times. Join with sl st in top of initial chain.

Theo
the Teddy Bear

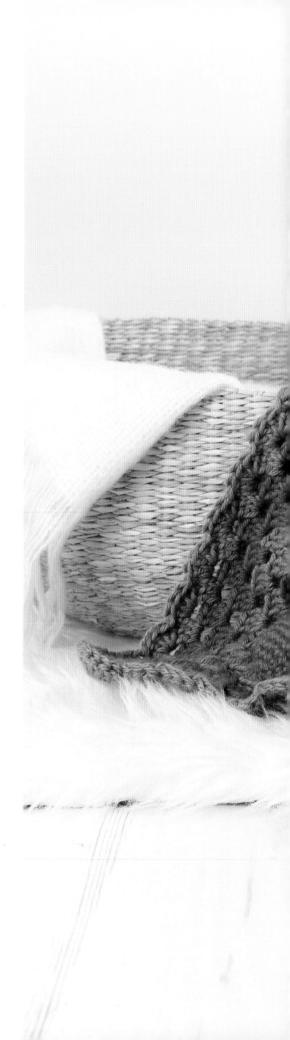

Skill level
Intermediate

You will need

- Worsted weight yarn: Brown, Dark Brown, Beige, Black, and Turquoise
- 4mm (G) hook
- Stitch marker
- Tapestry needle
- Stuffing
- 12mm amigurumi safety eyes
- Two small colored buttons
- Scissors

Stitch summary
ch, sc, sl st, sc2tog, surface sl st

Finished size
Teddy Bear: Approximately 10in (25cm) tall, including ears
Teddy Bear Lovey: Approximately 13in x 13in (33cm x 33cm)

CHART GUIDE

CHART	TEDDY BEAR	TEDDY BEAR LOVEY
Head	see chart	see chart
Body	see chart	n/a
Arm	see chart	see chart
Leg	see chart	n/a
Ear	see chart	same as Teddy Bear
Snout	see chart	same as Teddy Bear
Nose	see chart	same as Teddy Bear

All of the cookies have vanished
and Theo is wondering when
it will be time for dinner.

TEDDY BEAR PATTERN

Snout (beige)

Foundation ring: make a magic ring.

Round 1: work 6sc into ring.

Round 2: 2sc in all sts. (12 sts)

Round 3: (sc in next st, 2sc in next st) six times. (18 sts)

Round 4: (sc in next 2 sts, 2sc in next st) six times. (24 sts)

Rounds 5-6: sc in all sts. (24 sts)

Fasten off, leaving a long tail for sewing.

Nose (dark brown)

Foundation chain: ch4. Stitches are worked around both sides of this foundation chain.

Round 1: starting in second ch from hook, sc in next 2 sts, 3sc in last st. Continue on the other side of the foundation chain, sc in next st, 2sc in next st. (8 sts)

Round 2: 2sc in next st, sc in next st, 2sc in next 3 sts, sc in next st, 2sc in next 2 sts. (14 sts)

Round 3: sc in all sts. (14 sts)

Fasten off, leaving a long tail for sewing.

Stuff the nose and sew it to the snout between rounds 3 and 6. Ch3 from the bottom of the nose and attach it to the middle of the snout with your tapestry needle.

Ears (make 2 in brown)

Foundation ring: make a magic ring.

Round 1: work 6sc into ring.

Round 2: 2sc in all sts. (12 sts)

Round 3: (sc in next st, 2sc in next st) six times. (18 sts)

Round 4: (sc in next 2 sts, 2sc in next st) six times. (24 sts)

Rounds 5-8: sc in all sts. (24 sts)

The ears don't need to be stuffed. Flatten them and sew closed. Fasten off, leaving a long tail for sewing.

Head (brown)

Foundation ring: make a magic ring.

Round 1: work 6sc into ring.

Round 2: 2sc in all sts. (12 sts)

Round 3: (sc in next st, 2sc in next st) six times. (18 sts)

Round 4: (sc in next 2 sts, 2sc in next st) six times. (24 sts)

Round 5: (sc in next st, 2sc in next st, sc in next 2 sts) six times. (30 sts)

Round 6: (sc in next 4 sts, 2sc in next st) six times. (36 sts)

Round 7: (sc in next 2 sts, 2sc in next st, sc in next 3 sts) six times. (42 sts)

Round 8: (sc in next 6 sts, 2sc in next st) six times. (48 sts)

Round 9: sc in all sts. (48 sts)

Round 10: (sc in next 3 sts, 2sc in next st, sc in next 4 sts) six times. (54 sts)

Rounds 11-16: sc in all sts. (54 sts)

Round 17: (sc in next 3 sts, sc2tog, sc in next 4 sts) six times. (48 sts)

Round 18: sc in all sts. (48 sts)

Round 19: (sc in next 6 sts, sc2tog) six times. (42 sts)

Round 20: sc in all sts. (42 sts)

Stuff the head and continue stuffing as you go.

Round 21: (sc in next 2 sts, sc2tog, sc in next 3 sts) six times. (36 sts)

Round 22: sc in all sts. (36 sts)

Round 23: (sc in next 4 sts, sc2tog) six times. (30 sts)

Round 24: sc in all sts. (30 sts)

Round 25: (sc in next st, sc2tog, sc in next 2 sts) six times. (24 sts)

Round 26: (sc in next 2 sts, sc2tog) six times. (18 sts)

Fasten off.

Head assembly

Insert the safety eyes between rounds 14 and 15, with 1 stitch between them.

Using your tapestry needle and black yarn, make a diagonal stitch above each eye, between rounds 11 and 13, to give the teddy bear a more fun expression. Make each stitch about 3 crochet stitches long.

Sew the ears to the head between rounds 4 and 13. Place them evenly with 6 stitches between them on the top of the head.

Stuff the snout and sew it on the head between rounds 16 and 24.

TEDDY BEAR
SNOUT

TEDDY BEAR
NOSE

TEDDY BEAR
EAR

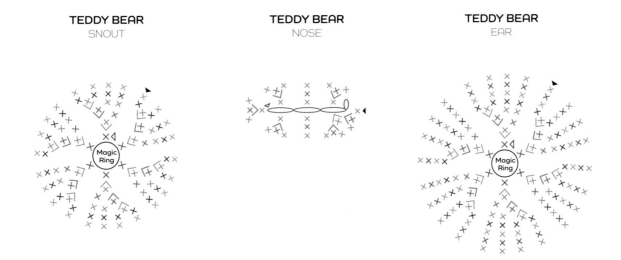

TEDDY BEAR
HEAD

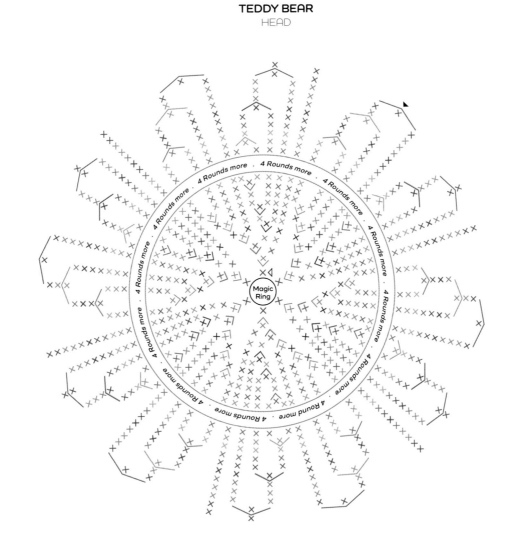

Body

Foundation ring: using brown yarn make a magic ring.

Round 1: work 6sc into ring.

Round 2: 2sc in all sts. (12 sts)

Round 3: (sc in next st, 2sc in next st) six times. (18 sts)

Round 4: (sc in next 2 sts, 2sc in next st) six times. (24 sts)

Round 5: (sc in next st, 2sc in next st, sc in next 2 sts) six times. (30 sts)

Round 6: (sc in next 4 sts, 2sc in next st) six times. (36 sts)

Round 7: sc in all sts. (36 sts)

Round 8: (sc in next 2 sts, 2sc in next st, sc in next 3 sts) six times. (42 sts)

Rounds 9-11: sc in all sts. (42 sts)

Round 12: (sc in next 2 sts, sc2tog, sc in next 3 sts) six times. (36 sts)

Rounds 13-14: sc in all sts. (36 sts)

Round 15: change to turquoise yarn. Sc in all sts. (36 sts)

Round 16: (sc in next 4 sts, sc2tog) six times. (30 sts)

Stuff the body and continue stuffing as you go.

Rounds 17-18: sc in all sts. (30 sts)

Round 19: (sc in next st, sc2tog, sc in next 2 sts) six times. (24 sts)

Rounds 20-21: sc in all sts. (24 sts)

Round 22: change to brown yarn. (Sc in next 2 sts, sc2tog) six times. (18 sts)

Fasten off, leaving a long tail for sewing.

Body detail

Pull up a loop of turquoise yarn between rounds 15 and 16 and do surface sl st in all 30 sts. Fasten off.

Pull up a loop of turquoise yarn between rounds 21 and 22 and do surface sl st in all 18 sts. These stitches define the top and bottom of the sweater. Fasten off.

Note: Don't make your surface slip stitch too tight.

Arms (make 2)

Foundation ring: using brown yarn make a magic ring.

Round 1: work 6sc into ring.

Round 2: 2sc in all sts. (12 sts)

Round 3: (sc in next st, 2sc in next st) six times. (18 sts)

Round 4: (sc in next 5 sts, 2sc in next st) three times. (21 sts)

Rounds 5-9: sc in all sts. (21 sts)

Round 10: sc in next 8 sts, sc2tog, sc in next 9 sts, sc2tog. (19 sts)

Round 11: sc in all sts. (19 sts)

Round 12: sc in next 7 sts, sc2tog, sc in next 8 sts, sc2tog. (17 sts)

Round 13: sc in all sts. (17 sts)

Round 14: sc in next 6 sts, sc2tog, sc in next 7 sts, sc2tog. (15 sts)

Round 15: sc in all sts. (15 sts)

Round 16: change to turquoise yarn. Sc in next 5 sts, sc2tog, sc in next 6 sts, sc2tog. (13 sts)

Rounds 17-18: sc in all sts. (13 sts)

Round 19: sc in next 4 sts, sc2tog, sc in next 5 sts, sc2tog. (11 sts)

Stuff the arms. Flatten the arms and sew them closed. Fasten off, leaving a long tail for sewing.

Arm detail

Pull up a loop of turquoise yarn between rounds 16 and 17 and do surface sl st in all 13 sts.

Legs (make 2 in brown)

Foundation ring: make a magic ring.

Round 1: work 6sc into ring.

Round 2: 2sc in all sts. (12 sts)

Round 3: (sc in next st, 2sc in next st) six times. (18 sts)

Round 4: (sc in next 5 sts, 2sc in next st) three times. (21 sts)

Rounds 5-7: sc in all sts. (21 sts)

Round 8: sc in next 8 sts, sc2tog, sc in next 9 sts, sc2tog. (19 sts)

Round 9: sc in all sts. (19 sts)

Round 10: sc in next 7 sts, sc2tog, sc in next 8 sts, sc2tog. (17 sts)

Round 11: sc in all sts. (17 sts)

Round 12: sc in next 6 sts, sc2tog, sc in next 7 sts, sc2tog. (15 sts)

Round 13: sc in all sts. (15 sts)

Round 14: sc in next 5 sts, sc2tog, sc in next 6 sts, sc2tog. (13 sts)

Round 15: sc in all sts. (13 sts)

Stuff the legs. Fasten off, leaving a long tail for sewing.

Toy assembly

Sew the head to the body.

Sew two little buttons onto the body.

Sew the arms to each side of the body between rounds 20 and 21.

Sew the legs at the bottom of the body between rounds 2 and 5.

TEDDY BEAR
ARM

TEDDY BEAR
LEG

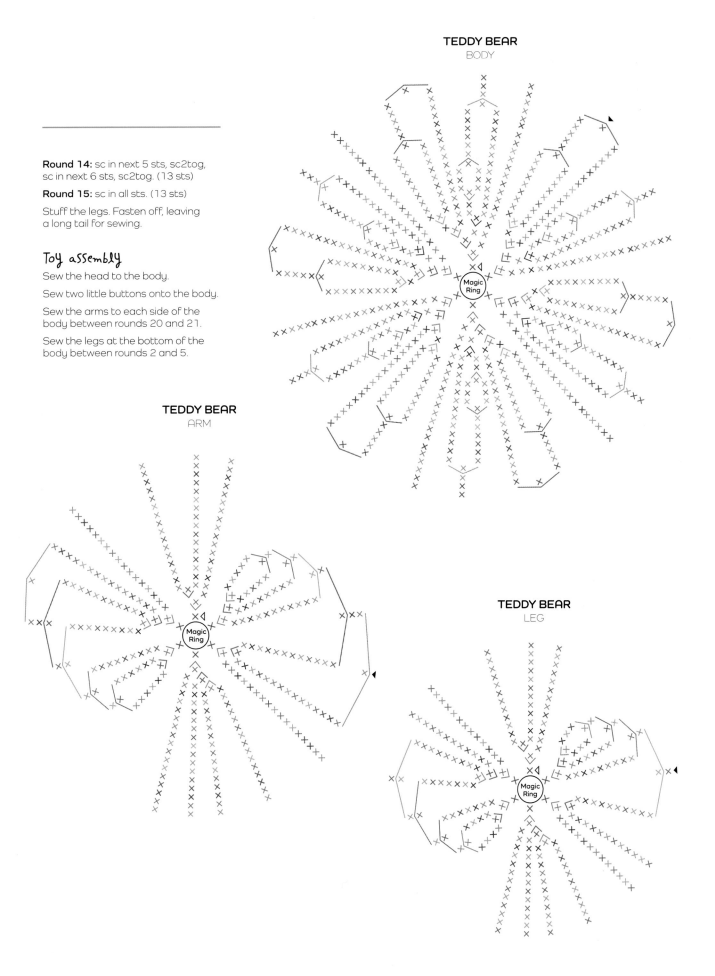

TEDDY BEAR LOVEY PATTERN

Snout (beige)

Follow the snout instructions from Theo the Teddy Bear.

Nose (dark brown)

Follow the nose instructions from Theo the Teddy Bear.

Ears (make 2 in brown)

Follow the ear instructions from Theo the Teddy Bear.

Head (brown)

Follow the head instructions from Theo the Teddy Bear, but add the following rounds:

Round 27: (sc in next st, sc2tog) six times. (12 sts)

Round 28: sc2tog six times. (6 sts)

Fasten off, leaving a long tail for sewing.

Head assembly

Follow the head assembly instructions from Theo the Teddy Bear.

Take the head and, using your tapestry needle, weave the yarn tail through each remaining stitch and pull it tight to close. Leave a long tail for sewing.

Arms (make 2)

Follow the arm instructions from Theo the Teddy Bear, but add the following rounds:

Rounds 20-21: sc in all sts. (11 sts)

Blanket

Make Granny Blanket using the following colors:

Rounds 1-3: brown.

Rounds 4-5: turquoise.

Rounds 6-7: brown.

Rounds 8-9: turquoise.

Rounds 10-11: brown.

Rounds 12-13: turquoise.

Lovey assembly

Sew the head on the center of the blanket, placing it so that the head faces one of the corners.

Sew the arms onto the blanket, just under each side of the head.

TEDDY BEAR LOVEY
HEAD

TEDDY BEAR LOVEY
ARM

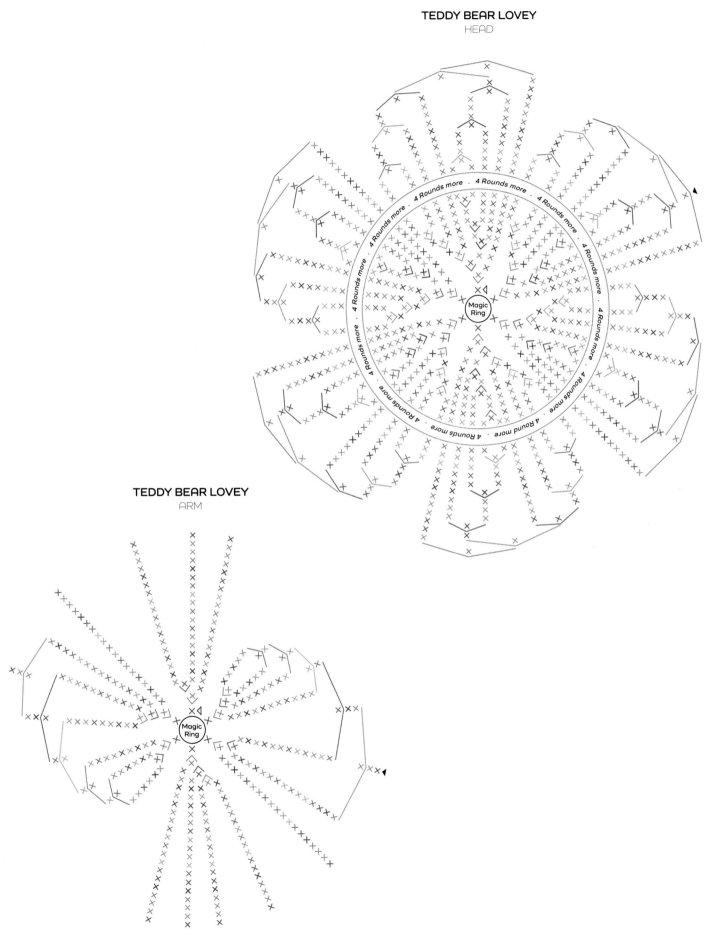

Clover
the Bunny

Skill level

Intermediate

You will need

- Worsted weight yarn: Gray, Yellow, Light Pink, and Black
- 4mm (G) hook
- Stitch marker
- Tapestry needle
- Stuffing
- 12mm amigurumi safety eyes
- Three small colored buttons
- Scissors

Stitch summary

ch, sc, sl st, sc2tog

Finished size

Bunny: Approximately 13in (33cm) tall, including ears
Bunny Lovey: Approximately 12in x 13in (30cm x 33cm)

CHART GUIDE

CHART	BUNNY	BUNNY LOVEY
Head	same as Teddy Bear	same as Teddy Bear Lovey
Body	same as Teddy Bear	n/a
Arm	same as Teddy Bear	same as Teddy Bear Lovey
Leg	same as Teddy Bear	n/a
Ear	see chart	same as Bunny
Tail	see chart	n/a

Clover is always getting into trouble for hopping around and making a mess.

BUNNY PATTERN

Left ear (yellow)

Foundation ring: make a magic ring.

Round 1: work 6sc into ring.

Round 2: sc in all sts. (6 sts)

Round 3: 2sc in all sts. (12 sts)

Round 4: sc in all sts. (12 sts)

Round 5: (sc in next st, 2sc in next st) six times. (18 sts)

Round 6: sc in all sts. (18 sts)

Round 7: (sc in next 5 sts, 2sc in next st) three times. (21 sts)

Rounds 8-13: sc in all sts. (21 sts)

Round 14: (sc in next 5 sts, sc2tog) three times. (18 sts)

Round 15: sc in all sts. (18 sts)

Round 16: (sc in next 7 sts, sc2tog) twice. (16 sts)

Round 17: (sc in next 6 sts, sc2tog) twice. (14 sts)

Round 18: (sc in next 5 sts, sc2tog) twice. (12 sts)

Round 19: sc in all sts. (12 sts)

The ears don't need to be stuffed. Flatten them and sew closed. Fasten off, leaving a long tail for sewing.

Right ear

This part is worked in joined rounds. Follow the left ear instructions using the following colors:

Rounds 1-3: yellow.

Rounds 4-5: gray.

Rounds 6-7: yellow.

Rounds 8-9: gray.

Rounds 10-11: yellow.

Rounds 12-13: gray.

Rounds 14-15: yellow.

Rounds 16-17: gray.

Rounds 18-19: yellow.

Head (gray)

Follow the head instructions from Theo the Teddy Bear.

Head assembly

Insert the safety eyes between rounds 14 and 15, with 1 stitch between them.

Using your tapestry needle and black yarn, make a diagonal stitch above each eye, between rounds 11 and 13, to give the rabbit a fun expression.

To make the nose, with light pink yarn make several horizontal stitches (2 sts in length) in the center, between rounds 15 and 16. Then make one long stitch down (3 sts in length).

Sew the ears to the head between rounds 2 and 7. Place them evenly, with 2 stitches between them on the top of the head.

Tail (gray)

Foundation ring: make a magic ring.

Round 1: work 6sc into ring.

Round 2: 2sc in all sts. (12 sts)

Round 3: (sc in next 3 sts, 2sc in next st) three times. (15 sts)

Round 4: sc in all sts. (15 sts)

Round 5: (sc in next st, sc2tog) five times. (10 sts)

Round 6: sc2tog five times. (5 sts)

Stuff the tail a little. Fasten off, leaving a long tail for sewing. Using your tapestry needle, weave the yarn tail through each remaining stitch and pull it tight to close.

Body (gray)

Follow the body instructions from Theo the Teddy Bear.

Sew the tail onto the back of the body. Place it in the center, on round 8. Sew three buttons randomly onto the body. I place them a little to the right, between rounds 10 and 14.

BUNNY LOVEY PATTERN

Right arm (yellow)

Follow the arm instructions from Theo the Teddy Bear.

Left arm

This part is worked in joined rounds. Follow the arm instructions from Theo the Teddy Bear using the following colors:

Rounds 1-3: yellow.

Rounds 4-5: gray.

Rounds 6-7: yellow.

Rounds 8-9: gray.

Rounds 10-11: yellow.

Rounds 12-13: gray.

Rounds 14-15: yellow.

Rounds 16-17: gray.

Rounds 18-19: yellow.

Left leg (yellow)

Follow the leg instructions from Theo the Teddy Bear.

Right leg

This part is worked in joined rounds. Follow the leg instructions from Theo the Teddy Bear using the following colors:

Rounds 1-3: yellow.

Rounds 4-5: gray.

Rounds 6-7: yellow.

Rounds 8-9: gray.

Rounds 10-11: yellow.

Rounds 12-13: gray.

Rounds 14-15: yellow.

Toy assembly

Sew the head to the body.

Sew the arms to each side of the body between rounds 20 and 21.

Sew the legs at the bottom of the body between rounds 1 and 6.

Ears

Follow the left and right ear instructions from Clover the Bunny.

Head (gray)

Follow the head instructions from Theo the Teddy Bear Lovey.

Head assembly

Follow the head assembly instructions from Clover the Bunny.

Take the head and, using your tapestry needle, weave the yarn tail through each remaining stitch and pull it tight to close. Leave a long tail for sewing.

Arms

Follow the arm instructions from Theo the Teddy Bear Lovey, using colors as for Clover the Bunny.

On left arm use gray yarn for rounds 20-21.

Blanket

Make Texture Blanket using the following colors:

Rounds 1-21: gray.

Rounds 22-25: yellow.

Lovey assembly

Sew the head in the center of the blanket, placing it so that it's facing one of the corners.

Sew the arms onto the blanket, just under either side of the head.

BUNNY
TAIL

BUNNY
EAR

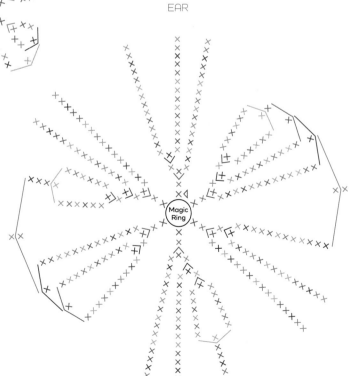

Dylan
the Dog

Skill level
Intermediate

You will need
- Worsted weight yarn: Light Brown, Brown, Dark Brown, Coral, and Black
- 4mm (G) hook
- 5mm (H) hook
- Stitch marker
- Tapestry needle
- Stuffing
- 12mm amigurumi safety eyes
- One small wooden button
- Scissors

Stitch summary
ch, sc, sl st, sc2tog

Finished size
Dog: Approximately 10½in (27cm) tall

Dog Lovey: Approximately 16in (40cm) diameter

CHART GUIDE

CHART	DOG	DOG LOVEY
Head	same as Teddy Bear	same as Teddy Bear Lovey
Body	same as Teddy Bear	n/a
Arm	same as Teddy Bear	same as Teddy Bear Lovey
Leg	same as Teddy Bear	n/a
Ear	see chart	same as Dog
Nose	see chart	same as Dog
Snout	same as Giraffe	same as Giraffe
Tail	same as Cat	n/a

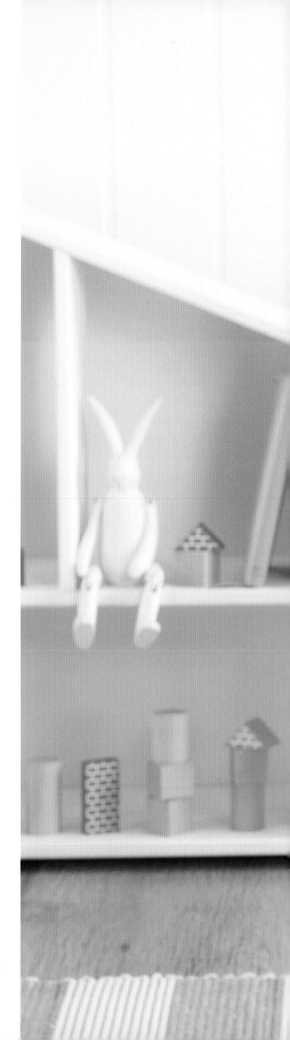

As soon as he hears the news,
Dylan can't wait to go
and tell his friends.

DOG PATTERN

Ears (make 2 in brown)

Foundation ring: make a magic ring.

Round 1: work 6sc into ring.

Round 2: 2sc in all sts. (12 sts)

Round 3: (sc in next st, 2sc in next st) six times. (18 sts)

Round 4: sc in all sts. (18 sts)

Round 5: (sc in next 2 sts, 2sc in next st) six times. (24 sts)

Round 6: sc in all sts. (24 sts)

Round 7: (sc in next st, 2sc in next st, sc in next 2 sts) six times. (30 sts)

Rounds 8-10: sc in all sts. (30 sts)

Round 11: (sc in next st, sc2tog, sc in next 2 sts) six times. (24 sts)

Round 12: sc in all sts. (24 sts)

Round 13: (sc in next 2 sts, sc2tog) six times. (18 sts)

Round 14: sc in all sts. (18 sts)

Round 15: (sc in next st, sc2tog) six times. (12 sts)

Rounds 16-19: sc in all sts. (12 sts)

The ears don't need to be stuffed. Flatten them and sew closed. Fasten off, leaving a long tail for sewing.

Snout (light brown)

Follow the snout instructions from Sefra the Giraffe.

Nose (dark brown)

Foundation chain: ch5.

Stitches will be worked around both sides of the foundation chain.

Round 1: starting in second ch from hook, sc in next 3 sts, 3sc in last st. Continue on the other side of the foundation chain, sc in next 2 sts, 2sc in next st. (10 sts)

Round 2: 2sc in next st, sc in next 2 sts, 2sc in next 3 sts, sc in next 2 sts, 2sc in next 2 sts. (16 sts)

Round 3: sc in all sts. (16 sts)

Fasten off, leaving a long tail for sewing.

Stuff the nose and sew it to the snout between rounds 2 and 6. Then sew a small vertical stitch downwards from the nose, covering about 2 crochet stitches.

Head (light brown)

Follow the head instructions from Theo the Teddy Bear.

Head assembly

Insert the safety eyes between rounds 14 and 15, with 3 stitches between them.

Using a tapestry needle and black yarn, make a diagonal stitch above each eye, between rounds 12 and 14, to give the dog a more fun expression. Make each stitch about 4 crochet stitches long.

Sew the ears to the head between rounds 7 and 8.

Stuff the snout and sew it to the head between rounds 16 and 24.

Tail

Follow the tail instructions from Liz the Cat using the following colors:

Rounds 1-4: brown.

Rounds 5-21: light brown.

Body (light brown)

Follow the body instructions from Theo the Teddy Bear.

Sew the tail on the back of the body between rounds 8 and 10.

Arms (make 2)

Follow the arm instructions from Theo the Teddy Bear using the following colors:

Rounds 1-6: brown.

Rounds 7-19: light brown.

Legs (make 2)

Follow the leg instructions from Theo the Teddy Bear using the following colors:

Rounds 1-6: brown.

Rounds 7-15: light brown.

DOG LOVEY PATTERN

Toy assembly

Sew the head to the body.

Sew the arms to each side of the body between rounds 20 and 21.

Sew the legs at the bottom of the body between rounds 3 and 5.

Scarf (coral)

Use 5mm (H) hook.

Foundation chain: ch89.

Row 1: starting in second ch from hook, sc in next 88 sts, ch1, turn. (88 sts)

Row 2: working with the third loop, sc in all sts. (88 sts)

Fasten off.

Place the scarf around the neck of the dog. If you like, you can sew a little wooden button on the knot of the scarf.

Ears (make 2 in brown)

Follow the ear instructions from Dylan the Dog.

Snout (light brown)

Follow the snout instructions from Sefra the Giraffe.

Nose (dark brown)

Follow the nose instructions from Dylan the Dog.

Head (light brown)

Follow the head instructions from Theo the Teddy Bear Lovey.

Head assembly

Follow the head assembly instructions from Dylan the Dog.

Take the head and, using your tapestry needle, weave the yarn tail through each remaining stitch and pull it tight to close. Leave a long tail for sewing.

Arms (make 2)

Follow the arm instructions from Theo the Teddy Bear Lovey using the following colors:

Rounds 1-6: brown.

Rounds 7-21: light brown.

Blanket

Make Peaks Blanket using the following colors:

Rounds 1-13: light brown.

Rounds 14-15: brown.

Lovey assembly

Sew the head on the center of the blanket.

Sew the arms onto the blanket, just under the right and left side of the head.

DOG
EAR

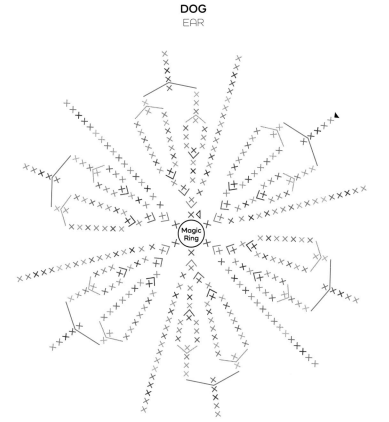

DOG
NOSE

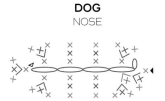

Liz
the Cat

Skill level
Intermediate

You will need
- Worsted weight yarn: White, Light Pink, Fuchsia, and Black
- 4mm (G) hook
- 5mm (H) hook
- Stitch marker
- Tapestry needle
- Stuffing
- 12mm amigurumi safety eyes
- One small wooden button
- Scissors

Stitch summary
ch, sc, sl st, sc2tog

Finished size
Cat: Approximately 11in (28cm) tall, including ears

Cat Lovey: Approximately 14½in x 14½in (37cm x 37cm)

CHART GUIDE

CHART	CAT	CAT LOVEY
Head	same as Teddy Bear	same as Teddy Bear Lovey
Body	same as Teddy Bear	n/a
Arm	same as Teddy Bear	same as Teddy Bear Lovey
Leg	same as Teddy Bear	n/a
Ear	see chart	same as Cat
Tail	see chart	n/a

Liz the Cat is very forgetful
and can't find her boots
when she wants to go out.

CAT PATTERN

EaRS (make 1 in white and 1 in light pink)

Foundation ring: make a magic ring.

Round 1: work 6sc into ring.

Round 2: sc in all sts. (6 sts)

Round 3: 2sc in all sts. (12 sts)

Round 4: sc in all sts. (12 sts)

Round 5: (sc in next st, 2sc in next st) six times. (18 sts)

Round 6: sc in all sts. (18 sts)

Round 7: (sc in next 5 sts, 2sc in next st) three times. (21 sts)

Rounds 8-9: sc in all sts. (21 sts)

The ears don't need to be stuffed. Flatten them and sew closed. Fasten off, leaving a long tail for sewing.

Head (light Pink)

Follow the head instructions from Theo the Teddy Bear.

Head assembly

Insert the safety eyes between rounds 15 and 16, with 2 stitches between them.

Using a tapestry needle and black yarn, make a diagonal stitch above each eye, between rounds 13 and 16, to give the cat a more fun expression. Make each stitch about 3 stitches long.

To make the nose, sew several horizontal stitches with fuchsia yarn in the middle of the face, between rounds 16 and 18 of the head. Then make some vertical stitches over the horizontal stitches you have just sewn. Then sew one long stitch down from the nose, covering 2 crochet sts. To make the mouth sew two little v-shaped stitches to the right and two to the left.

Sew the ears to the head between rounds 3 and 13.

Tail

Foundation ring: using white yarn make a magic ring.

Round 1: work 6sc into ring.

Round 2: (sc in next st, 2sc in next st) three times. (9 sts)

Rounds 3-21: change to pink yarn. Sc in all sts. (9 sts)

Stuff the tail a little. Fasten off, leaving a long tail for sewing.

Body (light Pink)

Follow the body instructions from Theo the Teddy Bear.

Sew the tail on the back of the body, between rounds 7 and 10.

ARmS (make 2)

Follow the arm instructions from Theo the Teddy Bear using the following colors:

Rounds 1-6: white.

Rounds 7-19: light pink.

Legs (make 2)

Follow the body instructions from Theo the Teddy Bear, using the following colors:

Rounds 1-6: white.

Rounds 7-15: light pink.

Toy assembly

Sew the head to the body.

Sew the arms to each side of the body between rounds 20 and 21.

Sew the legs at the bottom of the body between rounds 3 and 5.

ScaRf (fuchsia)

Use 5mm (H) hook.

Foundation chain: ch89.

Row 1: starting in second ch from hook, sc in next 88 sts, ch1, turn. (88 sts)

Row 2: Working with the third loop, sc in all sts. (88 sts)

Fasten off.

Place the scarf around the neck of the cat. If you like, you can sew a little wooden button on the knot of the scarf.

CAT LOVEY PATTERN

Ears (make 1 in white and 1 in light pink)

Follow the ear instructions from Liz the Cat.

Head (light pink)

Follow the head instructions from Theo the Teddy Bear Lovey.

Head assembly

Follow the head assembly instructions from Liz the Cat.

Take the head and, using your tapestry needle, weave the yarn tail through each remaining stitch and pull it tight to close. Leave a long tail for sewing.

Arms (make 2)

Follow the arm instructions from Theo the Teddy Bear Lovey using the following colors:

Rounds 1-6: white.

Rounds 7-21: light pink.

Blanket

Make Block Blanket using the following colors:

Odd Rounds: light pink.

Even Rounds: fuchsia.

Lovey assembly

Sew the head on the center of the blanket, placing it so that it's facing one of the corners.

Sew the arms onto the blanket, just under the right and left side of the head.

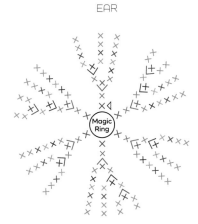

CAT
EAR

CAT
TAIL

Melvin
the Zebra

Skill level
Intermediate

You will need
- Worsted weight yarn: White and Black
- 4mm (G) hook
- Stitch marker
- Tapestry needle
- Stuffing
- 12mm amigurumi safety eyes
- Scissors

Stitch summary
ch, sc, sl st, sc2tog

Finished size
Zebra: Approximately 11in (28cm) tall

Zebra Lovey: Approximately 13in x 13in (33cm x 33cm)

CHART GUIDE

CHART	ZEBRA	ZEBRA LOVEY
Head	see chart	same as Zebra
Body	same as Teddy Bear	n/a
Arm	same as Teddy Bear	same as Teddy Bear Lovey
Leg	see chart	n/a
Ear	see chart	same as Zebra
Tail	same as Giraffe	n/a

Melvin is very proud
of his striped coat and
thinks he's the smartest
of all the animals.

ZEBRA PATTERN

EaRS (make 2 in black)

Foundation ring: make a magic ring.

Round 1: work 6sc into ring.

Round 2: sc in all sts. (6 sts)

Round 3: 2sc in all sts. (12 sts)

Round 4: sc in all sts. (12 sts)

Round 5: (sc in next st, 2sc in next st) six times. (18 sts)

Round 6: sc in all sts. (18 sts)

Round 7: (sc in next 5 sts, 2sc in next st) three times. (21 sts)

Rounds 8-9: sc in all sts. (21 sts)

Round 10: (sc in next 5 sts, sc2tog) three times. (18 sts)

Round 11: (sc in next st, sc2tog) six times. (12 sts)

Round 12: sc in all sts. (12 sts)

The ears don't need to be stuffed. Flatten them and sew closed. Fasten off, leaving a long tail for sewing.

Head

This part is worked in joined rounds. See Basic Techniques section for instructions.

Foundation ring: using black yarn make a magic ring.

Round 1: work 6sc into ring.

Round 2: 2sc in all sts. (12 sts)

Round 3: (sc in next st, 2sc in next st) six times. (18 sts)

Round 4: (sc in next 2 sts, 2sc in next st) six times. (24 sts)

Round 5: (sc in next st, 2sc in next st, sc in next 2 sts) six times. (30 sts)

Rounds 6-9: sc in all sts. (30 sts)

Round 10: change to white yarn. (Sc in next 4 sts, 2sc in next st) six times. (36 sts)

Round 11: sc in all sts. (36 sts)

Round 12: change to black yarn. Sc in all sts. (36 sts)

Round 13: (sc in next 2 sts, 2sc in next st, sc in next 3 sts) six times. (42 sts)

Rounds 14-15: change to white yarn. Sc in all sts. (42 sts)

Round 16: change to black yarn. (Sc in next 6 sts, 2sc in next st) six times. (48 sts)

Round 17: sc in all sts. (48 sts)

Rounds 18-19: change to white yarn. Sc in all sts. (48 sts)

Rounds 20-21: change to black yarn. Sc in all sts. (48 sts)

Round 22: change to white yarn. Sc in all sts. (48 sts)

Round 23: (sc in next 6 sts, sc2tog) six times. (42 sts)

Round 24: change to black yarn. Sc in all sts. (42 sts)

Stuff the head and continue stuffing as you go.

Round 25: (sc in next 2 sts, sc2tog, sc in next 3 sts) six times. (36 sts)

Round 26: change to white yarn. (Sc in next 4 sts, sc2tog) six times. (30 sts)

Round 27: (sc in next st, sc2tog, sc in next 2 sts) six times. (24 sts)

Round 28: change to black yarn. (Sc in next 2 sts, sc2tog) six times. (18 sts)

Round 29: (sc in next st, sc2tog) six times. (12 sts)

Round 30: sc2tog six times. (6 sts)

Fasten off, leaving a long tail for sewing.

To make the nostrils, with white yarn and using your tapestry needle, make a cross stitch on the right of the snout and another on the left. Place these stitches between rounds 4 and 5. Fasten off.

Head assembly

Apply tension to the eyes following the instructions in the Finishing Techniques section.

Insert the safety eyes between rounds 14 and 15, with 4 stitches between them.

Sew the ears to the head between rounds 20 and 21.

Take the head and, using your tapestry needle, weave the yarn tail through each remaining stitch and pull it tight to close. Weave in the yarn end.

Make the hairs following the instructions in the Finishing Techniques section. Make hairs from round 20 to round 27 on the back of the head, matching them to the color of the stripes.

Body

This part is worked in joined rounds. Follow the body instructions from Theo the Teddy Bear, using the following colors:

Rounds 1-2: black.

Rounds 3-4: white.

Rounds 5-6: black.

Rounds 7-8: white.

Rounds 9-10: black.

Rounds 11-12: white.

Rounds 13-14: black.

Rounds 15-16: white.

Rounds 17-18: black.

Rounds 19-20: white.

Rounds 21-22: black.

Tail (black)

Pull up a loop of yarn in the back of the body, on round 9. Ch 7.

Row 1: starting in second ch from hook, sl st in next 6 st.

Fasten off.

Make 3 hairs with black yarn following the instructions in the Finishing Techniques section.

Arms (make 2)

This part is worked in joined rounds. Follow instructions for Theo the Teddy Bear, with the following changes:

Round 5: work BLO.

Rounds 1-7: black.

Rounds 8-9: white.

Rounds 10-11: black.

Rounds 12-13: white.

Rounds 14-15: black.

Rounds 16-17: white.

Rounds 18-19: black.

Make the fingers following the instructions in the Finishing Techniques section.

Legs (make 2)

This part is worked in joined rounds.

Foundation ring: using black yarn, make a magic ring.

Round 1: work 6sc into ring.

Round 2: 2sc in all sts. (12 sts)

Round 3: (sc in next st, 2sc in next st) six times. (18 sts)

Round 4: (sc in next 5 sts, 2sc in next st) three times. (21 sts)

Round 5: BLO sc in all sts. (21 sts)

Rounds 6-7: sc in all sts. (21 sts)

Round 8: change to white yarn. Sc in next 8 sts, sc2tog, sc in next 9 sts, sc2tog. (19 sts)

Round 9: sc in all sts. (19 sts)

Round 10: change to black yarn. Sc in next 7 sts, sc2tog, sc in next 8 sts, sc2tog. (17 sts)

Round 11: sc in all sts. (17 sts)

ZEBRA LOVEY PATTERN

Round 12: change to white yarn. Sc in next 6 sts, sc2tog, sc in next 7 sts, sc2tog. (15 sts)

Round 13: sc in all sts. (15 sts)

Round 14: change to black yarn. Sc in next 5 sts, sc2tog, sc in next 6 sts, sc2tog. (13 sts)

Round 15: sc in all sts. (13 sts)

Round 16: change to white yarn. Sc in all sts. (13 sts)

Round 17: sc in next 4 st, sc2tog, sc in next 5 st, sc2tog. (11 sts)

Round 18-19: change to black yarn. Sc in all sts. (11 sts)

Stuff the legs. Fasten off, leaving a long tail for sewing.

Make the toes following the instructions in the Finishing Techniques section.

Toy assembly

Sew the head to the body.

Sew the arms to each side of the body between rounds 20 and 21.

Sew the legs at the bottom of the body between rounds 2 and 5.

Ears (make 2 in black)

Follow the ear instructions from Melvin the Zebra.

Head

Follow the head instructions from Melvin the Zebra.

Head assembly

Follow the head assembly instructions from Melvin the Zebra.

Arms (make 2)

Follow the arm instructions from Melvin the Zebra, but add the following rounds:

Rounds 20-21: change to white yarn. Sc in all sts. (11 sts)

Blanket

Make Granny Blanket using the following colors:

Rounds 1-2: white.

Rounds 3-4: black.

Rounds 5-6: white.

Rounds 7-8: black.

Rounds 9-10: white.

Rounds 11-12: black.

Round 13: white.

Lovey assembly

Sew the head on the center of the blanket, placing it so that it faces one of the corners.

Sew the arms onto the blanket, on either side of the head.

ZEBRA
LEG

ZEBRA
EAR

ZEBRA
HEAD

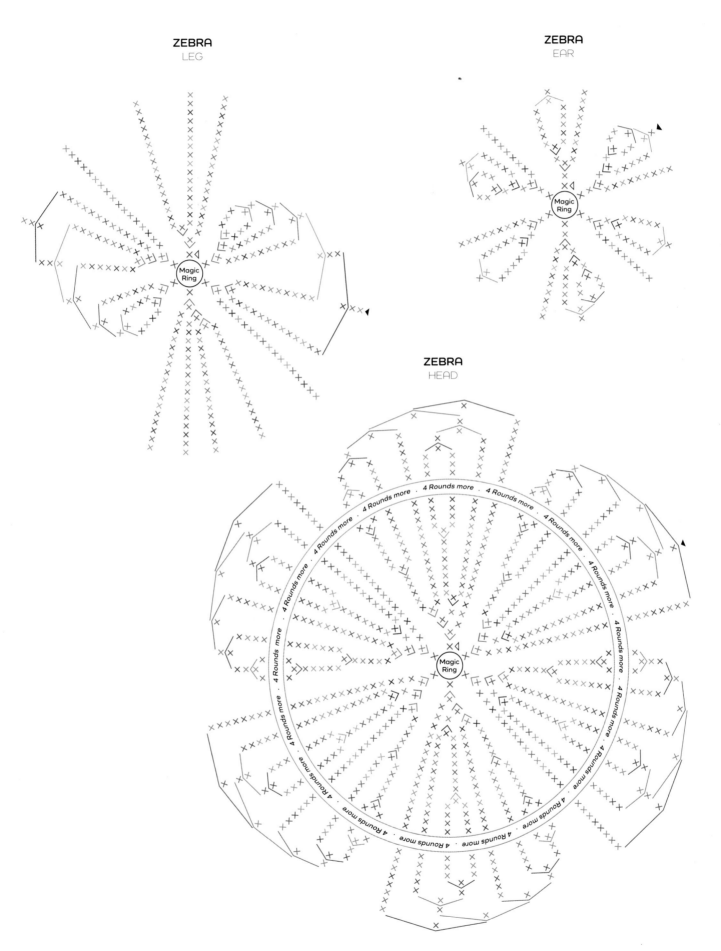

RoY
the Rhino

Skill level
Intermediate

You will need
- Worsted weight yarn: Dark Beige, Beige, Light Gray, and Black
- 4mm (G) hook
- Stitch marker
- Tapestry needle
- Stuffing
- 12mm amigurumi safety eyes
- Scissors

Stitch summary
ch, sc, sl st, sc2tog

Finished size
Rhino: Approximately 10in (25cm) tall
Rhino Lovey: Approximately 16in (40cm) diameter

CHART GUIDE

CHART	RHINO	RHINO LOVEY
Head	same as Zebra	same as Zebra
Body	same as Teddy Bear	n/a
Arm	same as Teddy Bear	same as Teddy Bear Lovey
Leg	same as Teddy Bear	n/a
Ear	see chart	same as Rhino
Big Horn	see chart	same as Rhino
Small Horn	see chart	same as Rhino

Roy the Rhino's favorite thing to do is to splash around in muddy water.

RHINO PATTERN

Ears (make 4 in dark beige)

Foundation ring: make a magic ring.

Round 1: work 6sc into ring.

Round 2: 2sc in all sts. (12 sts)

Round 3: (sc in next st, 2sc in next st) six times. (18 sts)

Round 4: (sc in next 2 sts, 2sc in next st) six times. (24 sts)

Make the Combined Ears following the instructions in the Finishing Techniques section.

Big horn (light gray)

Foundation ring: make a magic ring.

Round 1: work 6sc into ring.

Round 2: sc in next 3 sts, 2sc in next st, sc in next 2 sts. (7 sts)

Round 3: sc in next 4 sts, 2sc in next st, sc in next 2 sts. (8 sts)

Round 4: sc in next 5 sts, 2sc in next st, sc in next 2 sts. (9 sts)

Round 5: sc in next 6 sts, 2sc in next st, sc in next 2 sts. (10 sts)

Stuff the horn a little and fasten off, leaving a long tail for sewing.

Small horn (light gray)

Foundation ring: make a magic ring.

Round 1: work 6sc into ring.

Round 2: sc in next 3 sts, 2sc in next st, sc in next 2 sts. (7 sts)

Round 3: sc in next 4 sts, 2sc in next st, sc in next 2 sts. (8 sts)

Round 4: sc in next 5 sts, 2sc in next st, sc in next 2 sts. (9 sts)

Stuff the horn a little and fasten off, leaving a long tail for sewing.

Head (dark beige)

Follow the head instructions from Melvin the Zebra.

Head assembly

Apply tension to the eyes following the instructions in the Finishing Techniques section.

Insert the safety eyes between rounds 13 and 14, with 8 stitches between them.

Using a tapestry needle and black yarn, make a diagonal stitch above each eye, between rounds 16 and 18, to give the rhino a more fun expression. Make each stitch about 4 stitches long.

Sew the ears to the head between rounds 22 and 24.

Sew the big horn onto the head. Center it between rounds 4 and 7. Then sew the small horn between rounds 9 and 12.

Finally, take the head and using your tapestry needle, weave the yarn tail through each remaining stitch and pull it tight to close. Weave in the yarn end.

Body (dark beige)

Follow the body instructions from Theo the Teddy Bear.

Arms (make 2)

Follow the arm instructions from Theo the Teddy Bear, with the following changes:

Round 5: work BLO.

Rounds 1-7: beige.

Rounds 8-19: dark beige.

Make the fingers following the instructions in the Finishing Techniques section.

Legs (make 2)

Follow the leg instructions from Theo the Teddy Bear, using the following colors:

Round 5: work BLO.

Rounds 1-7: beige.

Rounds 8-15: dark beige.

Make the toes following the instructions in the Finishing Techniques section.

Toy assembly

Sew the head to the body.

Sew the arms to each side of the body between rounds 20 and 21.

Sew the legs at the bottom of the body between rounds 2 and 5.

RHINO LOVEY PATTERN

Big horn (light gray)

Follow the big horn instructions from Roy the Rhino.

Small horn (light gray)

Follow the small horn instructions from Roy the Rhino.

Ears (make 4 in dark beige)

Follow the ear instructions from Roy the Rhino.

Head (dark beige)

Follow the head instructions from Melvin the Zebra.

Head assembly

Follow the head assembly instructions from Roy the Rhino.

Arms (make 2)

Follow the arm instructions from Roy the Rhino but add the following rounds in dark beige:

Rounds 20-21: sc in all sts. (11 sts)

Blanket

Make Peaks Blanket using the following colors:

Rounds 1-13: dark beige.

Rounds 14-15: beige.

Lovey assembly

Sew the head on the center of the blanket, placing it so that it faces one of the peaks.

Sew the arms onto the blanket, on either side of the head.

RHINO
EAR

RHINO
SMALL HORN

RHINO
BIG HORN

SefRa
the Giraffe

Skill level
Intermediate

You will need
- Worsted weight yarn: Yellow, Brown, Beige, and Black
- 4mm (G) hook
- Stitch marker
- Tapestry needle
- Stuffing
- 12mm amigurumi safety eyes
- Scissors

Stitch summary
ch, sc, sl st, sc2tog

Finished size
Giraffe: Approximately 11½in (29cm) tall, including horns
Giraffe Lovey: Approximately 12in x 13in (30cm x 33cm)

CHART GUIDE

CHART	GIRAFFE	GIRAFFE LOVEY
Head	same as Teddy Bear	same as Teddy Bear Lovey
Body	see chart	n/a
Arm	same as Teddy Bear	same as Teddy Bear Lovey
Leg	same as Teddy Bear	n/a
Snout	see chart	same as Giraffe
Ear	see chart	same as Giraffe
Horn	see chart	same as Giraffe
Spot	see chart	same as Giraffe
Tail	see chart	n/a

GIRAFFE PATTERN

Snout (beige)

Foundation ring: make a magic ring.

Round 1: work 6sc into ring.

Round 2: 2sc in all sts. (12 sts)

Round 3: (sc in next st, 2sc in next st) six times. (18 sts)

Round 4: (sc in next 2 sts, 2sc in next st) six times. (24 sts)

Rounds 5-6: sc in all sts. (24 sts)

Fasten off, leaving a long tail for sewing.

To make the nostrils, using your tapestry needle and brown yarn, sew a cross stitch on either side of the snout, placing them on round 4 of the snout. Fasten off.

Ears (make 2 in yellow)

Foundation ring: make a magic ring.

Round 1: work 6sc into ring.

Round 2: sc in all sts. (6 sts)

Round 3: 2sc in all sts. (12 sts)

Round 4: sc in all sts. (12 sts)

Round 5: (sc in next st, 2sc in next st) six times. (18 sts)

Rounds 6-7: sc in all sts. (18 sts)

Round 8: (sc in next 7 sts, sc2tog) twice. (16 sts)

Round 9: (sc in next 6 sts, sc2tog) twice. (14 sts)

Round 10: (sc in next 5 sts, sc2tog) twice. (12 sts)

The ears don't need to be stuffed. Flatten them and sew closed. Fasten off, leaving a long tail for sewing.

Horns (make 2)

Foundation ring: using brown yarn make a magic ring.

Round 1: work 6sc into ring.

Round 2: 2sc in all sts. (12 sts)

Rounds 3-5: sc in all sts. (12 sts)

Round 6: (sc in next st, sc2tog) four times. (8 sts)

Rounds 7-10: change to yellow yarn. Sc in all sts. (8 sts)

Fasten off, leaving a long tail for sewing.

Head (yellow)

Follow the head instructions from Theo the Teddy Bear.

Head assembly

Insert the safety eyes between rounds 14 and 15, with 1 stitch between them.

Using your tapestry needle and brown yarn, make a diagonal stitch above each eye, between rounds 11 and 13, to give the giraffe a more fun expression. Make each stitch about 3 stitches long.

Sew the horns to the center of the head between rounds 4 and 6, placing them with 6 stitches between them.

Sew the ears to the head between rounds 9 and 14.

Stuff the snout and sew it on the head between rounds 16 and 24.

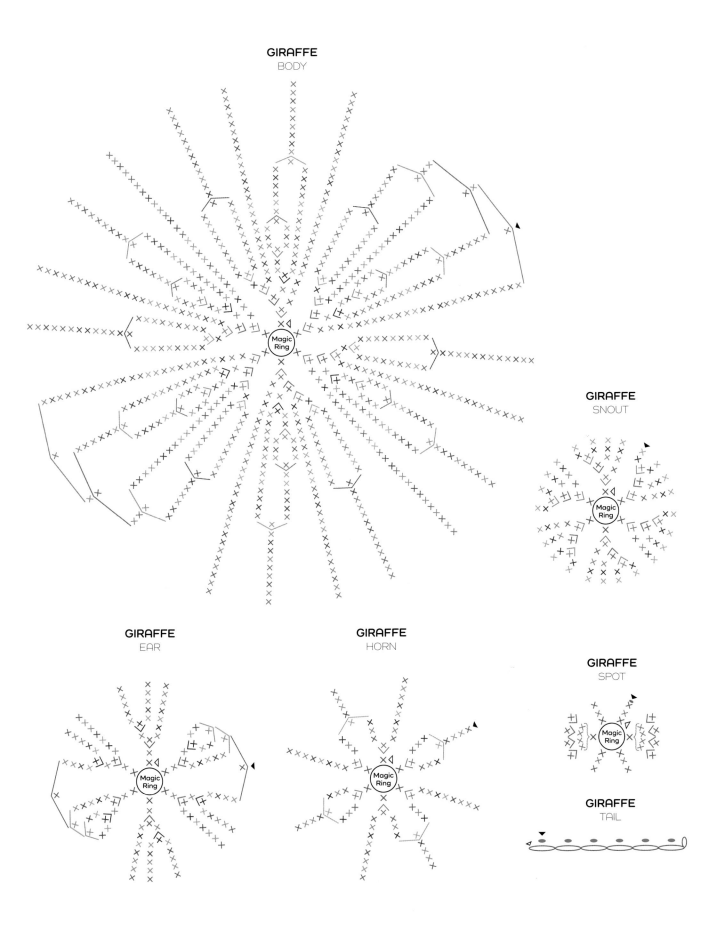

GIRAFFE
BODY

GIRAFFE
SNOUT

GIRAFFE
EAR

GIRAFFE
HORN

GIRAFFE
SPOT

GIRAFFE
TAIL

Spots (make 4 in brown)

Foundation ring: make a magic ring.

Round 1: work 6sc into ring.

Round 2: sc in next 2 sts, 4sc in next st, sc in next 2 sts, 4sc in next st. (12 sts)

Round 3: sc in next 2 sts, 2sc in next 4 sts, sc in next 2 sts, 2sc in next 4 sts. Join with sl st on first sc of this round. (20 sts)

Fasten off, leaving a long tail for sewing.

Body (Yellow)

Foundation ring: make a magic ring.

Round 1: work 6sc into ring.

Round 2: 2sc in all sts. (12 sts)

Round 3: (sc in next st, 2sc in next st) six times. (18 sts)

Round 4: (sc in next 2 sts, 2sc in next st) six times. (24 sts)

Round 5: (sc in next st, 2sc in next st, sc in next 2 sts) six times. (30 sts)

Round 6: (sc in next 4 sts, 2sc in next st) six times. (36 sts)

Round 7: sc in all sts. (36 sts)

Round 8: (sc in next 2 sts, 2sc in next st, sc in next 3 sts) six times. (42 sts)

Rounds 9-11: sc in all sts. (42 sts)

Round 12: (sc in next 2 sts, sc2tog, sc in next 3 sts) six times. (36 sts)

Rounds 13-15: sc in all sts. (36 sts)

Round 16: (sc in next 4 sts, sc2tog) six times. (30 sts)

Stuff the body and continue stuffing as you go.

Rounds 17-18: sc in all sts. (30 sts)

Round 19: (sc in next st, sc2tog, sc in next 2 sts) six times. (24 sts)

Rounds 20-22: sc in all sts. (24 sts)

Round 23: (sc in next 10 sts, sc2tog) twice. (22 sts)

Rounds 24-25: sc in all sts. (22 sts)

Round 26: (sc in next 9 sts, sc2tog) twice. (20 sts)

Round 27: sc in all sts. (20 sts)

Round 28: (sc in next 8 sts, sc2tog) twice. (18 sts)

Fasten off, leaving a long tail for sewing.

Sew the spots randomly onto the body.

Tail (Yellow)

Pull up a loop of yarn in the back of the body on round 9 and ch7.

Row 1: start in second ch from hook, sl st in next 6 sts.

Fasten off.

Make three hairs with brown yarn following the instructions in the Finishing Techniques section.

Arms (make 2)

Follow the arm instructions from Theo the Teddy Bear, but with the following changes:

Round 5: work BLO.

Rounds 1-7: brown.

Rounds 8-19: yellow.

Make the fingers following the instructions in the Finishing Techniques section.

Legs (make 2)

Follow the leg instructions from Theo the Teddy Bear, but with the following changes:

Round 5: work BLO.

Rounds 1-7: brown.

Rounds 8-15: yellow.

Make the toes following the instructions in the Finishing Techniques section.

Flatten the legs and sew them closed. Fasten off, leaving a long tail for sewing.

Toy assembly

Sew the head to the body.

Sew the arms to each side of the body between rounds 20 and 21.

Sew the legs on both sides of the body, left and right, between rounds 8 and 9.

GIRAFFE LOVEY PATTERN

Snout (beige)

Follow the snout instructions from Sefra the Giraffe.

Ears (make 2 in yellow)

Follow the ear instructions from Sefra the Giraffe.

Horns (make 2)

Follow the horn instructions from Sefra the Giraffe.

Head (yellow)

Follow the head instructions from Theo the Teddy Bear Lovey.

Head assembly

Follow the head assembly instructions from Sefra the Giraffe.

Take the head and using your tapestry needle, weave the yarn tail through each remaining stitch and pull it tight to close. Leave a long tail for sewing.

Arms (make 2)

Follow the arm instructions from Sefra the Giraffe, but add the following rounds in yellow:

Rounds 20-21: sc in all sts. (11 sts)

Spots (make 4 in brown)

Follow the spot instructions from Sefra the Giraffe, but use a 5mm (H) hook.

Note: Sew the spots neatly onto the lovey so that the stitches don't show on the reverse side.

Blanket

Make Texture Blanket using the following colors:

Rounds 1-21: yellow.

Rounds 22-25: brown.

Lovey assembly

Sew the head onto the center of the blanket, placing it so that the head faces one of the corners.

Sew the arms onto the blanket, just under each side of the head.

Sew the spots randomly onto the blanket.

Kenai
the Hippo

Skill level
Intermediate

You will need
- Worsted weight yarn: Gray, Light Pink, and Black
- 4mm (G) hook
- Stitch marker
- Tapestry needle
- Stuffing
- 12mm amigurumi safety eyes
- Scissors

Stitch summary
ch, sc, dc, hdc, 3dc cluster st, sl st, sc2tog

Finished size
Hippo: Approximately 11in (28cm) tall
Hippo Lovey: Approximately 13in x 13in (33cm x 33cm)

CHART GUIDE

CHART	HIPPO	HIPPO LOVEY
Head	same as Teddy Bear	same as Teddy Bear Lovey
Body	same as Teddy Bear	n/a
Arm	same as Teddy Bear	same as Teddy Bear Lovey
Leg	same as Teddy Bear	n/a
Ear	same as Rhino	same as Rhino
Snout	see chart	same as Hippo
Heart	see chart	n/a

Kenai the Hippo loves doing jigSaw PuzzleS. She jumpS foR joy when She PlaceS a Piece.

HIPPO PATTERN

EARS (make 2 in gray and 2 in light pink)

Follow the ear instructions from Roy the Rhino.

Make the Combined Ears following the instructions in the Finishing Techniques section, using one gray piece and one light pink piece for each ear.

Snout (gray)

Foundation ring: make a magic ring.

Round 1: work 6sc into ring.

Round 2: 2sc in all sts. (12 sts)

Round 3: (sc in next st, 2sc in next st) six times. (18 sts)

Round 4: (sc in next 2 sts, 2sc in next st) six times. (24 sts)

Round 5: (sc in next st, 2sc in next st, sc in next 2 sts) six times. (30 sts)

Round 6: sc in all sts. (30 sts)

Round 7: sc in next 10 sts, 3dc cluster stitch in next st, ch1, sc in next 4 sts, 3dc cluster stitch in next st, ch1, sc in next 14 sts. (30 sts – don't count the 2 chains)

Rounds 8-9: sc in all sts. (30 sts)

Fasten off, leaving a long tail for sewing.

Head (gray)

Follow the head instructions from Theo the Teddy Bear.

Head assembly

Insert the safety eyes between rounds 11 and 12, with 2 stitches between them.

Using a tapestry needle and black yarn, make a diagonal stitch above each eye, between rounds 8 and 10, to give the hippo a more fun expression. Make each stitch about 3 crochet stitches long.

Sew the ears to the head between rounds 7 and 9.

Stuff the snout and sew it to the head between rounds 13 and 23.

Body (gray)

Follow the body instructions from Theo the Teddy Bear.

Arms (make 2)

Follow the arm instructions from Theo the Teddy Bear using the following colors:

Rounds 1-4: light pink.

Rounds 5-19: gray.

Legs (make 2)

Follow the leg instructions from Theo the Teddy Bear using the following colors:

Rounds 1-4: light pink.

Rounds 5-15: gray.

Heart (light pink)

Foundation ring: make a magic ring.

Round 1: Ch3, 3dc, 2hdc, sc, ch2, sc, 2hdc, 3dc, ch2, sl st into the ring. Fasten off, leaving a long tail for sewing.

Toy assembly

Sew the head to the body.

Sew the arms to each side of the body between rounds 20 and 21.

Sew the legs to the bottom of the body between rounds 4 and 6.

Sew the heart to the body between rounds 8 and 12, placing it a little to the left.

HIPPO LOVEY PATTERN

Ears (make 2 in gray and 2 in light pink)

Follow the ear instructions from Kenai the Hippo.

Snout (gray)

Follow the snout instructions from Kenai the Hippo.

Head (gray)

Follow the head instructions from Theo the Teddy Bear Lovey.

Head assembly

Follow the head assembly instructions from Kenai the Hippo.

Take the head and, using your tapestry needle, weave the yarn tail through each remaining stitch and pull it tight to close. Leave a long tail for sewing.

Arms (make 2)

Follow the arm instructions from Theo the Teddy Bear Lovey using the following colors:

Rounds 1-4: light pink.

Rounds 5-21: gray.

Blanket

Make Block Blanket using the following colors:

Odd Rounds: gray.

Even Rounds: light pink.

Lovey assembly

Sew the head on the center of the blanket, placing it so that it's facing one of the corners.

Sew the arms onto the blanket, just under the right and left side of the head.

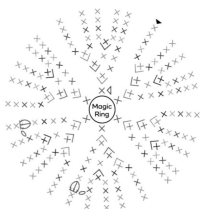

Luke
the Frog

Skill level
Intermediate

You will need
- Worsted weight yarn: Green, Turquoise, White, and Black
- 4mm (G) hook
- Stitch marker
- Tapestry needle
- Stuffing
- 12mm amigurumi safety eyes
- Scissors

Stitch summary
ch, sc, sl st, sc2tog

Finished size
Frog: Approximately 12in (30cm) tall, including ears
Frog Lovey: Approximately 14½in x 14½in (37cm x 37cm)

CHART GUIDE

CHART	FROG	FROG LOVEY
Head	same as Teddy Bear	same as Teddy Bear Lovey
Body	same as Teddy Bear	n/a
Arm	see chart	same as Frog
Leg	see chart	n/a
Eye	see chart	same as Frog
Foot	see chart	n/a

Luke loves to hop between
the beautiful lily pads that
are growing in his pond.

FROG PATTERN

Eyes (make 2 in white)

Foundation ring: make a magic ring.

Round 1: work 6sc into ring.

Round 2: 2sc in all sts. (12 sts)

Round 3: (sc in next 3 sts, 2sc in next st) three times. (15 sts)

Rounds 4-5: sc in all sts. (15 sts)

Fasten off, leaving a long tail for sewing.

Head (green)

Follow the head instructions from Theo the Teddy Bear.

Head assembly

Insert the safety eyes into the eyes, between rounds 4 and 5.

Stuff the eyes and sew onto the head between rounds 2 and 7, with 2 stitches between them.

To make the mouth, sew one straight stitch with black yarn, about 6 sts in length, one diagonal stitch 5 sts long and another little straight stitch 2 sts long. Place the mouth between rounds 11 and 15 of the head, and slightly to one side to make his expression more fun.

Body (green)

Follow the body instructions from Theo the Teddy Bear.

Arms (make 2)

Arms are made in joined rounds, not a continuous spiral, to keep stripes neat. See Basic Techniques section.

Foundation ring: using green yarn, make a magic ring.

Round 1: work 6sc into ring.

Round 2: 2sc in all sts. (12 sts)

Round 3: (sc in next st, 2sc in next st) six times. (18 sts)

Rounds 4-8: sc in all sts. (18 sts)

Round 9: (sc in next st, sc2tog) six times. (12 sts)

Round 10: sc in all sts. (12 sts)

Rounds 11-12: change to turquoise yarn. Sc in all sts. (12 sts)

Rounds 13-14: change to green yarn. Sc in all sts. (12 sts)

Rounds 15-16: change to turquoise yarn. Sc in all sts. (12 sts)

Rounds 17-18: change to green yarn. Sc in all sts. (12 sts)

Rounds 19-20: change to turquoise yarn. Sc in all sts. (12 sts)

Rounds 21-22: change to green yarn. Sc in all sts. (12 sts)

Rounds 23-24: change to turquoise yarn. Sc in all sts. (12 sts)

Rounds 25-26: change to green yarn. Sc in all sts. (12 sts)

Stuff the arms. Flatten them and sew closed. Fasten off, leaving a long tail for sewing.

Feet (make 2 in green)

Foundation ring: make a magic ring.

Round 1: work 6sc into ring.

Round 2: 2sc in all sts. (12 sts)

Round 3: sc in all sts. (12 sts)

Round 4: (sc in next st, 2sc in next st) six times. (18 sts)

Round 5: sc in all sts. (18 sts)

Round 6: (sc in next 2 sts, 2sc in next st) six times. (24 sts)

Rounds 7-12: sc in all sts. (24 sts)

Flatten the foot and work the next round by working into corresponding stitches from both sides of the foot to close it.

Round 13: (skip next st, 5dc in next st, skip next st, sl st in next st) three times. (18 sts)

Fasten off.

Legs (make 2)

Legs are made in joined rounds, not a continuous spiral, to keep stripes neat. See Basic Techniques section.

Foundation row: using green yarn ch12 and join with sl st to form a ring. Leave a long tail at the beginning.

For remaining rounds, sc in all sts using the following colors (12 sts):

Rounds 1-2: green.

Rounds 3-4: turquoise.

Rounds 5-6: green.

Rounds 7-8: turquoise.

Rounds 9-10: green.

Rounds 11-12: turquoise.

Rounds 13-14: green.

Rounds 15-16: turquoise.

Rounds 17-18: green.

Stuff the leg, fasten off and leave a long tail for sewing.

Foot assembly

Place the leg on the foot, between rounds 1 and 5 and sew it securely. Fasten off.

Toy assembly

Sew the head to the body.

Sew the arms to each side of the body between rounds 20 and 21.

Sew the legs to the bottom of the body between rounds 2 and 5.

FROG LOVEY PATTERN

Eyes (make 2 in white)

Follow the eye instructions from Luke the Frog.

Head (green)

Follow the head instructions from Theo the Teddy Bear Lovey.

Head assembly

Follow the head assembly instructions from Luke the Frog.

Take the head and, using your tapestry needle, weave the yarn tail through each remaining stitch and pull it tight to close. Leave a long tail for sewing.

Arms (make 2)

Follow the arm instructions from Luke the Frog.

Blanket

Make Block Blanket using the following colors:

Odd Rounds: green.

Even Rounds: turquoise.

Lovey assembly

Sew the head on the center of the blanket, placing it so that it's facing one of the corners.

Sew the arms onto the blanket, just under the right and left side of the head.

FROG
ARM

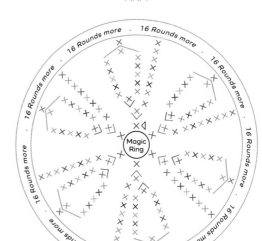

FROG
LEG

FROG
FOOT

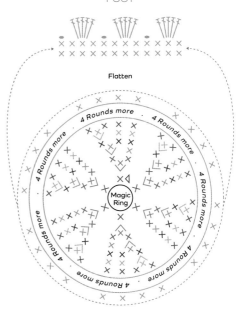

FROG
EYE

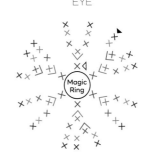

Zoe
the Sheep

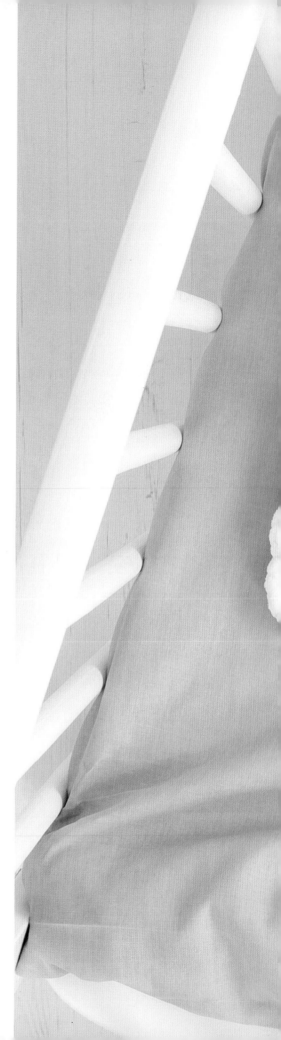

Skill level

Intermediate

You will need

- Worsted weight yarn: Beige, Dark Brown, and Black
- Super bulky yarn: White
- 4mm (G) hook
- 5mm (H) hook
- Stitch marker
- Tapestry needle
- Stuffing
- 12mm amigurumi safety eyes
- Scissors

Stitch summary

ch, sc, sl st, sc2tog

Finished size

Sheep: Approximately 10½in (27cm) tall, including ears
Sheep Lovey: Approximately 12in x 12in (30cm x 30cm)

CHART GUIDE

CHART	SHEEP	SHEEP LOVEY
Head	same as Teddy Bear	same as Teddy Bear Lovey
Body	see chart	n/a
Arm	same as Teddy Bear	same as Teddy Bear Lovey
Leg	same as Teddy Bear	n/a
Ear	same as Reindeer	same as Reindeer
Hair	see chart	same as Sheep
Tail	see chart	n/a

Zoe the sheep is very affectionate. She's always hugging and kissing her friends.

SHEEP PATTERN

Ears (make 2 in beige)

Follow the ear instructions from Clancy the Reindeer.

Hair (white super bulky)

Foundation ring: using 5mm (H) hook, make a magic ring. You may need to adjust your hook size if your super bulky yarn is too thick to manage with a 5mm (H) hook.

Round 1: work 6sc into ring.

Round 2: 2sc in all sts. (12 sts)

Round 3: (sc in next st, 2sc in next st) six times. (18 sts)

Round 4: (sc in next 2 sts, 2sc in next st) six times. (24 sts)

Round 5: (sc in next st, 2sc in next st, sc in next 2 sts) six times. (30 sts)

Round 6: (sc in next 4 sts, 2sc in next st) six times. (36 sts)

Round 7: (sc in next 2 sts, 2sc in next st, sc in next 3 sts) six times. (42 sts)

Rounds 8-11: sc in all sts. (42 sts)

Fasten off, leaving a long tail for sewing.

Note: Any textured yarn can be used for the hair, which will have different finished results.

Head (beige)

Follow the head instructions from Theo the Teddy Bear.

Head assembly

Insert the safety eyes between rounds 13 and 14, with 3 stitches between them.

Using a tapestry needle and black yarn, make a diagonal stitch above each eye, between rounds 11 and 13, to give the sheep a more fun expression. Make each stitch about 3 crochet stitches long.

To make the nose, sew one big v-shaped stitch with dark brown yarn, between rounds 17 and 19 of the head. Then sew one stitch down, about 4 crochet stitches long. To make the mouth, sew one little stitch to the right and another to the left.

Sew the hair to the head between rounds 9 and 24.

Sew the ears to the hair between rounds 9 and 11.

Tail (white super bulky)

Foundation ring: using 5mm (H) hook, make a magic ring.

Round 1: work 6sc into ring.

Round 2: 2sc in all sts. (12 sts)

Round 3: sc in all sts. (12 sts)

Stuff the tail a little. Fasten off, leaving a long tail for sewing.

Body (white super bulky)

Foundation ring: using 5mm (H) hook, make a magic ring.

Round 1: work 6sc into ring.

Round 2: 2sc in all sts. (12 sts)

Round 3: (sc in next st, 2sc in next st) six times. (18 sts)

Round 4: (sc in next 2 sts, 2sc in next st) six times. (24 sts)

Round 5: (sc in next st, 2sc in next st, sc in next 2 sts) six times. (30 sts)

Rounds 6-8: sc in all sts. (30 sts)

Round 9: (sc in next 3 sts, sc2tog) six times. (24 sts)

Rounds 10-11: sc in all sts. (24 sts)

Round 12: (sc in next 2 sts, sc2tog) six times. (18 sts)

Round 13: sc in all sts. (18 sts)

Stuff the body. Fasten off, leaving a long tail for sewing.

Sew the tail on the back of the body, between rounds 5 and 6.

Arms (make 2)

Follow the arm instructions from Theo the Teddy Bear, but with the following changes:

Round 5: work BLO.

Rounds 1-7: dark brown.

Rounds 8-19: beige.

Make the fingers following the instructions in the Finishing Techniques section.

Legs (make 2)

Follow the leg instructions from Theo the Teddy Bear, but with the following changes:

Round 5: work BLO.

Rounds 1-7: dark brown.

Rounds 8-15: beige.

Make the toes following the instructions in the Finishing Techniques section.

Toy assembly

Sew the head to the body.

Sew the arms to each side of the body between rounds 20 and 21.

Sew the legs to the bottom of the body between rounds 2 and 3.

SHEEP LOVEY PATTERN

Ears (make 2 in beige)

Follow the ear instructions from Clancy the Reindeer.

Hair (white super bulky)

Follow the hair instructions from Zoe the Sheep.

Head (beige)

Follow the head instructions from Theo the Teddy Bear Lovey.

Head assembly

Follow the head assembly instructions from Zoe the Sheep.

Take the head and, using your tapestry needle, weave the yarn tail through each remaining stitch and pull it tight to close. Leave a long tail for sewing.

Arms (make 2)

Follow the arm instructions from Zoe the Sheep but add the following rounds in beige:

Rounds 20-21: sc in all sts. (11 sts)

Blanket (white super bulky)

Work as for Granny Blanket using a 5mm (H) hook to round 8.

Round 9: sl st in next 2 dc, sl st in next ch2 corner space, ch3 (counts as first dc), 5dc, skip next st, sl st in next st, skip next st, [(3dc in next ch space, skip next st, sl st in next st, skip next st) seven times, 6dc in next ch2 corner space, skip next st, sl st in next st, skip next st] three times. (3dc in next ch space, skip next st, sl st in next st, skip next st) seven times. Join with sl st in top of initial ch3. Fasten off.

Lovey assembly

Sew the head on the center of the blanket, placing it so that it's facing one of the corners.

Sew the arms onto the blanket, just under the right and left side of the head.

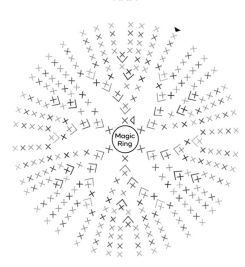

203

CeRi
the Panda

Skill level
Intermediate

You will need
- Worsted weight yarn: White, Black, and Fuchsia
- 4mm (G) hook
- Stitch marker
- Tapestry needle
- Stuffing
- 12mm amigurumi safety eyes
- Scissors

Stitch summary
ch, sc, tr, sl st, sc2tog

Finished size
Panda: Approximately 10in (25cm) tall, including ears
Panda Lovey: Approximately 16in (40cm) diameter

CHART GUIDE

CHART	PANDA	PANDA LOVEY
Head	same as Teddy Bear	same as Teddy Bear Lovey
Body	same as Teddy Bear	n/a
Arm	same as Teddy Bear	same as Teddy Bear Lovey
Leg	same as Teddy Bear	n/a
Spot	same as Giraffe	same as Giraffe
Snout	see chart	same as Panda
Ear	see chart	same as Panda
Bow	see chart	same as Panda

Ceri the Panda loves to travel and meet animals from far away places.

PANDA PATTERN

Eye Spots (make 2 in black)

Follow the spot instructions from Sefra the Giraffe.

Snout (white)

This part is worked in joined rounds. See Basic Techniques section for instructions.

Foundation ring: make a magic ring.

Round 1: work 6sc into ring.

Round 2: sc in next 2 sts, 4sc in next st, sc in next 2 sts, 4 sc in next st. (12 sts)

Round 3: sc in next 2 sts, (sc in next st, 2sc in next st) twice, sc in next 2 sts, (sc in next st, 2sc in next st) twice. (16 sts)

Round 4: sc in next 2 sts, (sc in next 2 sts, 2sc in next st) twice, sc in next 2 sts, (sc in next 2 st, 2sc in next st) twice. (20 sts)

Rounds 5-6: sc in all sts. (20 sts)

Fasten off, leaving a long tail for sewing.

To make the nose, sew several stitches into a triangle shape with black yarn in the center of the snout, between rounds 3 and 5. Then make a long straight stitch down from the nose, 4 crochet sts long.

Ears (make 2 in black)

Foundation ring: make a magic ring.

Round 1: work 6sc into ring.

Round 2: 2sc in all sts. (12 sts)

Round 3: (sc in next st, 2sc in next st) six times. (18 sts)

Round 4: (sc in next 2 sts, 2sc in next st) six times. (24 sts)

Rounds 5-7: sc in all sts. (24 sts)

Round 8: (sc in next 2 sts, sc2tog) six times. (18 sts)

The ears don't need to be stuffed. Flatten them and sew closed. Fasten off, leaving a long tail for sewing.

Bow (fuchsia)

Foundation ring: make a magic ring.

Round 1: (ch3, 4tr, ch3, sl st) twice into ring.

Fasten off, leaving a long tail for sewing.

Head (white)

Follow the head instructions from Theo the Teddy Bear.

Head assembly

Sew the eye spots onto the head, between rounds 8 and 14. Place them in the center, with 2 stitches between them. Place each spot at a slight angle, sloping down to the outside.

Insert the safety eyes between rounds 2 and 3 of the eye spot. Place them near the inside of each eye spot.

Stuff the snout and sew it on the head between rounds 19 and 25.

Sew the ears to the head between rounds 3 and 10. Place them evenly, with 6 stitches between them on the top of the head.

Sew the bow on the head, between the ears.

Body

Follow the body instructions from Theo the Teddy Bear, using the following colors:

Rounds 1-18: white.

Rounds 19-22: black.

With black yarn, make a cross stitch on the tummy. Place the stitch in the center, between rounds 8 and 9.

Arms (make 2 in black)

Follow the arm instructions from Theo the Teddy Bear.

Legs (make 2 in black)

Follow the leg instructions from Theo the Teddy Bear, but with the following changes:

Flatten the legs and sew them closed. Fasten off, leaving a long tail for sewing.

Toy assembly

Sew the head to the body.

Sew the arms to each side of the body between rounds 20 and 21.

Sew the legs on the sides of the body, between rounds 7 and 8.

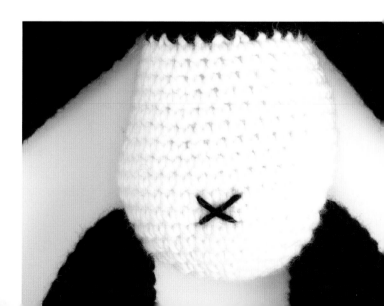

PANDA LOVEY PATTERN

Eye Spots (make 2 in black)

Follow the spot instructions from Ceri the Panda.

Snout (white)

Follow the snout instructions from Ceri the Panda.

Ears (make 2 in black)

Follow the ear instructions from Ceri the Panda.

Bow (fuchsia)

Follow the bow instructions from Ceri the Panda.

Head (white)

Follow the head instructions from Theo the Teddy Bear Lovey.

Head assembly

Follow the head assembly instructions from Ceri the Panda.

Take the head and, using your tapestry needle, weave the yarn tail through each remaining stitch and pull it tight to close. Leave a long tail for sewing.

Arms (make 2 in black)

Follow the arm instructions from Theo the Teddy Bear Lovey.

Blanket

Make Peaks Blanket using the following colors:

Rounds 1-5: black.

Rounds 6-15: white.

Lovey assembly

Sew the head on the center of the blanket, placing it so that it faces one of the peaks.

Sew the arms on the blanket, one on either side of the head.

TRish
the Cow

Skill level
Intermediate

You will need
- Worsted weight yarn: White, Brown, Light Pink, Beige and Black
- 4mm (G) hook
- Stitch marker
- Tapestry needle
- Stuffing
- 12mm amigurumi safety eyes
- Scissors

Stitch summary
ch, sc, sl st, 4dc cluster stitch, sc2tog

Finished size
Cow: Approximately 10½in (27cm) tall, including horns
Cow Lovey: Approximately 12in x 13in (30cm x 33cm)

CHART GUIDE

CHART	COW	COW LOVEY
Head	same as Teddy Bear	same as Teddy Bear Lovey
Body	same as Teddy Bear	n/a
Ear	same as Reindeer	same as Reindeer
Leg	same as Teddy Bear	n/a
Snout	see chart	same as Cow
Small Horn	same as Rhino	same as Rhino
Spot	same as Giraffe	same as Giraffe
Arm	same as Teddy Bear	same as Teddy Bear Lovey
Tail	see chart	n/a

TRish the Cow adoRes eating fResh GReen GRass. It gives her a lovely Shiny coat.

COW PATTERN

EaRS (make 1 in white and 1 in brown)

Follow the ear instructions from Clancy the Reindeer.

Small hoRns (make 2 in beige)

Follow the small horn instructions from Roy the Rhino.

Snout (light pink)

Foundation ring: make a magic ring.

Round 1: work 6sc into ring.

Round 2: 2sc in all sts. (12 sts)

Round 3: (sc in next st, 2sc in next st) six times. (18 sts)

Round 4: (sc in next 2 sts, 2sc in next st) six times. (24 sts)

Round 5: (sc in next st, 2sc in next st, sc in next 2 sts) six times. (30 sts)

Round 6: sc in all sts. (30 sts)

Round 7: sc in next 10 sts, 4dc cluster stitch in next st, ch 1, sc in next 4 sts, 4dc cluster stitch in next st, ch 1, sc in next 14 sts. (30 sts – don't count the 2 chains)

Rounds 8-9: sc in all sts. (30 sts)

Fasten off, leaving a long tail for sewing.

SPots (make 4 in brown)

Follow the spot instructions from Sefra the Giraffe.

Head (white)

Follow the head instructions from Theo the Teddy Bear.

Head assembly

Insert the safety eyes between rounds 11 and 12, with 2 stitches between them.

Using a tapestry needle and black yarn, make a diagonal stitch above each eye, between rounds 8 and 11, to give the cow a more fun expression. Make each stitch about 4 stitches long.

Sew the small horns to the head between rounds 4 and 6, with 6 stitches between them.

Sew the ears to the head between rounds 7 and 13.

Stuff the snout and sew it to the head between rounds 13 and 23.

Sew one spot on the head between rounds 4 and 11, placing it to one side above the eyebrow.

Body (white)

Follow the body instructions from Theo the Teddy Bear.

Sew 3 spots randomly on the body.

Tail (white)

Pull up a loop of yarn in the back of the body, on round 9. Ch 11.

Row 1: starting in second ch from hook, sl st in next 10 sts and fasten off.

Make 3 hairs with brown yarn following the instructions in the Finishing Techniques section.

COW
SNOUT

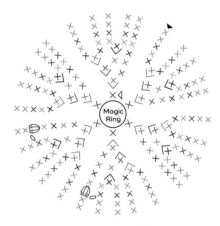

COW
TAIL

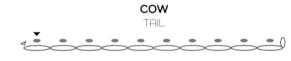

COW LOVEY PATTERN

ARmS (make 2)

Follow the arm instructions from Theo the Teddy Bear, but with the following changes:

Round 5: Work BLO.

Rounds 1-7: brown.

Rounds 8-19: white.

Make the fingers following the instructions in the Finishing Techniques section.

LegS (make 2)

Follow the leg instructions from Theo the Teddy Bear, but with the following changes:

Round 5: work BLO.

Rounds 1-7: brown.

Rounds 8-15: white.

Make the toes following the instructions in the Finishing Techniques section.

Toy assembly

Sew the head to the body.

Sew the arms to each side of the body between rounds 20 and 21.

Sew the legs at the bottom of the body between rounds 3 and 6.

EaRS (make 1 white and 1 in bROwn)

Follow the ear instructions from Clancy the Reindeer.

Small hORnS (beige)

Follow the small horn instructions from Roy the Rhino.

Snout (light Pink)

Follow the snout instructions from Trish the Cow.

Head (white)

Follow the head instructions from Theo the Teddy Bear Lovey.

Head assembly

Follow the head assembly instructions from Trish the Cow.

Take the head and, using your tapestry needle, weave the yarn tail through each remaining stitch and pull it tight to close. Leave a long tail for sewing.

ARmS (make 2)

Follow the arm instructions from Trish the Cow, but adding the following rounds in white:

Rounds 20-21: sc in all sts. (11 sts)

SPotS (make 3 in bROwn)

Follow the spot instructions from Sefra the Giraffe, but using a 5mm (H) hook.

Blanket

Make Texture Blanket using the following colors:

Rounds 1-21: white.

Rounds 22-25: brown.

Lovey assembly

Sew the head on the center of the blanket, placing it so that it's facing one of the corners.

Sew the arms onto the blanket, just under the right and left side of the head.

Sew the spots randomly on the blanket.

Sue
the Duck

Skill level
Intermediate

You will need
- Worsted weight yarn: Yellow, Orange, Turquoise, and Black
- 4mm (G) hook
- Stitch marker
- Tapestry needle
- Stuffing
- 12mm amigurumi safety eyes
- Scissors

Stitch summary
ch, sc, dc, sl st, sc2tog

Finished size
Duck: Approximately 10in (25cm) tall, including bow

Duck Lovey: Approximately 14in (35cm) diameter

CHART GUIDE

CHART	DUCK	DUCK LOVEY
Beak	see chart	same as Duck
Bow	see chart	same as Duck
Head	same as Teddy Bear	same as Teddy Bear Lovey
Body	same as Teddy Bear	n/a
Wing	see chart	see chart
Leg	see chart	n/a
Webbed Foot	see chart	n/a

There is nothing Sue likes more than splashing around in the water with her friends.

DUCK PATTERN

Beak (orange)

Foundation ring: make a magic ring.

Round 1: work 6sc into ring.

Round 2: 2sc in all sts. (12 sts)

Round 3: (sc in next st, 2sc in next st) six times. (18 sts)

Round 4: (sc in next 2 sts, 2sc in next st) six times. (24 sts)

Round 5: sc in all sts. (24 sts)

The beak doesn't need to be stuffed. Flatten it and sew closed. Fasten off, leaving a long tail for sewing.

Bow (turquoise)

Foundation ring: make a magic ring.

Round 1: (ch3, 3dc, ch2, sl st) twice into the ring.

To finish the bow, wrap another piece of turquoise yarn around the center several times. Fasten off and leave a long tail for sewing later.

Head (yellow)

Follow the head instructions from Theo the Teddy Bear.

Head assembly

Insert the safety eyes between rounds 16 and 17, with 4 stitches between them.

Using a tapestry needle and black yarn, make a diagonal stitch above each eye, between rounds 13 and 15. Sew the beak onto the head, just below the eyes, pinching it on top to give it some shape.

Sew the bow on top of the duck's head, on round 2.

Make 3 hairs with yellow yarn on round 1 of head, using the method in the Finishing Techniques section.

Body (yellow)

Follow the body instructions from Theo the Teddy Bear.

Wings (make 2 in yellow)

Foundation ring: make a magic ring.

Round 1: work 6sc into ring.

Round 2: (sc in next st, 2sc in next st) three times. (9 sts)

Round 3: (sc in next 2 sts, 2sc in next st) three times. (12 sts)

Round 4: (sc in next st, 2sc in next st, sc in next 2 sts) three times. (15 sts)

Round 5: (sc in next 4 sts, 2sc in next st) three times. (18 sts)

Round 6: (sc in next 2 sts, 2sc in next st, sc in next 3 sts) repeat three times. (21 sts)

Rounds 7-9: sc in all sts. (21 sts)

Round 10: (sc in next 2 sts, sc2tog, sc in next 3 sts) three times. (18 sts)

Round 11: sc in all sts. (18 sts)

Round 12: (sc in next 4 sts, sc2tog) three times. (15 sts)

Round 13: sc in all sts. (15 sts)

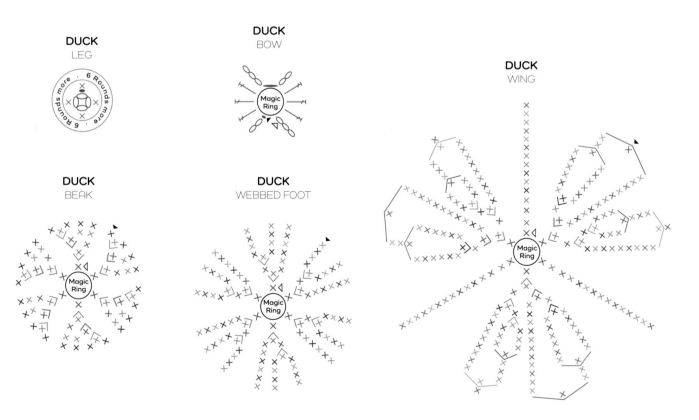

DUCK LEG

DUCK BOW

DUCK WING

DUCK BEAK

DUCK WEBBED FOOT

DUCK LOVEY PATTERN

Round 14: (sc in next st, sc2tog, sc in next 2 st) three times. (12 sts)

Round 15: (sc in next 2 sts, sc2tog) three times. (9 sts)

The wings don't need to be stuffed. Flatten them and sew closed. Fasten off, leaving a long tail for sewing.

Legs (make 2 in orange)

Foundation chain: Ch 4. Join with sl st to form a ring. Leave a long tail at the beginning.

Rounds 1-7: sc in all 4 sts. (4 sts)

Stuff the leg a little. Fasten off, leaving a long tail for sewing.

Webbed feet (make 2 in orange)

Foundation ring: make a magic ring.

Round 1: work 6 sc into ring.

Round 2: 2sc in all sts. (12 sts)

Round 3: sc in all sts. (12 sts)

Round 4: (sc in next st, 2sc in next st) six times. (18 sts)

Rounds 5-8: sc in all sts. (18 sts)

Flatten the feet (don't stuff them) and sew them closed. Fasten off.

Foot assembly

Place the leg on the webbed foot, between rounds 1 and 3 and sew it securely (1). Fasten off.

Toy assembly

Sew the head to the body.

Sew the wings to each side of the body between rounds 20 and 21.

Sew the legs at the bottom of the body between rounds 2 and 4.

1

Beak (orange)

Follow the beak instructions from Sue the Duck.

Bow (turquoise)

Follow the bow instructions from Sue the Duck.

Head (yellow)

Follow the head instructions from Theo the Teddy Bear Lovey.

Head assembly

Follow the head assembly instructions from Sue the Duck.

Take the head and, using your tapestry needle, weave the yarn tail through the remaining stitches and pull tight to close. Leave a long tail for sewing.

Wings (make 2 in yellow)

Work as for Sue the Duck to round 9.

Rounds 10-11: sc in all sts. (21 sts)

Round 12: (sc in next 2 sts, sc2tog, sc in next 3 sts) three times. (18 sts)

Round 13: sc in all sts. (18 sts)

Round 14: (sc in next 4 sts, sc2tog) three times. (15 sts)

Round 15: sc in all sts. (15 sts)

Round 16: (sc in next st, sc2tog, sc in next 2 sts) three times. (12 sts)

Round 17: (sc in next 2 sts, sc2tog) three times. (9 sts)

The wings don't need to be stuffed. Flatten them and sew closed. Fasten off, leaving a long tail for sewing.

Blanket

Make Round Blanket using the following colors:

Rounds 1-12: yellow.

Round 13: orange.

Lovey assembly

Sew the head on the center of the blanket.

Sew the arms on the blanket, one on either side of the head.

DUCK LOVEY
WING

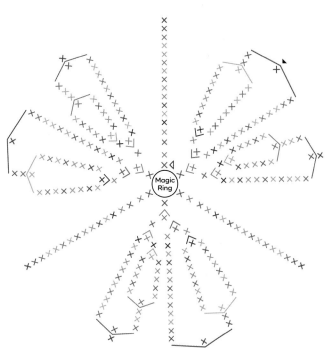

Jack
the Pig

Skill level

Intermediate

You will need

- Worsted weight yarn: Light Pink, Pink, Blue, and Black
- 4mm (G) hook
- Stitch marker
- Tapestry needle
- Stuffing
- 12mm amigurumi safety eyes
- One wooden button
- Scissors

Stitch summary

ch, sc, sl st, sc2tog, surface sl st

Finished size

Pig: Approximately 11in (28cm) tall, including ears

Pig Lovey: Approximately 16in x 16in (40cm x 40cm)

CHART GUIDE

CHART	PIG	PIG LOVEY
Head	same as Teddy Bear	same as Teddy Bear Lovey
Body	same as Teddy Bear	n/a
Arm	same as Teddy Bear	same as Teddy Bear Lovey
Leg	same as Teddy Bear	n/a
Ear	see chart	same as Pig
Snout	see chart	same as Pig
Tail	see chart	n/a

Jack the Pig wants to build a little house, but he doesn't know whether to make it out of straw, wooden sticks or bricks.

PIG PATTERN

Snout (Pink)

Foundation ring: make a magic ring.

Round 1: work 6sc into ring.

Round 2: 2sc in all sts. (12 sts)

Round 3: (sc in next st, 2sc in next st) six times. (18 sts)

Round 4: (sc in next 2 sts, 2sc in next st) six times. (24 sts)

Round 5: (sc in next st, 2sc in next st, sc in next 2 sts) six times. (30 sts)

Rounds 6-7: sc in all sts. (30 sts)

Fasten off, leaving a long tail for sewing.

To make the nostrils, use light pink yarn and your tapestry needle to sew a cross stitch on either side of the snout. Place these stitches between rounds 4 and 5 of the snout. Fasten off.

Ears (make 2 in Pink)

Foundation ring: make a magic ring.

Round 1: work 6sc into ring.

Round 2: (sc in next st, 2sc in next st) three times. (9 sts)

Round 3: (sc in next 2 sts, 2sc in next st) three times. (12 sts)

Round 4: (sc in next st, 2sc in next st, sc in next 2 sts) three times. (15 sts)

Round 5: (sc in next 4 sts, 2sc in next st) three times. (18 sts)

Round 6: sc in all sts. (18 sts)

Round 7: (sc in next 8 sts, 2sc in next st) twice. (20 sts)

Round 8: sc in all sts. (20 sts)

Round 9: (sc in next 9 sts, 2sc in next st) twice. (22 sts)

Rounds 10-11: sc in all sts. (22 sts)

The ears don't need to be stuffed. Flatten them and sew closed. Fold the tip of the ear over a little and make a tiny stitch so that it holds this shape (1). Fasten off, leaving a long tail for sewing (2).

Head (light Pink)

Follow the head instructions from Theo the Teddy Bear.

Head assembly

Insert the safety eyes between rounds 12 and 13, with 1 stitch between them.

Using a tapestry needle and black yarn, sew a diagonal stitch above each eye, between rounds 9 and 12, to give the pig a more fun expression. The length of each should be about 4 stitches.

Sew the ears to the head between rounds 3 and 12. Place them evenly, with 6 stitches between them on the top of the head.

Stuff the snout and sew it on the head between rounds 14 and 25.

Tail (light Pink)

Foundation chain: ch7.

Row 1: starting in second ch from hook, work 3sc in next 5 sts, sl st in next st.

Fasten off.

Body

Follow the body instructions from Theo the Teddy Bear, using the following colors:

Rounds 1-15: blue.

Rounds 16-22: light pink.

Sew the tail centrally on the back of the body, on round 7.

Body detail

Pull up a loop of blue yarn between rounds 15 and 16 and do surface sl st in all 30 sts. Fasten off.

Arms (make 2)

Follow the arm instructions from Theo the Teddy Bear, but with the following changes:

Round 5: work BLO.

Rounds 1-7: pink.

Rounds 8-19: light pink.

Make the fingers following the instructions in the Finishing Techniques section.

PIG LOVEY PATTERN

Legs (make 2)

Follow the leg instructions from Theo the Teddy Bear, but with the following changes:

Round 5: work BLO.

Rounds 1-7: pink.

Rounds 8-15: light pink.

Make the toes following the instructions in the Finishing Techniques section.

Toy assembly

Sew the head to the body.

Sew the arms to each side of the body between rounds 20 and 21.

Sew the legs at the bottom of the body between rounds 2 and 5.

Final detail

Make a strap with blue yarn by making a chain of 44 sts. Join the first and last ch with a sl st.

Sew the end on the back of the body, on round 15.

Sew a wooden button onto the front of the body, on round 15. Loop the strap around the button.

Snout (Pink)

Follow the snout instructions from Jack the Pig.

Ears (make 2 in Pink)

Follow the ear instructions from Jack the Pig.

Head (light Pink)

Follow the head instructions from Theo the Teddy Bear Lovey.

Head assembly

Follow the head assembly instructions from Jack the Pig.

Take the head and, using your tapestry needle, weave the yarn tail through the remaining stitches and pull tight to close. Leave a long tail for sewing.

Arms (make 2)

Follow the arm instructions from Jack the Pig, but add the following rounds in light pink:

Rounds 20-21: sc in all sts. (11 sts)

Blanket

Make Peaks Blanket using the following colors:

Rounds 1-11: light pink.

Round 12: pink.

Round 13: blue.

Rounds 14-15: pink.

Lovey assembly

Sew the head on the center of the blanket, placing it so that it faces one of the peaks.

Sew the arms onto the blanket, on either side of the head.

PIG
TAIL

1

2

PIG
EAR

PIG
SNOUT

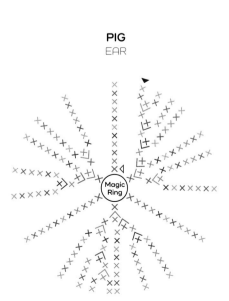

Clancy
the Reindeer

Skill level
Intermediate

You will need
- Worsted weight yarn: Beige, Red, Dark Brown, Green, White, and Black
- 4mm (G) hook
- 5mm (H) hook
- Stitch marker
- Tapestry needle
- Stuffing
- 12mm amigurumi safety eyes
- One snowflake button
- Scissors

Stitch summary
ch, sc, sl st, sc2tog

Finished size
Reindeer: Approximately 10½in (27cm) tall, including horns
Reindeer Lovey: Approximately 13in x 13in (33cm x 33cm)

CHART GUIDE

CHART	REINDEER	REINDEER LOVEY
Head	see chart	same as Reindeer
Body	same as Teddy Bear	n/a
Arm	same as Teddy Bear	same as Teddy Bear Lovey
Leg	same as Teddy Bear	n/a
Big Antler	see chart	same as Reindeer
Small Antler	see chart	same as Reindeer
Ear	see chart	same as Reindeer
Nose	see chart	same as Reindeer
Scarf	see chart	n/a

On a cold winter's night you'll never find Clancy without a cosy scarf.

REINDEER PATTERN

Nose (Red)

Foundation chain: ch5.

Stitches are worked around both sides of this foundation chain.

Round 1: starting in second ch from hook, sc in next 3 sts, 3sc in last st. Continue on other side of foundation chain, sc in next 2 sts, 2sc in next st. (10 sts)

Round 2: 2sc in next st, sc in next 2 sts, 2sc in next 3 sts, sc in next 2 sts, 2sc in next 2 sts. (16 sts)

Rounds 3-4: sc in all sts. (16 sts)

Fasten off, leaving a long tail for sewing.

Ears (make 2 in beige)

Foundation ring: make a magic ring.

Round 1: work 6sc into ring.

Round 2: sc in all sts. (6 sts)

Round 3: 2sc in all sts. (12 sts)

Round 4: (sc in next st, 2sc in next st) six times. (18 sts)

Round 5: sc in all sts. (18 sts)

Round 6: (sc in next 5 sts, 2sc in next st) three times. (21 sts)

Rounds 7-8: sc in all sts. (21 sts)

Round 9: (sc in next 5 sts, sc2tog) three times. (18 sts)

Round 10: (sc in next st, sc2tog) six times. (12 sts)

Round 11: sc in all sts. (12 sts)

The ears don't need to be stuffed. Flatten them and sew closed. Fasten off, leaving a long tail for sewing.

Small antlers (make 4 in dark brown)

Foundation ring: make a magic ring.

Round 1: work 6sc into ring.

Round 2: (sc in next st, 2sc in next st) three times. (9 sts)

Rounds 3-4: sc in all sts. (9 sts)

Fasten off, leaving a long tail for sewing.

Big antlers (make 2 in dark brown)

Foundation ring: make a magic ring.

Round 1: work 6sc into ring.

Round 2: (sc in next st, 2sc in next st) three times. (9 sts)

Rounds 3-10: sc in all sts. (9 sts)

Fasten off, leaving a long tail for sewing.

Antler assembly

Take two small antlers and sew them onto the sides of one of the big antlers at angles. Attach the first antler to the head between rounds 3 and 6, and the second between rounds 5 and 8.

Head (beige)

Foundation ring: make a magic ring.

Round 1: work 6sc into ring.

Round 2: 2sc in all sts. (12 sts)

Round 3: (sc in next st, 2sc in next st) six times. (18 sts)

Round 4: (sc in next 2 st, 2sc in next st) six times. (24 sts)

Round 5: (sc in next st, 2sc in next st, sc in next 2 sts) six times. (30 sts)

Rounds 6-8: sc in all sts. (30 sts)

Round 9: (sc in next 4 sts, 2sc in next st) six times. (36 sts)

Rounds 10-11: sc in all sts. (36 sts)

Round 12: (sc in next 2 sts, 2sc in next st, sc in next 3 sts) six times. (42 sts)

Rounds 13-14: sc in all sts. (42 sts)

Round 15: (sc in next 6 sts, 2sc in next st) six times. (48 sts)

REINDEER
HEAD

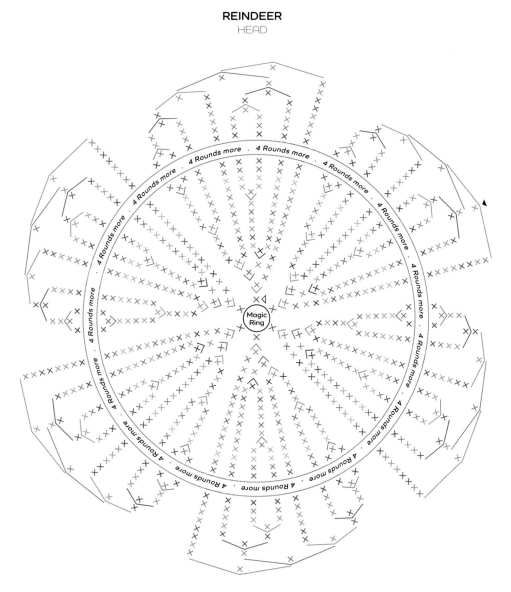

REINDEER
BIG ANTLER

REINDEER
SMALL ANTLER

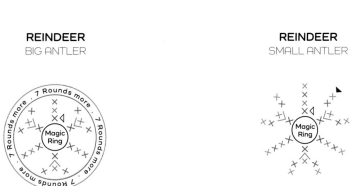

Rounds 16-21: sc in all sts. (48 sts)

Round 22: (sc in next 6 sts, sc2tog) six times. (42 sts)

Round 23: sc in all sts. (42 sts)

Stuff the head and continue stuffing as you go.

Round 24: (sc in next 2 sts, sc2tog, sc in next 3 sts) six times. (36 sts)

Round 25: (sc in next 4 sts, sc2tog) six times. (30 sts)

Round 26: (sc in next st, sc2tog, sc in next 2 sts) six times. (24 sts)

Round 27: (sc in next 2 sts, sc2tog) six times. (18 sts)

Round 28: (sc in next st, sc2tog) six times. (12 sts)

Rnd 29: sc2tog six times. (6 sts)

Fasten off, leaving a long tail for sewing.

Head assembly

Apply tension to the eyes following the instructions in the Finishing Techniques section.

Insert the safety eyes between rounds 11 and 12, with 4 stitches between them.

Using a tapestry needle and black yarn, sew a diagonal stitch above each eye, between rounds 14 and 15, to give the reindeer a more fun expression. Make each stitch about 3 stitches long.

Stuff the nose and sew it to the head between rounds 4 and 6.

Sew the antlers to the head between rounds 19 and 21. Place them evenly with 9 stitches between them.

Sew the ears to the head between rounds 20 and 21.

Take the head and, using your tapestry needle, weave the yarn tail through the remaining stitches and pull tight to close. Weave in the yarn end.

Body (beige)

Follow the body instructions from Theo the Teddy Bear.

Arms (make 2)

Follow the arm instructions from Theo the Teddy Bear, but with the following changes:

Round 5: work BLO.

Rounds 1-7: dark brown.

Rounds 8-19: beige.

Make the fingers following the instructions in the Finishing Techniques section.

Legs (make 2)

Work as leg from Theo the Teddy Bear, but with the following changes:

Round 5: work BLO.

Rounds 1-7: dark brown.

Rounds 8-15: beige.

Make the toes following the instructions in the Finishing Techniques section.

Toy assembly

Sew the head to the body.

Sew the arms to the sides of the body between rounds 20 and 21.

Sew the legs to the bottom of the body, between rounds 2 and 5.

Scarf (green)

Foundation chain: with a 5mm (H) hook, ch6.

Row 1: starting in second ch from hook, sc in next 5 sts, ch1, turn. (5 sts)

Rows 2-68: sc in all sts, ch1 and turn. (5 sts)

Fasten off.

Place the scarf around the neck of the reindeer. You can sew a snowflake button on the knot of the scarf if you like.

REINDEER LOVEY PATTERN

Nose (Red)

Follow the nose instructions from Clancy the Reindeer.

Ears (make 2 in beige)

Follow the ear instructions from Clancy the Reindeer.

Small antlers (make 4 in dark brown)

Follow the small antler instructions from Clancy the Reindeer.

Big antlers (make 2 in dark brown)

Follow the big antler instructions from Clancy the Reindeer.

Antler assembly

Follow the complete antler assembly instructions from Clancy the Reindeer.

Head (beige)

Follow the head instructions from Clancy the Reindeer.

Head assembly

Follow the head assembly instructions from Clancy the Reindeer.

Arms (make 2)

Follow the arm instructions from Clancy the Reindeer, adding the following rounds in beige:

Rounds 20-21: sc in all sts. (11 sts)

Blanket

Make Granny Blanket using the following colors:

Rounds 1-3: red.

Rounds 4-5: white.

Rounds 6-7: red.

Rounds 8-9: white.

Rounds 10-11: red.

Rounds 12-13: green.

Lovey assembly

Sew the head on the center of the blanket, placing it so that it faces one of the corners.

Sew the arms onto the blanket, on either side of the head.

REINDEER
EAR

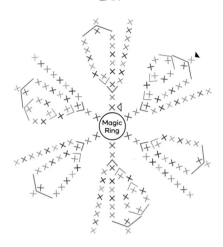

REINDEER
NOSE

REINDEER
SCARF

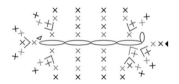

225

Cindy
the Mouse

Skill level
Intermediate

You will need
- Worsted weight yarn: Gray, Fuchsia, Light Pink, and Black
- 4mm (G) hook
- Stitch marker
- Tapestry needle
- Stuffing
- 12mm amigurumi safety eyes
- Scissors

Stitch summary
ch, sc, sl st, sc2tog, tr, surface sl st

Finished size
Mouse: Approximately 10½in (27cm) tall, including ears
Mouse Lovey: Approximately 14in (35cm) diameter

CHART GUIDE

CHART	MOUSE	MOUSE LOVEY
Head	see chart	same as Mouse
Body	same as Teddy Bear	n/a
Arm	same as Teddy Bear	same as Teddy Bear Lovey
Leg	same as Teddy Bear	n/a
Ear	see chart	same as Mouse
Bow	see chart	same as Mouse
Skirt	see chart	n/a

Cindy is a little bit shy and often hides behind bits of furniture so nobody can see her.

MOUSE PATTERN

Ears (make 2 in gray)

Foundation ring: make a magic ring.

Round 1: work 6sc into ring.

Round 2: 2sc in all sts. (12 sts)

Round 3: (sc in next st, 2sc in next st) six times. (18 sts)

Round 4: (sc in next 2 sts, 2sc in next st) six times. (24 sts)

Rounds 5-10: sc in all sts. (24 sts)

Round 11: (sc in next 2 sts, sc2tog) six times. (18 sts)

Round 12: sc in all sts. (18 sts)

The ears don't need to be stuffed. Flatten them and sew closed. Fasten off, leaving a long tail for sewing.

Bow (fuchsia)

Foundation ring: make a magic ring.

Round 1: (ch4, 3tr, ch3, sl st) twice into ring.

Take a piece of fuchsia yarn and tie around the center several times. Fasten off, leaving a for sewing later.

Head (gray)

Foundation ring: make a magic ring.

Round 1: work 6sc into ring.

Round 2: sc in all sts. (6 sts)

Round 3: 2sc in all sts. (12 sts)

Round 4: sc in all sts. (12 sts)

Round 5: (sc in next st, 2sc in next st) six times. (18 sts)

Round 6: sc in all sts. (18 sts)

Round 7: (sc in next 2 sts, 2sc in next st) six times. (24 sts)

Round 8: sc in all sts. (24 sts)

Round 9: sc in next 9 sts, 2sc in next 6 sts, sc in next 9 sts. (30 sts)

Round 10: sc in all sts. (30 sts)

Round 11: sc in next 9 sts, (sc in next st, 2sc in next st) six times, sc in next 9 sts. (36 sts)

Round 12: sc in all sts. (36 sts)

Round 13: sc in next 9 sts, (sc in next 2 sts, 2sc in next st) six times, sc in next 9 sts. (42 sts)

MOUSE
EAR

MOUSE
BOW

MOUSE
HEAD

Rounds 14-21: sc in all sts. (42 sts)

Stuff the head and continue stuffing as you go.

Round 22: (sc in next 2 sts, sc2tog, sc in next 3 sts) six times. (36 sts)

Round 23: sc in all sts. (36 sts)

Round 24: (sc in next 4 sts, sc2tog) six times. (30 sts)

Round 25: sc in all sts. (30 sts)

Round 26: (sc in next st, sc2tog, sc in next 2 sts) six times. (24 sts)

Round 27: (sc in next 2 sts, sc2tog) six times. (18 sts)

Round 28: (sc in next st, sc2tog) six times. (12 sts)

Round 29: sc2tog six times. (6 sts)

Fasten off, leaving a tail for sewing.

Head assembly

Insert the safety eyes between rounds 9 and 10, with 4 stitches between them.

Using a tapestry needle and black yarn, make a diagonal stitch above each eye, between rounds 12 and 13, about 4 stitches long.

To make the nose, use light pink yarn and sew several triangle-shaped stitches in the center of the head between rounds 1 and 2.

Sew the ears to the head between rounds 19 and 20.

Sew the bow in front of the left ear.

Body

Follow the body instructions from Theo the Teddy Bear, but with the following changes:

Round 14: work BLO.

Rounds 1-8: white.

Rounds 9-22: fuchsia.

Body detail

Pull up a loop of light pink yarn on the front of the body between rounds 13 and 14 (leaving a long tail at the beginning) and do surface sl st in all 36 sts around. Leave a long tail. Make a little bow with both ends of body detail yarn.

Note: Tie a knot in each end of the yarn on the belt so that it doesn't fray.

Skirt

Pull up a loop of fuchsia yarn at the front of round 13 and work as follows:

Round 1: sc in all sts. (36 sts)

Round 2: (sc in next 2 sts, 2sc in next st, sc in next 3 sts) six times. (42 sts)

Rounds 3-7: sc in all sts. (42 sts)

Round 8: change to light pink yarn. (sc, ch, sc in next st, skip next st) twenty-one times. (42 sts)

Join with a sl st in first sc of this round. Fasten off.

Arms (make 2 in gray)

Follow the arm instructions from Theo the Teddy Bear.

Legs (make 2 in gray)

Follow the leg instructions from Theo the Teddy Bear.

Flatten the legs and sew closed. Fasten off, leaving a tail for sewing.

Toy assembly

Sew the head to the body.

Sew the arms to each side of the body between rounds 20 and 21.

Sew the legs on the sides of the body, between rounds 6 and 7.

MOUSE
SKIRT

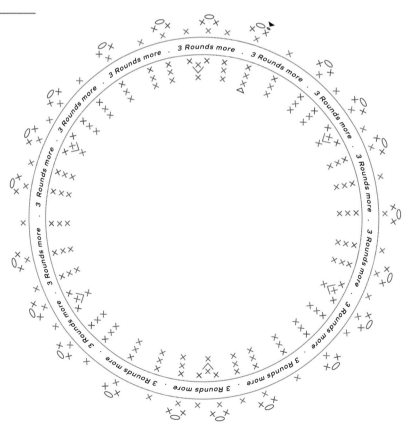

MOUSE LOVEY PATTERN

Ears (make 2 in gray)

Follow the ear instructions from Cindy the Mouse.

Bow (fuchsia)

Follow the bow instructions from Cindy the Mouse.

Head (gray)

Follow the head instructions from Cindy the Mouse.

Head assembly

Follow the head assembly instructions from Cindy the Mouse.

Arms (make 2 in gray)

Follow the arm instructions from Theo the Teddy Bear Lovey.

Blanket

Make Round Blanket using the following colors:

Round 1: gray.

Rounds 2-12: fuchsia.

Round 13: light pink.

Lovey assembly

Sew the head on the center of the blanket.

Sew the arms onto the blanket, just under each side of the head.

Cooper
the Fox

Skill level
Intermediate

You will need
- Worsted weight yarn: Orange, White, and Black
- 4mm (G) hook
- Stitch marker
- Tapestry needle
- Stuffing
- 12mm amigurumi safety eyes
- Scissors

Stitch summary
ch, sc, sl st, sc2tog

Finished size
Fox: Approximately 10in (25cm) tall

Fox Lovey: Approximately 13in x 13in (33cm x 33cm)

CHART GUIDE

CHART	FOX	FOX LOVEY
Head	same as Mouse	same as Mouse
Body	same as Teddy Bear	n/a
Arm	same as Teddy Bear	same as Teddy Bear Lovey
Leg	same as Teddy Bear	n/a
Ear	see chart	same as Fox
Tail	see chart	n/a

COOPER is a very cunning boy and loves nothing more than playing tricks on his friends.

FOX PATTERN

Ears (make 2)

Foundation ring: using black yarn make a magic ring.

Round 1: work 6sc into ring.

Round 2: sc in all sts. (6 sts)

Round 3: 2sc in all sts. (12 sts)

Round 4: change to orange yarn. Sc in all sts. (12 sts)

Round 5: (sc in next st, 2sc in next st) six times. (18 sts)

Round 6: sc in all sts. (18 sts)

Round 7: (sc in next 2 sts, 2sc in next st) six times. (24 sts)

Rounds 8-10: sc in all sts. (24 sts)

The ears don't need to be stuffed. Flatten them and sew closed. Fasten off, leaving a long tail for sewing.

Head

Follow the instructions from Cindy the Mouse, but in the following colors:

Rounds 1-8: white.

Rounds 9-29: orange.

Head assembly

Insert the safety eyes between rounds 9 and 10, with 4 stitches between them.

Using a tapestry needle and black yarn, make a diagonal stitch above each eye, between rounds 12 and 13, to give it a more fun expression. The length of each stitch is about 4 stitches.

To make the nose, with black yarn, do several triangle-shaped stitches. Place them in the center, between rounds 1 and 2 of the head.

Sew the ears to the head between rounds 19 and 23. Place them evenly with 2 stitches between them on the top of the head.

Take the head and using your tapestry needle, weave the yarn tail through the remaining stitches and pull tight to close. Weave in the yarn end.

Tail

Foundation ring: using white yarn make a magic ring.

Round 1: work 6sc into ring.

Round 2: (sc in next 2 sts, 2sc in next st) twice. (8 sts)

Round 3: (sc in next 3 sts, 2sc in next st) twice. (10 sts)

Round 4: (sc in next 4 sts, 2sc in next st) twice. (12 sts)

Round 5: change to orange yarn. Sc in all sts. (12 sts)

Round 6: (sc in next 2 sts, 2sc in next st) four times. (16 sts)

Round 7: (sc in next st, 2sc in next st, sc in next 2 sts) four times. (20 sts)

Round 8: sc in all sts. (20 sts)

Round 9: (sc in next st, sc2tog, sc in next 2 sts) four times. (16 sts)

Round 10: sc in all sts. (16 sts)

Round 11: (sc in next 2 sts, sc2tog) four times. (12 sts)

Round 12: sc in all 12 sts. (12 sts)

Round 13: (sc in next 4 sts, sc2tog) twice. (10 sts)

Round 14: sc in all 10 sts. (10 sts)

Round 15: (sc in next st, sc2tog, sc in next 2 st) twice. (8 sts)

Rounds 16-17: sc in all sts. (8 sts)

Stuff the tail, flatten the end and sew it closed. Fasten off, leaving a long tail for sewing.

Body (orange)

Follow the instructions for Theo the Teddy Bear.

Sew the tail on the back of the body, between rounds 6 and 9, leaning a little to one side.

FOX LOVEY PATTERN

ARMS (make 2)

Follow the instructions for Theo the Teddy Bear, using the following colors:

Rounds 1-7: black.

Rounds 8-19: orange.

Legs (make 2)

Follow the instructions for Theo the Teddy Bear, using the following colors:

Rounds 1-6: black.

Rounds 7-15: orange.

Toy assembly

Sew the head to the body.

Sew the arms to each side of the body between rounds 20 and 21.

Sew the legs at the bottom of the body between rounds 2 and 5.

Ears (make 2)

Follow the ear instructions from Cooper the Fox.

Head

Follow the head instructions from Cooper the Fox.

Head assembly

Follow the head assembly instructions from Cooper the Fox.

ARMS (make 2)

Follow the arm instructions from Theo the Teddy Bear Lovey using the following colors:

Rounds 1-7: black.

Rounds 8-21: orange.

Blanket

Make Granny Blanket using the following colors:

Rounds 1-9: orange.

Rounds 10-11: white.

Rounds 12-13: black.

Lovey assembly

Sew the head on the center of the blanket.

Sew the arms onto the blanket, on either side of the head.

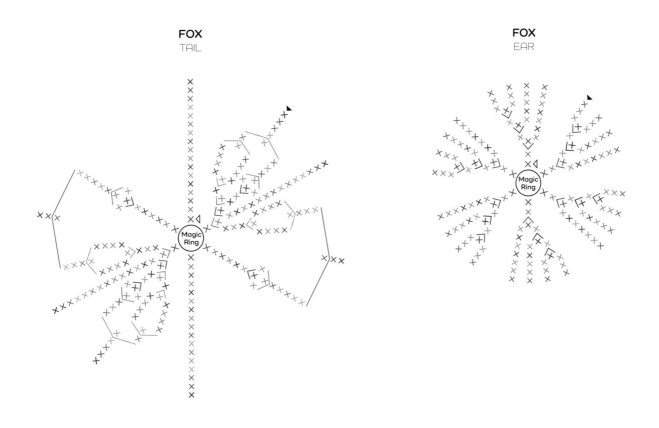

FOX
TAIL

FOX
EAR

Maverick
the Monkey

Skill level
Intermediate

You will need
- Worsted weight yarn: Beige, Brown, and Black
- 4mm (G) hook
- Stitch marker
- Tapestry needle
- Stuffing
- 12mm amigurumi safety eyes
- Scissors

Stitch summary
ch, sc, sl st, 4dc cluster st, sc2tog

Finished size
Monkey: Approximately 11½in (29cm) tall

Monkey Lovey: Approximately 12in x 13in (30cm x 33cm)

CHART GUIDE

CHART	MONKEY	MONKEY LOVEY
Head	same as Teddy Bear	same as Teddy Bear Lovey
Body	same as Teddy Bear	n/a
Snout	see chart	same as Monkey
Arm	see chart	same as Monkey
Leg	see chart	n/a
Ear	see chart	same as Monkey
Tail	see chart	n/a

Maverick has the
funniest laugh
that sends all his
friends off into
fits of giggles.

MONKEY PATTERN

Snout (beige)

Foundation chain: ch 12.

Stitches are worked along both sides of the foundation chain.

Round 1: start in second ch from hook, sc in next 10 sts, 3 sc in last st. Continue on the other side of the foundation chain, sc in next 9 sts, 2sc in next st. (24 sts)

Round 2: 2sc in next st, sc in next 9 sts, 2sc in next 3 sts, sc in next 9 sts, 2sc in next 2 sts. (30 sts)

Rounds 3-5: sc in all sts. (30 sts)

Fasten off, leaving a long tail for sewing.

To make the nostrils, using brown yarn and your tapestry needle, make a cross stitch on each side of the snout, on round 1. Fasten off.

Note: Line up the nose stitches carefully under the eyes for the perfect expression.

EaRS (make 2 in brown)

Foundation ring: make a magic ring.

Round 1: work 6sc into ring.

Round 2: 2sc in all sts. (12 sts)

Round 3: (sc in next st, 2sc in next st) six times. (18 sts)

Round 4: (sc in next 5 sts, 2sc in next st) three times. (21 sts)

Rounds 5-7: sc in all sts. (21 sts)

Round 8: (sc in next 5 sts, sc2tog) three times. (18 sts)

Round 9: sc in all sts. (18 sts)

Round 10: (sc in next st, sc2tog) six times. (12 sts)

The ears don't need to be stuffed. Flatten them and sew closed. Fasten off, leaving a long tail for sewing.

Head (brown)

Follow the head instructions from Theo the Teddy Bear.

Head assembly

Insert the safety eyes between rounds 14 and 15, with 3 stitches between them.

Using a tapestry needle and black yarn, make a diagonal stitch above each eye, between rounds 11 and 13, to give the monkey a more fun expression. Make each stitch about 4 stitches long.

Stuff the snout and sew it onto the head, between rounds 16 and 24.

Sew the ears to the head between rounds 11 and 17.

Tail (brown)

Foundation ring: make a magic ring.

Round 1: work 6sc into ring.

Round 2: (sc in next st, 2sc in next st) three times. (9 sts)

Round 3-24: sc in all sts. (9 sts)

Stuff the tail a little. Fasten off, leaving a long tail for sewing.

Body (brown)

Follow the body instructions from Theo the Teddy Bear.

With beige yarn, make a cross stitch on the center of the body, between rounds 8 and 9.

Sew the tail on the back of the body, between rounds 6 and 8, leaning a little to one side.

ARmS (make 2)

Foundation ring: using beige yarn make a magic ring.

Round 1: work 6sc into ring.

Round 2: 2sc in all sts. (12 sts)

Round 3: (sc in next st, 2sc in next st) six times. (18 sts)

Rounds 4-7: sc in all sts. (18 sts)

Round 8: 4dc cluster stitch in first st, ch1, sc in next 17 sts. (18 sts)

Round 9: (sc in next st, sc2tog) six times. (12 sts)

Round 10: sc in all sts. (12 sts)

Round 11-24: change to brown yarn. sc in all sts. (12 sts)

Stuff the arms. Flatten them and sew closed. Fasten off, leaving a long tail for sewing.

Legs (make 2)

Foundation ring: using beige yarn make a magic ring.

Round 1: work 6sc into ring.

Round 2: 2sc in all sts. (12 sts)

Round 3: (sc in next st, 2sc in next st) six times. (18 sts)

Round 4: (sc in next 2 sts, 2sc in next st) six times. (24 sts)

Rounds 5-8: sc in all sts. (24 sts)

Round 9: (sc in next 2 sts, sc2tog) six times. (18 sts)

Round 10: (sc in next st, sc2tog) six times. (12 sts)

Round 11: sc in all sts. (12 sts)

Rounds 12-26: Change to brown yarn. Sc in all sts. (12 sts)

Stuff the legs. Flatten them and sew closed. Fasten off, leaving a long tail for sewing.

Toy assembly

Sew the head to the body.

Sew the arms to each side of the body between rounds 20 and 21.

Sew the legs at the bottom of the body between rounds 2 and 5.

MONKEY LOVEY PATTERN

Snout (beige)

Follow the snout instructions from Maverick the Monkey.

Ears (make 2 in brown)

Follow the ear instructions from Maverick the Monkey.

Head (brown)

Follow the head instructions from Theo the Teddy Bear Lovey.

Head assembly

Follow the head assembly instructions from Maverick the Monkey.

Take the head and using your tapestry needle, weave the yarn tail through each remaining stitch and pull it tight to close. Leave a long tail for sewing.

Arms (make 2)

Follow the arm instructions from Maverick the Monkey.

Blanket

Make Texture Blanket using the following colors:

Rounds 1-21: brown.

Rounds 22-25: beige.

Lovey assembly

Sew the head onto the center of the blanket, placing it so that the head faces one of the corners.

Sew the arms onto the blanket, just under each side of the head.

MONKEY
EAR

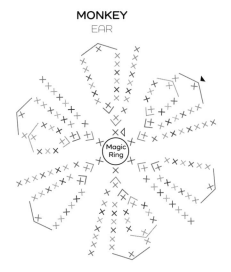

MONKEY
SNOUT

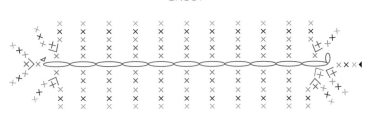

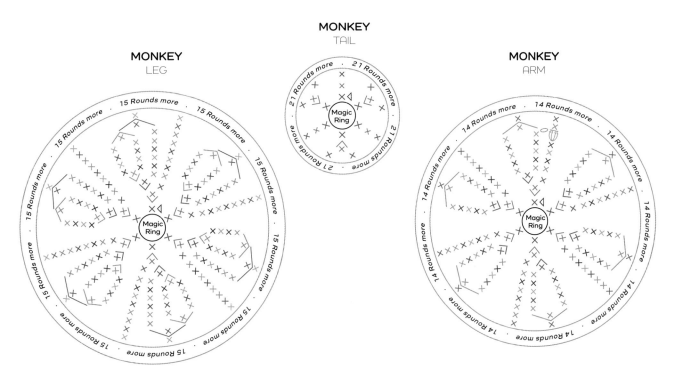

MONKEY
LEG

MONKEY
TAIL

MONKEY
ARM

Ava
the Girl

Skill level
Intermediate

You will need
- Worsted weight yarn: Beige, Yellow, Coral, White, and Black
- 4mm (G) hook
- 5mm (H) hook
- Stitch marker
- Tapestry needle
- Stuffing
- 12mm amigurumi safety eyes
- Two small buttons
- Scissors

Stitch summary
ch, sc, hdc, dc, sl st, 4dc cluster st, sc2tog

Finished size
Girl: Approximately 10½in (27cm) tall
Girl Lovey: Approximately 14in (35cm) diameter

CHART GUIDE

CHART	GIRL	GIRL LOVEY
Head	same as Teddy Bear	same as Teddy Bear Lovey
Body	same as Teddy Bear	n/a
Arm	same as Monkey	same as Monkey
Leg	same as Teddy Bear	n/a
Hair	see chart	same as Girl
Bow	same as Duck	same as Duck
Bun	see chart	same as Girl
Skirt	see chart	n/a

Ava is very funny
and always makes
her friends laugh.

GIRL PATTERN

Hair (yellow)

Foundation ring: using 5mm (H) hook, make a magic ring.

Round 1: work 6sc into ring.

Round 2: 2sc in all sts. (12 sts)

Round 3: (sc in next st, 2sc in next st) six times. (18 sts)

Round 4: (sc in next 2 sts, 2sc in next st) six times. (24 sts)

Round 5: (sc in next st, 2sc in next st, sc in next 2 sts) six times. (30 sts)

Round 6: (sc in next 4 sts, 2sc in next st) six times. (36 sts)

Round 7: (sc in next 2 sts, 2sc in next st, sc in next 3 sts) six times. (42 sts)

Round 8: (sc in next 6 sts, 2sc in next st) six times. (48 sts)

Rounds 9-14: sc in all sts. (48 sts)

Round 15: (skip next st, 5hdc in next st, skip next st, sc in next st) twelve times. (72 sts)

Fasten off, leaving a long tail for sewing.

Bun (make 2 in yellow)

Foundation ring: using 5mm (H) hook, make a magic ring.

Round 1: work 6sc into ring.

Round 2: 2sc in all sts. (12 sts)

Round 3: (sc in next st, 2sc in next st) six times. (18 sts)

Round 4: (sc in next 5 sts, 2sc in next st) three times. (21 sts)

Rounds 5-6: sc in all sts. (21 sts)

Round 7: (sc in next 5 sts, sc2tog) three times. (18 sts)

Round 8: (sc in next st, sc2tog) six times. (12 sts)

Stuff the buns. Fasten off, leaving a long tail for sewing.

Sew the buns on the hair between rounds 7 and 11.

Bow (make 2 in coral)

Follow the bow instructions from Sue the Duck.

Sew one bow just in front of each bun.

Head (beige)

Follow the head instructions from Theo the Teddy Bear.

Head assembly

Insert the safety eyes between rounds 14 and 15, with 2 stitches between them.

Using a tapestry needle and black yarn, make a diagonal stitch above each eye, between rounds 12 and 14, to give the girl a more fun expression. Make each stitch about 3 stitches long.

To make the nose, sew several horizontal stitches with beige yarn in the center of the head, between rounds 16 and 17. Then make some vertical stitches over the horizontal stitches.

To make the mouth, use black yarn and sew one straight stitch across 2 crochet sts, one diagonal stitch across 2 stitches and another little straight stitch, working between rounds 20 and 21 of the head. You can position it a little to the right to make her expression more fun.

Place the hair on the head and stitch it on, working along round 14 of the hair.

Body

Follow the body instructions from Theo the Teddy Bear, but with the following changes:

Round 15: work BLO.

Rounds 1-12: white.

Rounds 13-22: coral.

Sew two little buttons on the body on rounds 16 and 19.

GIRL
SKIRT

242

GIRL LOVEY PATTERN

Skirt (coral)

Pull up a loop of coral yarn at the front of round 14 and work as follows:

Round 1: sc in all sts. (36 sts)

Round 2: (sc in next 2 sts, 2sc in next st, sc in next 3 sts) six times. (42 sts)

Rounds 3-6: sc in all sts. (42 sts)

Round 7: (sc, ch1, sc in next st, skip next st) twenty-one times. (42 sts)

Join with a sl st in first sc of this round. Fasten off.

Arms (make 2 in beige)

Follow the instructions from Maverick the Monkey.

Legs (make 2 in beige)

Follow the instructions from Theo the Teddy Bear.

Toy assembly

Sew the head to the body.

Sew the arms to each side of the body between rounds 20 and 21.

Sew the legs to the bottom of the body between rounds 3 and 5.

Hair (yellow)

Follow the hair instructions from Ava the Girl.

Bun (make 2 in yellow)

Follow the bun instructions from Ava the Girl.

Bow (make 2 in coral)

Follow the bow instructions from Sue the Duck.

Sew one bow just in front of each bun.

Head (beige)

Follow the head instructions from Theo the Teddy Bear Lovey.

Head assembly

Follow the head assembly instructions from Ava the Girl.

Take the head and, using your tapestry needle, weave the yarn tail through each remaining stitch and pull it tight to close. Leave a long tail for sewing.

Arms (make 2 in beige)

Follow the arm instructions from Maverick the Monkey.

Blanket

Make Round Blanket using the following colors:

Rounds 1-12: coral

Rounds 13: white

Lovey assembly

Sew the head on the center of the blanket.

Sew the arms onto the blanket, just under the right and left side of the head.

GIRL
HAIR

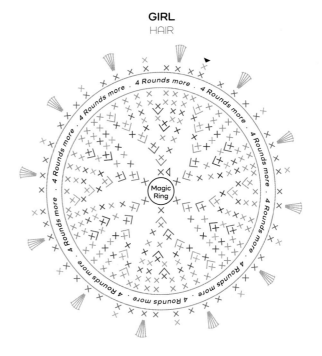

GIRL
BUN

243

Ethan
the Boy

Skill level
Intermediate

You will need
- Worsted weight yarn: Beige, Green, Dark Blue, Brown, and Black
- 4mm (G) hook
- 5mm (H) hook
- Stitch marker
- Tapestry needle
- Stuffing
- 12mm amigurumi safety eyes
- Scissors

Stitch summary
ch, sc, dc, hdc, sl st, 4dc cluster st, sc2tog, surface sl st

Finished size
Boy: Approximately 10½in (27cm) tall

Boy Lovey: Approximately 14in (35cm) diameter

CHART GUIDE

CHART	BOY	BOY LOVEY
Head	same as Teddy Bear	same as Teddy Bear Lovey
Body	same as Teddy Bear	n/a
Arm	same as Monkey	same as Monkey
Leg	same as Teddy Bear	n/a
Hair	see chart	same as Boy
Bow Tie	same as Bow from Duck	n/a

Ethan loves making
things and creating
funny inventions.

245

BOY PATTERN

Hair (brown)

Foundation ring: using 5mm (H) hook, make a magic ring.

Round 1: work 6sc into ring.

Round 2: 2sc in all sts. (12 sts)

Round 3: (sc in next st, 2sc in next st) six times. (18 sts)

Round 4: (sc in next 2 sts, 2sc in next st) six times. (24 sts)

Round 5: (sc in next st, 2sc in next st, sc in next 2 sts) six times. (30 sts)

Round 6: (sc in next 4 sts, 2sc in next st) six times. (36 sts)

Round 7: (sc in next 2 sts, 2sc in next st, sc in next 3 sts) six times. (42 sts)

Round 8: (sc in next 6 sts, 2sc in next st) six times. (48 sts)

Rounds 9-16: sc in all sts. (48 sts)

Round 17: sc in next 35 sts, hdc in next st, 2dc in next st, 6dc in next st, skip next 3 sts, sc in next 7 sts. (51 sts)

Fasten off, leaving a long tail for sewing.

Head (beige)

Follow the body instructions from Theo the Teddy Bear.

Head assembly

Insert the safety eyes between rounds 14 and 15, with 2 stitches between them.

Using a tapestry needle and black yarn, make a diagonal stitch above each eye, between rounds 13 and 15, to give the boy a more fun expression. Make each stitch about 3 stitches long.

To make the nose, sew several horizontal stitches with beige yarn in the center of the head, between rounds 16 and 18. Then make some vertical stitches over the horizontal stitches.

To make the mouth, use black yarn and sew one straight stitch across 2 crochet sts, one diagonal stitch across 2 stitches and another little straight stitch, working between rounds 20 and 21 of the head. You can position it a little to the right to make his expression more fun.

Place the hair on the head with the fringe above the boy's face. Stitch the hair on, working along round 16 of the hair.

Note: The boy looks better if you don't sew his fringe to his head.

BOY
HAIR

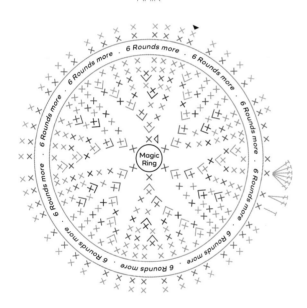

BOY LOVEY PATTERN

Body

Follow the body instructions from Theo the Teddy Bear, but with the following changes:

Round 14: work BLO.

Rounds 1-13: dark blue.

Rounds 14-21: green.

Round 22: beige.

Bow tie (dark blue)

Follow the bow instructions from Sue the Duck.

Sew the bow tie onto the body. Place it in the center on round 21.

Arms (make 2)

Follow the instructions from Maverick the Monkey, but with the following changes:

Rounds 1-18: beige.

Round 19: work the first 3 sts with beige yarn, then change to green.

Rounds 20-24: green.

Arm detail

Pull up a loop of green yarn between rounds 19 and 20 and do surface sl st in all 12 st.

Legs (make 2)

Follow the instructions from Theo the Teddy Bear, but with the following changes:

Rounds 1-7: beige.

Rounds 8-15: dark blue.

Leg detail

Pull up a loop of dark blue yarn between rounds 7 and 8 and do surface sl st in all 21 sts.

Toy assembly

Sew the head to the body.

Sew the arms to each side of the body between rounds 20 and 21.

Sew the legs at the bottom of the body between rounds 2 and 3.

Hair (brown)

Follow the hair instructions from Ethan the Boy.

Head (beige)

Follow the head instructions from Theo the Teddy Bear Lovey.

Head assembly

Follow the head assembly instructions from Ethan the Boy.

Take the head and, using your tapestry needle, weave the yarn tail through each remaining stitch and pull it tight to close. Leave a long tail for sewing.

Arms (make 2)

Follow the arm instructions from Ethan the Boy.

Blanket

Make Round Blanket using the following colors:

Rounds 1-5: green.

Rounds 6-13: dark blue.

Lovey assembly

Sew the head on the center of the blanket.

Sew the arms onto the blanket, just under the right and left side of the head.

BASIC TECHNIQUES

CHANGING COLOR

To change yarn color while working in continuous rounds of single crochet, work until you have one stitch left of the last round of the first color.

Insert hook into the last stitch, yarn over and pull up a loop. Then yarn over with the new color and pull through both loops on the hook, leaving one loop in the new color.

For any other stitch, work in the first color until the last yarn over, then do the last yarn over in the new color. Your final loop left on the hook should be in the new color yarn.

FASTENING OFF

To fasten off your yarn, complete the final stitch, then cut your yarn, leaving a tail of at least 6in (15cm). Thread the tail end of the yarn onto your tapestry needle and make a couple of stitches on the reverse side of the crochet piece, working into stitches of the same color and making them as invisible as you can.

Make another couple of stitches, working over the first two to really secure the yarn end. Cut the yarn as close to the work as possible, taking care not to cut into any of your crochet stitches!

USING STITCH MARKERS

When working in continuous spirals, which you'll be doing for most of the patterns in this section, using a stitch marker will make it much easier to see where your round starts and finishes.

Choose a split ring marker and push it through the first stitch of the round, just underneath the hook after you have made the stitch.

Continue with the pattern – you'll know you've finished the round when you reach the last stitch before the marker. Work this last stitch. You can now count the stitches between your hook and the marker to make sure you have the correct number.

Work the first stitch of the next round and move the marker up.

SPIRAL VS JOINED ROUNDS

Most of the patterns in this section are worked in spiral rounds.

To do this you work each round continuously, moving straight onto the first stitch of the new round after working the last stitch of the previous round.

Use your stitch markers to keep track of which round you are working on.

If you work in continuous spirals, you'll find that you won't see a seam in your finished work.

To work in joined rounds, finish the round you are on and make a slip stitch into the first stitch of the round.

Place a stitch marker into the slip stitch. Work one chain, then start the next round.

CROCHETING IN ROWS

The texture blanket is worked in straight rows. To do this follow the pattern to the end of the row and then turn your work, so the other side is facing you.

You'll be instructed to make a number of chain at the end of each row, which takes you up to the right point for starting the next row and keeps the sides of your piece straight and neat.

Continue to turn your work each time you reach the end of a row.

THIRD LOOP

For some of the patterns you'll have to work with the third loop. To find this loop, look behind the back loop on the back side of the stitch. The third loop is the loop directly underneath the back loop.

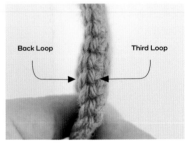

STITCHES

ABBREVIATIONS

ch	chain
sl st	slip stitch
sc	single crochet
dc	double crochet
hdc	half double crochet
tr	treble crochet
st(s)	stitch(es)
sc2tog	single crochet 2 together (decrease by one stitch)
BLO	back loop only

CHART SYMBOLS

 magic ring

 start

 end

 ch

 sl st

 sc

 2sc

 sc2tog

 hdc

 dc

tr

 3dc cluster stitch

 4dc cluster stitch

US AND UK CROCHET STITCHES

Be aware that crochet terms in the US differ from those in the UK. The crochet patterns in this section are written in US terms, but if you are used to working with UK terms here is a useful conversion chart to explain the difference:

US TERM	UK TERM
Single Crochet (sc)	Double Crochet (dc)
Double Crochet (dc)	Treble Crochet (tr)
Half Double Crochet (hdc)	Half Treble Crochet (htr)
Treble Crochet (tr)	Double Treble Crochet (dtr)
3dc Cluster	3tr Cluster
4dc Cluster	4tr Cluster

SINGLE CROCHET (SC)

Called Double Crochet (dc) in UK.

Insert hook into work where indicated, yarn over and pull up a loop, yarn over and pull through both loops on hook, one loop remaining.

HALF DOUBLE CROCHET (HDC)

Called Half Treble Crochet (htr) in UK.

Yarn over and insert hook into work where indicated, yarn over and pull up a loop, yarn over and pull through all three loops on hook, one loop remaining.

DOUBLE CROCHET (DC)

Called Treble Crochet (tr) in UK.

Yarn over and insert hook into work where indicated, yarn over and pull up a loop. Yarn over and pull through two loops on the hook, yarn over and pull through the remaining two loops on the hook, one loop remaining.

TREBLE CROCHET (TR)

Called Double Treble (dtr) in UK.

Yarn over twice and insert hook into work where indicated, yarn over and pull up a loop. Yarn over and pull through two loops on the hook, repeat twice more, one loop remaining.

SINGLE CROCHET 2 TOGETHER (SC2TOG)

Use this to method to decrease by one stitch.

Insert hook into front loop of next two stitches as indicated, yarn over and pull through those two loops (two loops on hook). Yarn over and pull through both loops.

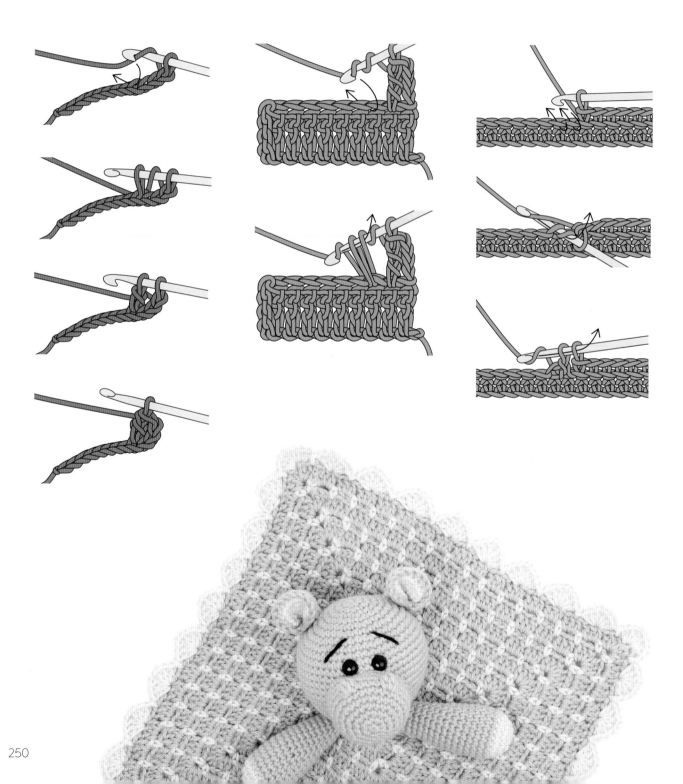

250

REVERSE SINGLE CROCHET (REVERSE SC)

Also Called Crab Stitch.

Reverse single crochet is worked exactly like regular single crochet except you work from left to right instead of right to left. Insert hook into the stitch to the right of the hook, yarn over and pull up a loop, yarn over and pull though both loops on the hook as you would with a regular single crochet.

Keep working in this manner in each stitch to the right of the hook.

3DC CLUSTER

Yarn over, insert hook into the next stitch, yarn over and pull up a loop, yarn over and pull through two loops, leaving last two loops on the hook.

Yarn over, insert hook into the same stitch, yarn over and pull up a loop, yarn over and pull through two loops on the hook, leaving the last loop of this dc on the hook (there are now three loops on the hook).

Yarn over, insert hook into the same stitch, yarn over and pull up a loop, yarn over and pull through two loops on the hook, leaving the last loop of this dc on the hook (there are now four loops on the hook).

Yarn over and pull loop through all the loops on the hook to complete the cluster.

4DC CLUSTER

Yarn over, insert hook into the next stitch, yarn over and pull up a loop, yarn over and pull through two loops, leaving last two loops on the hook.

Yarn over, insert hook into the same stitch, yarn over and pull up a loop, yarn over and pull through two loops on the hook, leaving the last loop of this dc on the hook (there are now three loops on the hook).

Yarn over, insert hook into the same stitch, yarn over and pull up a loop, yarn over and pull through two loops on the hook, leaving the last loop of this dc on the hook (there are now four loops on the hook).

Yarn over, insert hook into the same stitch, yarn over and pull up a loop, yarn over and pull through two loops on the hook, leaving the last loop of this dc on the hook (there are now five loops on the hook).

Yarn over and pull loop through all the loops on the hook to complete the cluster.

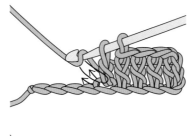

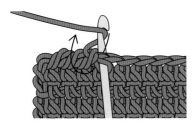

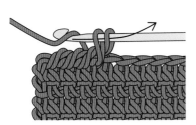

SLIP STITCH (SL ST)

Insert hook into work where indicated, yarn over and pull loop through stitch and loop on hook, one loop remaining.

SURFACE SLIP STITCH

Insert hook into work where indicated, yarn over and pull loop through stitch and loop on hook, one loop remaining. Repeat, working along a round of crochet so that slip stitches lie on the surface of the piece already worked.

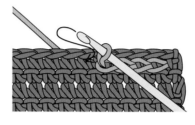

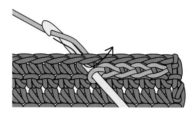

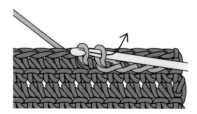

MAGIC RING

Make a loop with your yarn, and hold it closed with the working end held over the forefinger of your left hand. Insert hook into the ring and pull up a loop through the ring.

Yarn over and pull a loop through both loops on the hook (one sc made). Continue until you have made the number of sc specified in the pattern. Take the yarn end and pull the ring tight.

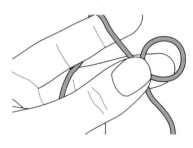

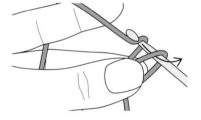

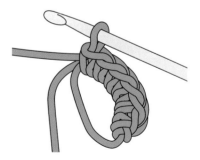

FINISHING TECHNIQUES

SEW EDGES

Sewing the edges is straightforward. Just take your project, flatten it out and sew the open edges closed (1). The pattern will tell you whether you should fasten off your yarn or leave a long tail. Images show the bottom edge of one ear (2).

ADDING TENSION TO THE EYES

When you add tension to the eyes, the head will take shape, but for this to happen, the head must first be stuffed. Follow the steps below:

Thread a needle with a new piece of yarn in the same color as the head and make a knot at one end.

Insert the needle inside the head and pull it out where one of the eyes will be. Push the needle back into the head, close to where it came out (3), and bring it out through the hole at the base of the head (4). Remember that the placement of the eyes will be indicated in each pattern.

Repeat this process with a new piece of yarn for the other eye.

Push the amigurumi safety eyes into the head, where you made the stitches (5).

Apply tension to the two bits of yarn to get the desired shape. Tie them together in a knot (6) and cut the ends of the yarn.

Push the knot into the head with the help of your crochet hook (7).

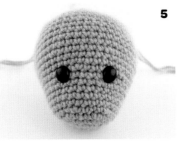

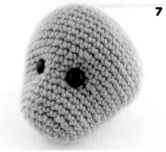

FINGERS/TOES

With the start of the round at the back of the arm/leg, find the center of the round.

Use yarn in the same color that you started the arm/leg with.

To make the finger/toe, thread your tapestry needle and insert it into the arm/leg, bringing it out through the center of the magic ring (8).

Insert the needle back through the arm/leg, just below the color change round and bring it out again in the same place (9). Pull the thread tight.

Repeat this process to make more stitches in the same place (10).

Fasten off the yarn.

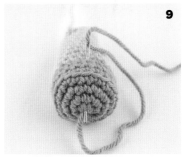

COMBINED EARS

To make one combined ear, crochet two pieces following the pattern instructions and fasten off just one of them (11).

Place the pieces wrong sides together (12).

Insert your hook back into the live stitch and through the corresponding stitch in the other piece (13) and work a sc. Now work 1 sc in each

stitch around the edge, working through both pieces (14).

Now fold the ear together at the bottom (15) and make several stitches to secure it (16). Fasten off.

HAIR

To make the hair, cut several pieces of yarn, approximately 3in (8cm) long. The number of pieces you need depends on the project you are making.

Insert the hook through one stitch on the head, loop the center of the yarn piece over the hook (1) and draw it through the stitch. Wrap both ends of yarn over the hook again (2) and pull them through the loop.

Using a needle to help you, unwind the strands of yarn (3).

Repeat this process to make more hair – the pattern will tell you where to place the hair. Finally, cut the hair to the desired length.

CLOSING ARMS AND ATTACHING TO BODY

Once you have finished crocheting the arm, stuff lightly with toy stuffing and thread your tapestry needle. Pinch the top of the arm shut and with a couple of small stitches sew it closed.

Use the yarn end to sew the arm to the top of the body, placing it on the row indicated on the pattern. Position it so that the flat edge of the arm runs from front to back.

JOINING LEGS TO BODY

Once you have made the legs, fill them with toy stuffing.

When you attach the legs to the base of the body, don't pinch them closed. Sew around the leg with small, neat stitches using the tail end of matching yarn.

The pattern will tell you where to position the legs.

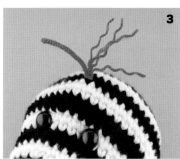

ASSEMBLING THE LOVEYS

Place the head in the center of the blanket, facing it towards one of the corners if the blanket is not circular (4).

Secure the head to the blanket with pins (5).

Thread your tapestry needle and stitch the head securely to the blanket (6).

Stitch each arm securely to the blanket, one on either side of the head (7).

Fasten off all ends neatly.

ABOUT THE AUTHOR

Hi, I'm Carolina!

I live in a beautiful city in the south of Spain, with my husband and two daughters, Clara and Alicia. I'm a nurse, and I'm passionate about crochet. My journey with a hook and yarn has been slow but exciting – from a very young age I learnt from my mother and grandmother, who taught me the foundations of this wonderful world. Little by little, I learnt about techniques and patterns, developing my own colorful and fun style.

After my daughter Clara was born, I had a moment of reflection and started thinking about selling my patterns. I wanted to share my creativity with others and have an incentive to keep on developing new toys and characters. This was the moment when "One and Two Company", my small pattern shop, was born.

My daughters are my main source of inspiration. Clara is super creative and keeps coming up with stories full of incredible characters. My little Alice loves everything her mommy does. She plays with my creations and fills them with life, although she's very demanding. She's my best quality control!

It's comforting to be able to work on something I love and to see how other people, far away, crochet my creations and enjoy them. I love seeing the ideas I put into my designs come alive when people make my patterns.

ACKNOWLEDGMENTS

First of all I want to say a huge thank you to all the people who have trusted in my work every day from the beginning, supporting me and helping me move forwards. Without you all my efforts would not make sense.

Thanks to Ame Verso for thinking of me for this book, for trusting in my work, and for all your time and help during this wonderful project.

Thanks to Jeni Hennah for all your help preparing the book, for your understanding and support.

Thanks to Caroline Voaden for your continuous reviews of the patterns, text, charts... everything!

Thanks to Courtney Knorr-Warriner, Linda Woodthrope, Shannon Kishbaugh and Lisa Fox, my testers, or rather my friends who always help me by testing my patterns, giving me ideas, and being a fundamental part of my work.

And a special thanks to my family, my parents who always trusted me, my husband who always encourages me and helps me in every project, and my daughters Clara and Alicia, who are the best part of my life. You are One and Two Company. I love you!

Little Happy Circus

TINE NIELSEN

Roll up, roll up, the circus has come to town! It's not just any circus, but the "Little Happy Circus".

This collection of crochet circus characters features all your favorites including a friendly clown, sleepy elephant, show pony, handsome strongman, pretty ballerina, juggling walrus, and even the popcorn to enjoy while you watch the performance!

The toys all have their own quirky personalities. and there's step-by-step photography alongside the crochet patterns so you can get stitching straight away.

If you wonder why this little circus is something quite unique, come and see it with your very own eyes. I promise you won't regret it!

WHAT YOU WILL NEED

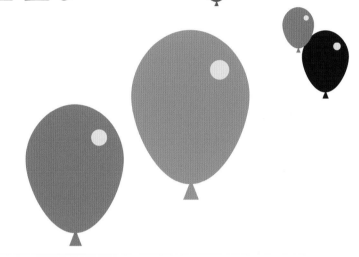

· Yarn
· Crochet hook
· Polyester stuffing
· Safety eyes
· Scissors
· Tapestry needles
· Pins
· Feathers
· Black sewing thread

YARN

I've chosen to use Drops yarn for all of the characters in my section of this book, mainly Drops Safran and Drops Loves You 6. Yarnliving.com has been so kind to supply all of the yarn I've used to make this section.

You can use any yarn and any color to make the characters. The choice of yarn is completely up to you and your preference.

I recommend that you use cotton yarn if the dolls are for children.

You can also differ the size of the dolls by using a thicker or thinner yarn. Just remember to use a crochet hook that fits the yarn. If you choose a different kind of yarn, be aware that the measurements of the dolls may change.

CROCHET HOOKS

There are so many crochet hooks available – I recommend that you use whichever one suits you. I prefer to use Clover Soft Touch crochet hooks and highly recommend them.

STITCH MARKER

Use a stitch marker or a long strand of yarn in a contrasting color to mark the beginning of every round.

BEFORE YOU GET STARTED

THE PATTERNS

Below, you'll find a list of the abbreviations used in this section.

You'll also find some helpful techniques over the following pages.
I've chosen not to show you the common stitches, such as chain, single crochet, etc. They have been well covered in the previous sections of this book and there are plenty of instructions and video tutorials available on the internet and Youtube.

All of the patterns in this section start with a description of the materials and abbreviations used in the particular pattern.

You are more than welcome to send me an email if you have any questions or if you need help following a pattern.

If there should be an error in any of the patterns, please let me know. You'll find the corrections on my website at www.littlehappycrochet.dk

ABBREVIATIONS

· Chain stitch (ch)
· Slip stitch (sl st)
· Single crochet (sc)
· Half double crochet (hdc)
· Double crochet (dc)
· Double treble crochet (dtr)
· Increase (2i1)
· Decrease (2»1)
· Round (R)
· Row (RW)

POMPOM

Wrap the yarn around a fork until it's nice and thick. The more yarn you wrap, the thicker the pompom.

Cut a piece of yarn and insert it between the middle tines of the fork. Tie tightly around the wrapped yarn.

Remove from the fork. Cut all of the ends of the loops.

Now shake and roll the pompom between your hands. Trim it to make it nice and round.

CHANGING COLOR

Color changes are always difficult when crocheting in spiral. In my experience, color changes will never be completely invisible.

This is how I change color in spiral - it's often possible to hide the color changes under an arm or on the back of the doll when sewing parts together.

In the last stitch before the color change, you must use both the old and the new color.

Insert your crochet hook in the last stitch before the color change. You'll now have 2 loops on your hook.

Yarn over with the new color.

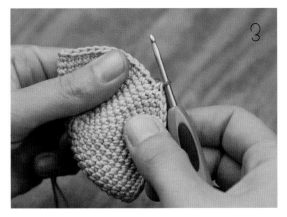

Pull the new yarn through the 2 loops. You're now set to continue with the new color.

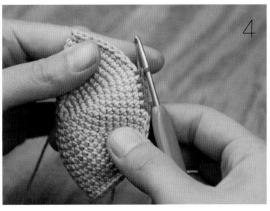

This is how I do a color change.

DOUBLE TREBLE CROCHET

The double treble crochet is used for the lion's mane, amongst others.

Yarn over 3 times.

Insert your crochet hook into the stitch indicated, yarn over and pull a loop through. You'll now have 5 loops on your hook.

Yarn over and pull through the first 2 loops. You'll now have 4 loops on your hook.

Yarn over and pull through the next 2 loops. You'll now have 3 loops on your hook.

Yarn over and pull through the next 2 loops. You'll now have 2 loops on your hook.

Yarn over and pull through the last 2 loops. You've now made a double treble crochet.

For the lion's mane, you shift between double treble crochet and single crochet. Make a single crochet in the next stitch. Make sure that the "bump" is on the front of your work.

This is how it should look when you are alternating between double treble crochet and single crochet.

JOINING LEGS

For most of the dolls in this section, you need to join the legs together. It might seem a bit difficult at first if you haven't done this before, so I've included a photo tutorial to make it easier for you.

The photos below are of the circus director, however I use this technique to join the legs for all my dolls.

Don't break the yarn on the second leg. Chain 9.

Insert your crochet hook into any stitch on the first leg.

Crochet around the leg with 1 sc in each stitch.
For the circus director you'll end up with 18 sc in total.

You've now reached the chain stitches.
Crochet 1 sc in each of the chain stitches = 9 sts

Crochet around the other leg with 1 sc in each stitch = 18 sts.

You've now reached the other side of the chain stitches. Crochet 1 sc in each of the chain stitches = 9 sts.

This is what the legs should look like now. For the circus director you should have 54 stitches in total.

ASSEMBLING

If you need to stuff the body parts as you go, the pattern will say so.

Please make sure you don't over-stuff your doll as the stuffing will be visible through your work. Make sure to stuff the body parts evenly.

You can use pins to attach the body parts to make sure they're placed exactly as you wish. When you're happy with the look, sew the parts together.

Every pattern has a guide for assembling to help you end up with a nice result.

Please be sure to attach the parts securely. You don't want the dolls to lose an arm or a leg during play. Personality comes from fine details – be patient and don't be afraid to have two or three tries before the result is satisfying to you.

LITTLE MR. BEAR

WHAT YOU WILL NEED

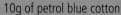

MATERIALS
80g of brown cotton
· Drops Safran, color 23

10g of petrol blue cotton
· Drops Safran, color 51

A small amount of beige cotton
· Drops Safran, color 21

2 safety eyes, size 6mm
Stuffing

ABBREVIATIONS
Chain stitch (ch)
Slip stitch (sl st)
Single crochet (sc)
Increase (2i1)
Decrease (2»1)
Round (R)

Little Mr. Bear will measure
approx. 12in (30cm) in height.

MR. BEAR IS THE NICEST
BEAR YOU'LL EVER
MEET. HE'S ALWAYS
UP FOR A CUDDLE.

LITTLE MR. BEAR

LEGS
· brown yarn (make 2)
Stuff as you go!
R1: 6 sc in a magic ring
= 6 sts
R2: (2i1) x 6 = 12 sts
R3: (3 sc, 2i1) x 3 = 15 sts
R4-7: sc around = 15 sts
R8: (4 sc, 2i1) x 3 = 18 sts
R9-12: sc around = 18 sts
R13: (2 sc, 2i1) x 6 = 24 sts
R14-15: sc around = 24 sts
Finish with a slip stitch. Break
the yarn and crochet the other
leg. Don't break the yarn on
the 2nd leg but continue
crocheting the body.

BODY
· brown yarn
Chain 5 and insert your hook in any
stitch on the first leg.
Crochet around that leg and continue
by crocheting around both the chain
stitches and the legs. You can find a
description on how to join legs on
page 266.

R16: 24 sc, 1 sc in each of the 5 chain
stitches, 24 sc, 1 sc in each of the
5 chain stitches = (58 sts)
R17: (28 sc, 2i1) x 2 = 60 sts
R18: (9 sc, 2i1) x 6 = 66 sts
R19: (10 sc, 2i1) x 6 = 72 sts
R20: (11 sc, 2i1) x 6 = 78 sts
R21: (12 sc, 2i1) x 6 = 84 sts
R22-31: sc around = 84 sts
R32: (12 sc, 2»1) x 6 = 78 sts
R33-34: sc around = 78 sts
R35: (11 sc, 2»1) x 6 = 72 sts
R36-37: sc around = 72 sts
R38: (10 sc, 2»1) x 6 = 66 sts
R39-40: sc around = 66 sts
R41: (9 sc, 2»1) x 6 = 60 sts
R42-43: sc around = 60 sts
R44: (8 sc, 2»1) x 6 = 54 sts
R45-47: sc around = 54 sts
R48: (7 sc, 2»1) x 6 = 48 sts
R49-51: sc around = 48 sts
R52: (6 sc, 2»1) x 6 = 42 sts
R53-55: sc around = 42 sts
R56: (5 sc, 2»1) x 6 = 36 sts
R57-59: sc around = 36 sts
R60: (4 sc, 2»1) x 6 = 30 sts
R61-63: sc around = 30 sts
R64: (3 sc, 2»1) x 6 = 24 sts
R65: sc around = 24 sts

R66: in the back loop only, sc around
= 24 sts
Finish with a slip stitch. Break the
yarn but leave enough yarn to sew
the head and the body together.

COLLAR
· petrol blue yarn
In round 66 you crocheted only
in the back loops. Now you'll
have to start the collar in the
front loop on round 66.
Hold the bear so the legs are
pointing away from you. Make a
loop and insert your hook in any
stitch on the round.
R1: sc around = 24 sts
R2: (2i1) x 24 = 48 sts
R3: (2i1) x 48 = 96 sts
R4-9: sc around = 96 sts
Finish with a slip stitch. Break the
yarn and fasten off.

HEAD
· brown yarn
R1: 6 sc in a magic ring
= 6 sts
R2: (2i1) x 6 = 12 sts
R3: (1 sc, 2i1) x 6 = 18 sts
R4: (2 sc, 2i1) x 6 = 24 sts
R5: (3 sc, 2i1) x 6 = 30 sts
R6: (4 sc, 2i1) x 6 = 36 sts
R7: (5 sc, 2i1) x 6 = 42 sts
R8: (6 sc, 2i1) x 6 = 48 sts
R9: (7 sc, 2i1) x 6 = 54 sts
R10: (8 sc, 2i1) x 6 = 60 sts
R11: (9 sc, 2i1) x 6 = 66 sts
R12: (10 sc, 2i1) x 6 = 72 sts
R13-24: sc around = 72 sts
Insert your safety eyes at this
point. They should be placed
between rounds 13 and 14 and
with 7 sc between them.
R25: (10 sc, 2»1) x 6 = 66 sts
R26: (9 sc, 2»1) x 6 = 60 sts
R27: (8 sc, 2»1) x 6 = 54 sts
R28: (7 sc, 2»1) x 6 = 48 sts
R29: (6 sc, 2»1) x 6 = 42 sts
R30: (5 sc, 2»1) x 6 = 36 sts
R31: (4 sc, 2»1) x 6 = 30 sts
R32: (3 sc, 2»1) x 6 = 24 sts
Finish with a slip stitch and break
the yarn.

MUZZLE
· beige yarn
R1: 6 sc in a magic ring = 6 sts
R2: (2i1) x 6 = 12 sts
R3: (1 sc, 2i1) x 6 = 18 sts
R4: (2 sc, 2i1) x 6 = 24 sts
R5: (3 sc, 2i1) x 6 = 30 sts
R6: (4 sc, 2i1) x 6 = 36 sts
Finish with a slip stitch. Break
the yarn but leave enough to
sew the muzzle onto the head.

ARMS
· brown yarn (make 2)
R1: 6 sc in a magic ring = 6 sts
R2: (2i1) x 6 = 12 sts
R3: (2 sc, 2i1) x 4 = 16 sts
R4-24: sc around = 16 sts
R25: (6 sc, 2»1) x 2 = 14 sts
R26: sc around = 14 sts
Finish with a slip stitch. Break
the yarn but leave enough to
sew the arm onto the body.

TAIL
· brown yarn
R1: 6 sc in a magic ring = 6 sts
R2: (2i1) x 6 = 12 sts
R3-5: sc around = 12 sts
R6: (2»1) x 6 = 6 sts
Finish with a slip stitch. Break
the yarn but leave enough to
sew the tail onto the body.

EARS
· brown yarn (make 2)
R1: 6 sc in a magic ring = 6 sts
R2: (2i1) x 6 = 12 sts
R3: (1 sc, 2i1) x 6 = 18 sts
R4: (2 sc, 2i1) x 6 = 24 sts
R5-8: sc around = 24 sts
R9: (2 sc, 2»1) x 6 = 18 sts
R10: sc around = 18 sts
Finish with a slip stitch. Break
the yarn but leave enough to
sew the ear onto the head.

ASSEMBLING

1.
Stuff the head and embroider the nose and the mouth on the muzzle.
See picture A.
Pin the muzzle to the head and sew it on.

2.
Bend the ears a bit and sew them onto the top of the head. They should be placed between rounds 7 and 15. See picture B.

3.
Sew the head and the body together. Make sure to stuff the neck before sewing all the way around. It'll keep the head from dangling.

A

B

4.
Stuff the arms but not all the way to the top. Sew them onto each side of the body, 3 rounds from the collar.
See picture C.

5.
Stuff the tail and sew it onto the back of the body. Place it between round 29 and round 31. See picture D.

C

D

LITTLE
MR. BEAR

MR. HAPPY CIRCUS

WHAT YOU WILL NEED

MATERIALS

18g of jeans blue cotton
· Drops Safran, color 06

35g of black cotton
· Drops Safran, color 16

20g of off white cotton
· Drops Safran, color 18

A small amount of curry yellow cotton
· Drops Loves You 6, color 105

2 safety eyes, size 6mm
Stuffing
Cardboard/plastic to stabilize the hat
8 safety eyes for the rows of buttons (optional)

2.5-3mm

ABBREVIATIONS

Chain stitch (ch)
Slip stitch (sl st)
Single crochet (sc)
Half double crochet (hdc)
Double crochet (dc)
Increase (2i1)
Decrease (2»1)
Round (R)
Row (RW)

Mr. Happy Circus will measure
approx. 12in (30cm) in height.

WITH HIS HAT SLIGHTLY
TILTED AND HIS
MOUSTACHE PERFECTLY
TRIMMED, MR. HAPPY
CIRCUS WELCOMES
EVERYONE TO THE
HAPPIEST CIRCUS
OF THEM ALL.

MR. HAPPY CIRCUS

Double row of buttons: I've chosen to use safety eyes as buttons with embroidery in between. You can also embroider French knots as buttons.
If you choose to use safety eyes, you'll have to insert them as you go. The first two safety eyes should be placed between rounds 36 and 37 and with 6 sc between them. Place each remaining set of 2 buttons 5 rounds above the last.

LEGS
· jeans blue yarn (make 2)
Stuff as you go!
R1: 6 sc in a magic ring = 6 sts
R2: (2i1) x 6 = 12 sts
R3: (1 sc, 2i1) x 6 = 18 sts
R4-15: sc around = 18 sts
Finish with a slip stitch. Break the yarn and crochet the other leg. Don't break the yarn on the 2nd leg but continue crocheting the body.

BODY
· jeans blue yarn
Chain 9 and insert your hook in any stitch on the first leg.
Crochet around that leg and continue by crocheting around both the chain stitches and the legs. You can find a description on page 266 on how to join legs.
R16: 18 sc, 1 sc in each of the 9 chain stitches, 18 sc, 1 sc in each of the 9 chain stitches = 54 sts
R17: (8 sc, 2i1) x 6 = 60 sts
R18: sc around = 60 sts
R19: (9 sc, 2i1) x 6 = 66 sts
R20: sc around = 66 sts
R21: (10 sc, 2i1) x 6 = 72 sts
R22: sc around = 72 sts
R23: (11 sc, 2i1) x 6 = 78 sts
R24: sc around = 78 sts
R25: (12 sc, 2i1) x 6 = 84 sts
R26-28: sc around = 84 sts
Change to black yarn
R29: sc around = 84 sts
R30: in the back loop only, sc around = 84 sts
R31-38: sc around = 84 sts
R39: (12 sc, 2»1) x 6 = 78 sts
R40: sc around = 78 sts
R41: (11 sc, 2»1) x 6 = 72 sts
R42: sc around = 72 sts
R43: (10 sc, 2»1) x 6 = 66 sts
R44: sc around = 66 sts
R45: (9 sc, 2»1) x 6 = 60 sts
R46: sc around = 60 sts
R47: (8 sc, 2»1) x 6 = 54 sts
R48: sc around = 54 sts
R49: (7 sc, 2»1) x 6 = 48 sts
R50: sc around = 48 sts
R51: (6 sc, 2»1) x 6 = 42 sts
R52: sc around = 42 sts
R53: (5 sc, 2»1) x 6 = 36 sts
R54-55: sc around = 36 sts
R56: (4 sc, 2»1) x 6 = 30 sts
R57: sc around = 30 sts
R58: sc around = 30 sts
Finish with a slip stitch. Break the yarn but leave enough to sew the body and head together.

EDGE, JACKET
· black yarn
In round 30 on the body you crocheted only in the back loops.
Now you'll have to crochet in the front loops. Turn the legs away from you.
Insert your hook in any stitch and sc around = 84 sts

HEAD
· off-white yarn
R1: 6 sc in a magic ring = 6 sts
R2: (2i1) x 6 = 12 sts
R3: (1 sc, 2i1) x 6 = 18 sts
R4: (2 sc, 2i1) x 6 = 24 sts
R5: (3 sc, 2i1) x 6 = 30 sts
R6: (4 sc, 2i1) x 6 = 36 sts
R7: (5 sc, 2i1) x 6 = 42 sts

R8: (6 sc, 2i1) x 6 = 48 sts
R9: (7 sc, 2i1) x 6 = 54 sts
R10: (8 sc, 2i1) x 6 = 60 sts
R11: (9 sc, 2i1) x 6 = 66 sts
R12: (10 sc, 2i1) x 6 = 72 sts
R13-23: sc around = 72 sts
Insert your safety eyes at this
point. They should be placed
between rounds 15 and 16 and
with 5 sc between them.
R24: (10 sc, 2»1) x 6 = 66 sts
R25: sc around = 66 sts
R26: (9 sc, 2»1) x 6 = 60 sts
R27: sc around = 60 sts
R28: (8 sc, 2»1) x 6 = 54 sts
R29: (7 sc, 2»1) x 6 = 48 sts
R30: (6 sc, 2»1) x 6 = 42 sts
R31: (5 sc, 2»1) x 6 = 36 sts
R32: (4 sc, 2»1) x 6 = 30 sts
Finish with a slip stitch and break
the yarn.

ARMS
· off-white yarn (make 2)
Stuff as you go!
R1: 6 sc in a magic ring = 6 sts
R2: (2i1) x 6 = 12 sts
R3-5: sc around = 12 sts
Change to black yarn
R6: sc around = 12 sts
R7: in the back loop only,
sc around = 12 sts
R8-37: sc around = 12 sts
Finish with a slip stitch. Break the
yarn but leave enough to sew the
arm onto the body.

EDGE, SLEEVE
· black yarn (make 2)
In round 7 on the arm you
crocheted only in the back loops.
Now you'll have to crochet in the
front loop. Turn the hand away
from you.
Insert your hook in any stitch and
sc around = 12 sts

MOUSTACHE
· black yarn
Chain 17. Start at the 2nd chain
stitch from the hook.
Rw1: 2 sl st, 1 sc, 1 hdc, 2
dc, 1 hdc, 1 sc, 1 sl st, 1
hdc, 2 dc, 1 hdc, 1 sc, 2
sl st = 16 sts
Break the yarn but leave enough
to sew the moustache to the
head.

HAT
· black yarn
R1: 6 sc in a magic ring = 6 sts
R2: (2i1) x 6 = 12 sts
R3: (1 sc, 2i1) x 6 = 18 sts
R4: (2 sc, 2i1) x 6 = 24 sts
R5: (3 sc, 2i1) x 6 = 30 sts
Before continuing, draw the
circle onto a piece of cardboard/
plastic. You'll need it to stabilize
the bottom of the hat.

R6: in the back loop only,
sc around = 30 sts
R7-8: sc around = 30 sts
R9: (3 sc, 2»1) x 6 = 24 sts
R10-11: sc around = 24 sts
R12: (3 sc, 2i1) x 6 = 30 sts
R13-14: sc around = 30 sts
R15: in the front loop only,
sc around = 30 sts
R16: (4 sc, 2i1) x 6 = 36 sts
R17: (5 sc, 2i1) x 6 = 42 sts
Finish with a slip stitch. Break
the yarn but leave enough to
sew the hat onto the head.

WHIP
· black yarn
The whip is crocheted in rows and
each row is turned with 1 chain
stitch.
Chain 16. Start in the 2nd chain
stitch from the hook.
Rw1-3: sc to end = 15 sts
Finish with a slip stitch. Break
the yarn but leave about 16in
(40cm). Fold the whip and sew
it together along the edge.
Fasten off and use the end of
the yarn as the whip itself.

ASSEMBLING

1.
Stuff the head. Pin the moustache to the head and sew it on. The moustache should be placed one round below the eyes. See picture A.

2.
Sew the head and the body together, Make sure to stuff the neck properly before sewing all the way around. It keeps the head from dangling.

3.
Sew the arms onto each side of the body at the neck. See picture B.

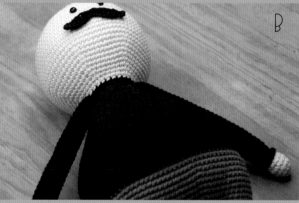

4.
Place the cardboard/plastic in the bottom of the hat and stuff it. Pin the hat to the head slightly tilted and sew it on. See picture C.

5.
Embroider cross stitches between the safety eyes with curry yellow yarn. See picture D. If you don't want to use safety eyes as buttons, you can embroider French knots instead.

THE ADORABLE BALLERINA

WHAT YOU WILL NEED

MATERIALS
45g of off-white cotton
· Drops Safran, color 18

75g of light pink cotton
· Drops Safran, color 01

15g of brown cotton
· Drops Safran, color 23

A small amount of black cotton
· Drops Safran, color 16

2 safety eyes, size 6mm
Stuffing

2.5-3mm

ABBREVIATIONS
Chain stitch (ch)
Slip stitch (sl st)
Single crochet (sc)
Half double crochet (hdc)
Double crochet (dc)
Increase (2i1)
Decrease (2»1)
Round (R)

The Adorable Ballerina will measure approx. 16in (40cm) in height and 10in (25cm) when sitting.

WHEN THE ADORABLE BALLERINA IS BALANCING ON THE WIRE, JUST BELOW THE CEILING OF THE CIRCUS TENT, SHE'S SO HAPPY. SHE CAN'T IMAGINE LIFE WITHOUT THE LITTLE HAPPY CIRCUS.

THE ADORABLE BALLERINA

HEAD
· off-white
Stuff as you go!
R1: 6 sc in a magic ring = 6 sts
R2: (2i1) x 6 = 12 sts
R3: (1 sc, 2i1) x 6 = 18 sts
R4: (2 sc, 2i1) x 6 = 24 sts
R5: (3 sc, 2i1) x 6 = 30 sts
R6: (4 sc, 2i1) x 6 = 36 sts
R7: (5 sc, 2i1) x 6 = 42 sts
R8: (6 sc, 2i1) x 6 = 48 sts
R9: (7 sc, 2i1) x 6 = 54 sts
R10: (8 sc, 2i1) x 6 = 60 sts
R11: (9 sc, 2i1) x 6 = 66 sts
R12-22: sc around = 66 sts
Insert your safety eyes at this point. They should be placed between rounds 13 and 14 and with 6 sc between them.
R23: (9 sc, 2»1) x 6 = 60 sts
R24: (8 sc, 2»1) x 6 = 54 sts
R25: (7 sc, 2»1) x 6 = 48 sts
R26: (6 sc, 2»1) x 6 = 42 sts
R27: (5 sc, 2»1) x 6 = 36 sts
R28: (4 sc, 2»1) x 6 = 30 sts
R29: (3 sc, 2»1) x 6 = 24 sts
R30: sc around = 24 sts
Finish with a slip stitch and break the yarn.

BODY
· light pink yarn
Stuff as you go!
R1: 6 sc in a magic ring = 6 sts
R2: (2i1) x 6 = 12 sts
R3: (1 sc, 2i1) x 6 = 18 sts
R4: (2 sc, 2i1) x 6 = 24 sts
R5: (3 sc, 2i1) x 6 = 30 sts
R6: (4 sc, 2i1) x 6 = 36 sts
R7: (5 sc, 2i1) x 6 = 42 sts
R8: (6 sc, 2i1) x 6 = 48 sts
R9: (7 sc, 2i1) x 6 = 54 sts
R10: (8 sc, 2i1) x 6 = 60 sts
R11: (9 sc, 2i1) x 6 = 66 sts
R12: (10 sc, 2i1) x 6 = 72 sts
R13-20: sc around = 72 sts
R21: (10 sc, 2»1) x 6 = 66 sts
R22-23: sc around = 66 sts
R24: in the back loop only, sc around = 66 sts
R25: sc around = 66 sts
R26: (9 sc, 2»1) x 6 = 60 sts
R27-30: sc around = 60 sts
R31: (8 sc, 2»1) x 6 = 54 sts
R32-35: sc around = 54 sts
R36: (7 sc, 2»1) x 6 = 48 sts
R37-40: sc around = 48 sts
R41: (6 sc, 2»1) x 6 = 42 sts
R42-44: sc around = 42 sts
Change to off-white yarn

R45: in the back loop only, sc around = 42 sts
R46: (5 sc, 2»1) x 6 = 36 sts
R47-49: sc around = 36 sts
R50: (4 sc, 2»1) x 6 = 30 sts
R51: (3 sc, 2»1) x 6 = 24 sts
Finish with a slip stitch. Break the yarn but leave enough to sew the body and the head together.

SKIRT
· light pink yarn
You crocheted in the back loop only in round 24 on the body. Now you'll have to crochet in the front loop. Hold the bottom of the body away from you. Insert your hook in any stitch on the body and sc around = 66 sts
R1: sc around = 66 sts
R2: (2i1) x 66 = 132 sts
R3: sc around = 132 sts
R4: (1 sc, 2i1) x 66 = 198 sts
R5-10: sc around = 198 sts
Finish with a slip stitch. Break the yarn and fasten off.

HAIR

· brown yarn

R1: 6 sc in a magic ring = 6 sts
R2: (2i1) x 6 = 12 sts
R3: (1 sc, 2i1) x 6 = 18 sts
R4: (2 sc, 2i1) x 6 = 24 sts
R5: (3 sc, 2i1) x 6 = 30 sts
R6: (4 sc, 2i1) x 6 = 36 sts
R7: (5 sc, 2i1) x 6 = 42 sts
R8: (6 sc, 2i1) x 6 = 48 sts
R9: (7 sc, 2i1) x 6 = 54 sts
R10: (8 sc, 2i1) x 6 = 60 sts
R11: (9 sc, 2i1) x 6 = 66 sts
R12-20: sc around = 66 sts
R21: 57 sc, 1 hdc, 5 dc, 1 hdc, 1 sc, 1 sl st = 66 sts
Finish with a slip stitch. Break the yarn but leave enough to sew the hair onto the head.

BUN

· brown yarn

R1: 6 sc in a magic ring = 6 sts
R2: (2i1) x 6 = 12 sts
R3: (1 sc, 2i1) x 6 = 18 sts
R4: (2 sc, 2i1) x 6 = 24 sts
R5: (3 sc, 2i1) x 6 = 30 sts
R6: (4 sc, 2i1) x 6 = 36 sts
R7: (5 sc, 2i1) x 6 = 42 sts
R8: (6 sc, 2i1) x 6 = 48 sts
R9-13: sc around = 48 sts
R14: (6 sc, 2»1) x 6 = 42 sts
Finish with a slip stitch. Break the yarn but leave enough to sew the bun onto the hair.

ARMS

· off-white yarn (make 2)

Stuff as you go but make sure not to stuff all the way to the top.
R1: 6 sc in a magic ring = 6 sts
R2: (2i1) x 6 = 12 sts
R3-46: sc around = 12 sts
Finish with a slip stitch. Break the yarn but leave enough to sew the arm to the body.

LEGS

· black yarn (make 2)

Stuff as you go!
R1: 6 sc in a magic ring = 6 sts
R2: (2i1) x 6 = 12 sts
R3-6: sc around = 12 sts
Change to off-white yarn
R7-46: sc around = 12 sts
Change to light pink yarn
R47-50: sc around = 12 sts
Finish with a slip stitch. Break the yarn but leave enough to sew the leg to the body.

ASSEMBLING

1.
Pin the hair to the head and place it so she will get a side parting. Sew the hair all the way around. Please be aware not to sew it too tight as the edge of the hair might get uneven. See picture A.

2.
Stuff the bun and pin it to the hair, 12 rounds from the edge. Sew it on all the way around.

3.
Embroider a little nose with off-white yarn by stitching 2–5 times over 2 stitches. Embroider the nose 3 rounds below the eyes. See picture B.

4.
Sew the head and the body together. Make sure to stuff the neck properly before sewing all the way around. It keeps the head from dangling.

5.
Sew the arms onto each side of the body, 2 rounds below the neck. Thread a needle with a long string of light pink yarn and sew the straps of the dress. See picture C.

6.
Pin the legs onto the bottom of the body and sew them on. Thread a needle with black yarn and embroider the straps on the legs. See picture D.

THE ADORABLE
BALLERINA

SHINY MISS HORSE

WHAT YOU WILL NEED

MATERIALS

120g of coal gray cotton
· Drops Loves You 6, color 118

 2.5-3mm

30g of off-white cotton
· Drops Loves You 6, color 101

A small amount of light gray cotton
· Drops Loves You 6, color 103

Some silver thread for the halter
2 safety eyes, size 12mm
Feathers
Stuffing

ABBREVIATIONS

Chain stitch (ch)
Slip stitch (sl st)
Single crochet (sc)
Increase (2i1)
Decrease (2»1)
Round (R)
Row (RW)

Shiny Miss Horse will measure
approx. 14in (35cm) in height.

SHINY MISS HORSE BRINGS
SHINE AND COLOR TO THE
CIRCUS. SHE LOVES FRINGES,
FEATHERS AND FIREWORKS.
EVERY DAY IS A GIFT AND
MUST BE CELEBRATED.

SHINY MISS HORSE

LEGS

· coal gray yarn (make 2)
Stuff as you go!
R1: 6 sc in a magic ring = 6 sts
R2: (2i1) x 6 = 12 sts
R3: (3 sc, 2i1) x 3 = 15 sts
R4-7: sc around = 15 sts
R8: (4 sc, 2i1) x 3 = 18 sts
R9-12: sc around = 18 sts
R13: (2 sc, 2i1) x 6 = 24 sts
R14-15: sc around = 24 sts
Finish with a slip stitch. Break the yarn and crochet the other leg. Don't break the yarn on the 2nd leg but continue crocheting the body.

BODY

· coal gray yarn
Chain 5 and insert your hook in any stitch on the first leg. Crochet around that leg and continue by crocheting around both the chain stitches and the legs. You can find a description on page 266 on how to join legs.
R16: 24 sc, 1 sc in each of the 5 chain stitches, 24 sc, 1 sc in each of the 5 chain stitches = 58 sts
R17: (28 sc, 2i1) x 2 = 60 sts
R18: (9 sc, 2i1) x 6 = 66 sts

R19: (10 sc, 2i1) x 6 = 72 sts
R20: (11 sc, 2i1) x 6 = 78 sts
R21: (12 sc, 2i1) x 6 = 84 sts
R22-31: sc around = 84 sts
R32: (12 sc, 2»1) x 6 = 78 sts
R33-34: sc around = 78 sts
R35: (11 sc, 2»1) x 6 = 72 sts
R36-37: sc around = 72 sts
R38: (10 sc, 2»1) x 6 = 66 sts
R39-40: sc around = 66 sts
R41: (9 sc, 2»1) x 6 = 60 sts
R42-43: sc around = 60 sts
R44: (8 sc, 2»1) x 6 = 54 sts
R45-47: sc around = 54 sts
R48: (7 sc, 2»1) x 6 = 48 sts
R49-51: sc around = 48 sts
R52: (6 sc, 2»1) x 6 = 42 sts
R53-55: sc around = 42 sts
R56: (5 sc, 2»1) x 6 = 36 sts
R57-59: sc around = 36 sts
R60: (4 sc, 2»1) x 6 = 30 sts
R61-63: sc around = 30 sts
R64: (3 sc, 2»1) x 6 = 24 sts
R65-66: sc around = 24 sts
Finish with a slip stitch. Break the yarn but leave enough to sew the body and the head together.

HEAD

· off-white yarn
Stuff as you go!
R1: 6 sc in a magic ring = 6 sts
R2: (2i1) x 6 = 12 sts
R3: (1 sc, 2i1) x 6 = 18 sts
R4: (2 sc, 2i1) x 6 = 24 sts
R5: (3 sc, 2i1) x 6 = 30 sts
R6: (4 sc, 2i1) x 6 = 36 sts
R7: (5 sc, 2i1) x 6 = 42 sts
R8-10: sc around = 42 sts
Change to coal gray yarn
R11-12: sc around = 42 sts
R13: (6 sc, 2i1) x 6 = 48 sts
R14-16: sc around = 48 sts
R17: (7 sc, 2i1) x 6 = 54 sts
R18-20: sc around = 54 sts
R21: (8 sc, 2i1) x 6 = 60 sts
R22-24: sc around = 60 sts
R25: (9 sc, 2i1) x 6 = 66 sts
R26-35: sc around = 66 sts
Insert your safety eyes at this point. They should be placed between rounds 26 and 27 and with 15 sc between them.
R36: (9 sc, 2»1) x 6 = 60 sts
R37: sc around = 60 sts
R38: (8 sc, 2»1) x 6 = 54 sts
R39: (7 sc, 2»1) x 6 = 48 sts
R40: (6 sc, 2»1) x 6 = 42 sts
R41: (5 sc, 2»1) x 6 = 36 sts

R42: (4 sc, 2»1) x 6 = 30 sts
R43: (3 sc, 2»1) x 6 = 24 sts
R44: (2 sc, 2»1) x 6 = 18 sts
R45: (1 sc, 2»1) x 6 = 12 sts
R46: (2»1) x 6 = 6 sts
Finish with a slip stitch. Break the yarn but leave enough to sew the hole together. Sew the hole by stitching in the front loop of the 5 sc. Pull the thread so the hole closes in. Fasten off.

EARS
· coal gray yarn (make 2)
R1: 6 sc in a magic ring = 6 sts
R2: sc around = 6 sts
R3: (2i1) x 6 = 12 sts
R4-5: sc around = 12 sts
R6: (1 sc, 2i1) x 6 = 18 sts
R7-10: sc around = 18 sts
Finish with a slip stitch. Break the yarn but leave enough to sew the ear onto the head.

ARMS
· coal gray yarn (make 2)
R1: 6 sc in a magic ring = 6 sts
R2: (2i1) x 6 = 12 sts
R3: (2 sc, 2i1) x 4 = 16 sts
R4-24: sc around = 16 sts
R25: (6 sc, 2»1) x 2 = 14 sts
R26: sc around = 14 sts
Finish with a slip stitch. Break the yarn but leave enough to sew the arm to the body.

HALTER
The halter is crocheted in both light gray yarn and the silver thread. The halter is crocheted in rows. Turn each row with 1 chain stitch.

HALTER
MUZZLE PIECE
· light gray yarn and silver thread
Chain 45 with both the light grey yarn and the silver thread. Start in the 2nd chain stitch from the hook.
Rw1: sc to end = 44 sts
Fasten off, leaving enough to sew the halter onto the muzzle.

HALTER
NECK PIECE
· light gray yarn and silver thread
Chain 65 with both the light grey yarn and the silver thread. Start in the 2nd chain stitch from the hook.
Rw1: sc to end = 64 sts
Fasten off, leaving enough to sew the halter onto the head.

HALTER
FOREHEAD PIECE
· light gray yarn and silver thread
Chain 29 with both the light grey yarn and the silver thread. Start in the 2nd chain stitch from the hook.
Rw1: sc to end = 28 sts
Fasten off, leaving enough to sew the halter onto the forehead.

FEATHER HOLDER
· light gray yarn
R1: 6 sc in a magic ring = 6 sts
R2-7: sc around = 6 sts
Finish with a slip stitch. Break the yarn but leave enough to sew the holder onto the head.

ASSEMBLING

1.
Pin the head to the body to make sure it's placed correctly. Sew the head and body together. Stuff the neck before sewing all the way around to keep the head from dangling.

2.
Sew the ears onto the top of the head. Attach them at round 35 and with 11 stitches between them. See picture A.

3.
Stuff the arms but not all the way to the top. Sew them onto each side of the body, 5 rounds below the neck.

4.
It's now time to attach the halter. Place the strap around the muzzle right where the color changes. Sew the 2 ends together. I've also given it a few stitches below the muzzle, so the halter doesn't move.
Sew the strap for the neck onto each side of the halter and sew the strap for the forehead on, just below the ears.
Sew in all ends.
See picture B.

5.
Giving the horse a mane: cut a bunch of long strands of yarn, approx. 12in (30cm) long. Use pins to mark where you want the mane to be placed. Start between the ears and continue until 6 rounds above the neck. Crochet one strand of hair at a time from between the ears to the neck. Continue with another 3 rows of hair on each side of the beginning row, or until you think there's enough hair. See picture C.
Trim the hair if you're going for a more groomed look.

6.
Cut a bunch of strands of yarn for the tail, approx. (20in (50cm) long. Attach each strand of yarn at the back of the horse, at round 30 from the legs. Make a braid. See picture D.

7.
Sew the feather holder onto the head right between the ears. Place the feathers in the holder.

SHINY
MISS HORSE

MR. ELEPHANT SLEEPYHEAD

WHAT YOU WILL NEED

MATERIALS
170g of light gray cotton
· Drops Loves You 6, color 103

A small amount of coal gray cotton
· Drops Loves You 6, color 118

2.5-3mm

A small amount of sea green cotton
· Drops Loves You 6, color 112

A small amount of jeans blue cotton
· Drops Loves You 6, color 117

Stuffing

ABBREVIATIONS
Chain stitch (ch)
Slip stitch (sl st)
Single crochet (sc)
Increase (2i1)
Decrease (2»1)
Round (R)

Mr. Elephant Sleepyhead will measure
approx. 12in (30cm) in height.

I MEAN, IT'S NOT
THAT MR. ELEPHANT
SLEEPYHEAD FINDS THE
CIRCUS LIFE BORING -
ON THE CONTRARY.
IT'S JUST THAT THERE'S
ALWAYS A NAP THAT'S
CALLING FOR HIM.

MR. ELEPHANT SLEEPYHEAD

LEGS

· light gray yarn (make 2)
Stuff as you go!
R1: 6 sc in a magic ring = 6 sts
R2: (2i1) x 6 = 12 sts
R3: (3 sc, 2i1) x 3 = 15 sts
R4-7: sc around = 15 sts
R8: (4 sc, 2i1) x 3 = 18 sts
R9-12: sc around = 18 sts
R13: (2 sc, 2i1) x 6 = 24 sts
R14-15: sc around = 24 sts
Finish with a slip stitch. Break
the yarn and crochet the other
leg. Don't break the yarn on the
2nd leg but continue crocheting
the body.

BODY

· light gray yarn
Chain 5 and insert your hook in any
stitch on the first leg.
Crochet around that leg and continue
by crocheting around both the chain
stitches and the legs. You can find
a description on page 266 on how to
join legs.
R16: 24 sc, 1 sc in each of the 5 chain
stitches, 24 sc, 1 sc in each of the
5 chain stitches = 58 sts

R17: (28 sc, 2i1) x 2 = 60 sts
R18: (9 sc, 2i1) x 6 = 66 sts
R19: (10 sc, 2i1) x 6 = 72 sts
R20: (11 sc, 2i1) x 6 = 78 sts
R21: (12 sc, 2i1) x 6 = 84 sts
R22-31: sc around = 84 sts
R32: (12 sc, 2»1) x 6 = 78 sts
R33-34: sc around = 78 sts
R35: (11 sc, 2»1) x 6 = 72 sts
R36-37: sc around = 72 sts
R38: (10 sc, 2»1) x 6 = 66 sts
R39-40: sc around = 66 sts
R41: (9 sc, 2»1) x 6 = 60 sts
R42-43: sc around = 60 sts
R44: (8 sc, 2»1) x 6 = 54 sts
R45-47: sc around = 54 sts
R48: (7 sc, 2»1) x 6 = 48 sts
R49-51: sc around = 48 sts
R52: (6 sc, 2»1) x 6 = 42 sts
R53-55: sc around = 42 sts
R56: (5 sc, 2»1) x 6 = 36 sts
R57-59: sc around = 36 sts
R60: (4 sc, 2»1) x 6 = 30 sts
R61-63: sc around = 30 sts
R64: (3 sc, 2»1) x 6 = 24 sts
R65-66: sc around = 24 sts
Finish with a slip stitch. Break
the yarn but leave enough to
sew the body and the head
together.

HEAD

· light gray yarn
Stuff as you go!
R1: 6 sc in a magic ring = 6 sts
R2: (2i1) x 6 = 12 sts
R3-20: sc around = 12 sts
R21: (5 sc, 2i1) x 2 = 14 sts
R22-23: sc around = 14 sts
R24: (6 sc, 2i1) x 2 = 16 sts
R25-26: sc around = 16 sts
R27: (7 sc, 2i1) x 2 = 18 sts
R28-29: sc around = 18 sts
R30: (2 sc, 2i1) x 6 = 24 sts
R31-32: sc around = 24 sts
R33: (3 sc, 2i1) x 6 = 30 sts
R34-35: sc around = 30 sts
R36: (4 sc, 2i1) x 6 = 36 sts
R37: sc around = 36 sts
R38: (5 sc, 2i1) x 6 = 42 sts
R39: (6 sc, 2i1) x 6 = 48 sts
R40: (7 sc, 2i1) x 6 = 54 sts
R41: (8 sc, 2i1) x 6 = 60 sts
R42: (9 sc, 2i1) x 6 = 66 sts
R43: (10 sc, 2i1) x 6 = 72 sts
R44-55: sc around = 72 sts
R56: (10 sc, 2»1) x 6 = 66 sts
R57: sc around = 66 sts
R58: (9 sc, 2»1) x 6 = 60 sts
R59: sc around = 60 sts

R60: (8 sc, 2»1) x 6 = 54 sts
R61: sc around = 54 sts
R62: (7 sc, 2»1) x 6 = 48 sts
R63: (6 sc, 2»1) x 6 = 42 sts
R64: (5 sc, 2»1) x 6 = 36 sts
R65: (4 sc, 2»1) x 6 = 30 sts
R66: (3 sc, 2»1) x 6 = 24 sts
R67: (2 sc, 2»1) x 6 = 18 sts
R68: (1 sc, 2»1) x 6 = 12 sts
R69: (2»1) x 6 = 6 sts
Finish with a slip stitch. Break the yarn but leave enough to sew the hole together. Sew the hole together by stitching through the front loop of the 6 sc and pull the yarn. Fasten off.

EARS

· light gray yarn (make 2)
R1: 6 sc in a magic ring = 6 sts
R2: (2i1) x 6 = 12 sts
R3: (1 sc, 2i1) x 6 = 18 sts
R4: (2 sc, 2i1) x 6 = 24 sts
R5: (3 sc, 2i1) x 6 = 30 sts
R6: (4 sc, 2i1) x 6 = 36 sts
R7: (5 sc, 2i1) x 6 = 42 sts
R8: (6 sc, 2i1) x 6 = 48 sts
R9: (7 sc, 2i1) x 6 = 54 sts
R10: (8 sc, 2i1) x 6 = 60 sts
R11-24: sc around = 60 sts

R25: (8 sc, 2»1) x 6 = 54 sts
R26: sc around = 54 sts
R27: (7 sc, 2»1) x 6 = 48 sts
R28: (6 sc, 2»1) x 6 = 42 sts
Finish with a slip stitch. Break the yarn but leave enough to sew the ears onto the head.

ARMS

· light gray yarn (make 2)
R1: 6 sc in a magic ring = 6 sts
R2: (2i1) x 6 = 12 sts
R3: (1 sc, 2i1) x 6 = 18 sts
R4-7: sc around = 18 sts
R8: (7 sc, 2»1) x 2 = 16 sts
R9-15: sc around = 16 sts
R16: (6 sc, 2»1) x 2 = 14 sts
R17-30: sc around = 14 sts
Finish with a slip stitch. Break the yarn but leave enough to sew the arm onto the body.

CIRCUS HAT

· sea green yarn
R1: 6 sc in a magic ring = 6 sts
R2: (1 sc, 2i1) x 3 = 9 sts
R3-4: sc around = 9 sts
R5: (2 sc, 2i1) x 3 = 12 sts
R6-7: sc around = 12 sts
R8: (3 sc, 2i1) x 3 = 15 sts
R9: sc around = 15 sts
R10: (4 sc, 2i1) x 3 = 18 sts
Finish with a slip stitch. Break the yarn but leave enough to sew the hat onto the head.

ASSEMBLING

1.
Pin the head to the body to make sure it's placed correctly. The trunk should point downwards. Sew the head and body together. Make sure to stuff the neck properly to keep the head from dangling.

2.
Fold the ears and sew them onto each side of the head. The ears should be placed ¾in (2cm) above the neck, and they should bend a little. See picture A.

3.
Stuff the arms but not all the way to the top. Sew them onto each side of the body, 3 rounds from the neck.

4.
Embroider the eyes and eyelashes on each side of the head with coal gray yarn. Embroider 5 lines on the trunk with coal gray yarn. See picture B.

5.
Cut three long pieces of yarn and sew them on the back of the body, at round 29 from the feet. Make a braid. See picture C.

6.
Make a pompom for the circus hat. You can find a description for making a pompom on page 262.
Sew the pompom onto the top of the hat. Stuff the hat and sew it onto the head. See picture D.

LITTLE MISS MAGIC

WHAT YOU WILL NEED

MATERIALS - BUNNY
75g of white cotton
· Drops Safran, color 17

 2.5-3mm

A small amount of gray cotton
· Drops Safran, color 07

A small amount of light pink yarn
· Drops Safran, color 01

2 safety eyes, size 12mm
Stuffing

MATERIALS - MAGICIAN'S HAT
300g of black cotton 8/8
· Drops Paris, color 15

 4mm

Cardboard/plastic for the bottom of the hat

ABBREVIATIONS
Chain stitch (ch)
Slip stitch (sl st)
Single crochet (sc)
Increase (2i1)
Decrease (2»1)
Round (R)
Row (RW)

Little Miss Magic will measure approx. 7in (17cm) in height and 11in (28cm) with her ears stretched. The magician's hat will measure approx. 8in (20cm) in height.

THE CUTEST MEMBER OF LITTLE HAPPY CIRCUS IS LITTLE MISS MAGIC. SHE'S A BIT SHY AND HER FAVORITE HIDING SPOT IS INSIDE THE BIG MAGICIAN'S HAT. HERE SHE CAN HIDE UNTIL THE SPOTLIGHT REACHES HER CUTE FACE.

LITTLE MISS MAGIC

HEAD

· white yarn
R1: 6 sc in a magic ring = 6 sts
R2: (2i1) x 6 = 12 sts
R3: (1 sc, 2i1) x 6 = 18 sts
R4: (2 sc, 2i1) x 6 = 24 sts
R5: (3 sc, 2i1) x 6 = 30 sts
R6: (4 sc, 2i1) x 6 = 36 sts
R7: (5 sc, 2i1) x 6 = 42 sts
R8: (6 sc, 2i1) x 6 = 48 sts
R9: (7 sc, 2i1) x 6 = 54 sts
R10: (8 sc, 2i1) x 6 = 60 sts
R11: (9 sc, 2i1) x 6 = 66 sts
R12: (10 sc, 2i1) x 6 = 72 sts
R13: (11 sc, 2i1) x 6 = 78 sts
R14-24: sc around = 78 sts
Insert your safety eyes at this
point. They should be placed
between rounds 17 and 18 and
with 10 sc between them.
R25: (11 sc, 2»1) x 6 = 72 sts
R26: (10 sc, 2»1) x 6 = 66 sts
R27: (9 sc, 2»1) x 6 = 60 sts
R28: (8 sc, 2»1) x 6 = 54 sts
R29: (7 sc, 2»1) x 6 = 48 sts
R30: (6 sc, 2»1) x 6 = 42 sts
R31: (5 sc, 2»1) x 6 = 36 sts
R32: (4 sc, 2»1) x 6 = 30 sts
Finish with a slip stitch and break
the yarn.

BODY

· white yarn
R1: 6 sc in a magic ring = 6 sts
R2: (2i1) x 6 = 12 sts
R3: (1 sc, 2i1) x 6 = 18 sts
R4: (2 sc, 2i1) x 6 = 24 sts
R5: (3 sc, 2i1) x 6 = 30 sts
R6: (4 sc, 2i1) x 6 = 36 sts
R7: (5 sc, 2i1) x 6 = 42 sts
R8: (6 sc, 2i1) x 6 = 48 sts
R9: (7 sc, 2i1) x 6 = 54 sts
R10: (8 sc, 2i1) x 6 = 60 sts
R11: (9 sc, 2i1) x 6 = 66 sts
R12-20: sc around = 66 sts
R21: (9 sc, 2»1) x 6 = 60 sts
R22: sc around = 60 sts
R23: (8 sc, 2»1) x 6 = 54 sts
R24: sc around = 54 sts
R25: (7 sc, 2»1) x 6 = 48 sts
R26: sc around = 48 sts
R27: (6 sc, 2»1) x 6 = 42 sts
R28: sc around = 42 sts
R29: (5 sc, 2»1) x 6 = 36 sts
R30: sc around = 36 sts
R31: (4 sc, 2»1) x 6 = 30 sts
Finish with a slip stitch. Break
the yarn but leave enough
to sew the body and the
head together.

EARS

· white yarn (make 2)
R1: 6 sc in a magic ring = 6 sts
R2: (2i1) x 6 = 12 sts
R3: sc around = 12 sts
R4: (1 sc, 2i1) x 6 = 18 sts
R5: sc around = 18 sts
R6: (2 sc, 2i1) x 6 = 24 sts
R7-16: sc around = 24 sts
R17: (10 sc, 2»1) x 2 = 22 sts
R18-20: sc around = 22 sts
R21: (9 sc, 2»1) x 2 = 20 sts
R22-24: sc around = 20 sts
R25: (8 sc, 2»1) x 2 = 18 sts
R26-28: sc around = 18 sts
R29: (7 sc, 2»1) x 2 = 16 sts
R30-39: sc around = 16 sts
Finish with a slip stitch. Break the
yarn but leave enough to sew the
ear onto the head.

LEGS

· light gray yarn (make 2)

Chain 6 and crochet around these chain stitches. Start in the 2nd chain stitch from the hook.

R1: 4 sc, 3i1, 3 sc, 2i1 = 12 sts
R2: 2i1, 3 sc, 2i1, 1 sc, 2i1, 3 sc, 2i1, 1 sc = 16 sts
R3: 2i1, 5 sc, 2i1, 1 sc, 2i1, 5 sc, 2i1, 1 sc = 20 sts
R4: 2i1, 7 sc, 2i1, 1 sc, 2i1, 7 sc, 2i1, 1 sc = 24 sts
R5: (3 sc, 2i1) x 6 = 30 sts
Change to white yarn.
R6-10: sc around = 30 sts
R11: 13 sc, (2»1) x 3, 11 sc = 27 sts
R12: 9 sc, (1 sc, 2»1) x 3, 9 sc = 24 sts
R13-15: sc around = 24 sts
Finish with a slip stitch. Break the yarn but leave enough to sew the leg onto the body.

ARMS

· white yarn (make 2)

R1: 6 sc in a magic ring = 6 sts
R2: (2i1) x 6 = 12 sts
R3: (1 sc, 2i1) x 6 = 18 sts
R4-7: sc around = 18 sts
R8: (7 sc, 2»1) x 2 = 16 sts
R9: sc around = 16 sts
R10: (6 sc, 2»1) x 2 = 14 sts
R11: sc around = 14 sts
R12: (5 sc, 2»1) x 2 = 12 sts
R13-20: sc around = 12 sts
Finish with a slip stitch. Break the yarn but leave enough to sew the arm onto the body.

TAIL

· white yarn

Make a pompom. See description on page 262.

MAGICIAN'S HAT

· black yarn

R1: 6 sc in a magic ring = 6 sts
R2: (2i1) x 6 = 12 sts
R3: (1 sc, 2i1) x 6 = 18 sts
R4: (2 sc, 2i1) x 6 = 24 sts
R5: (3 sc, 2i1) x 6 = 30 sts
R6: (4 sc, 2i1) x 6 = 36 sts
R7: (5 sc, 2i1) x 6 = 42 sts
R8: (6 sc, 2i1) x 6 = 48 sts
R9: (7 sc, 2i1) x 6 = 54 sts
R10: (8 sc, 2i1) x 6 = 60 sts
R11: (9 sc, 2i1) x 6 = 66 sts
R12: (10 sc, 2i1) x 6 = 72 sts
R13: (11 sc, 2i1) x 6 = 78 sts
R14: (12 sc, 2i1) x 6 = 84 sts
R15: (13 sc, 2i1) x 6 = 90 sts
R16: (14 sc, 2i1) x 6 = 96 sts
R17: (15 sc, 2i1) x 6 = 102 sts
R18: (16 sc, 2i1) x 6 = 108 sts
R19: in the backloop only, sc around = 108 sts
R20-56: sc around = 108 sts
R57: in the front loop only, (17 sc, 2i1) x 6 = 114 sts
R58: (18 sc, 2i1) x 6 = 120 sts
R59: (19 sc, 2i1) x 6 = 126 sts
R60: (20 sc, 2i1) x 6 = 132 sts
R61: (21 sc, 2i1) x 6 = 138 sts
R62: (22 sc, 2i1) x 6 = 144 sts
R63: (23 sc, 2i1) x 6 = 150 sts
Finish with a slip stitch and break the yarn. Fasten off.

ASSEMBLING

1.
Stuff the head and the body and sew them together. Embroider the nose with light pink yarn. See picture A.

2.
Stuff the legs and pin them to the body. Make sure the bunny sits properly before sewing the legs on. I've sewn the legs onto the body between rounds 9 and 11 and with 6 stitches in between them. See picture B.

3.
Stuff the arms but not all the way to the top. Sew them onto each side of the body at the neck.

4.
Sew the ears onto the head with 11 stitches between them. See picture C.

5.
Sew the tail onto the back of the body. See picture D.

6.
You can put a round circle of cardboard or plastic at the bottom of the magician's hat if you wish to stabilize the bottom.

LITTLE YELLOW LION

WHAT YOU WILL NEED

MATERIALS

110g of curry yellow cotton
· Drops Loves You 6, color 105

50g of off-white cotton
· Drops Loves You 6, color 101

6g of light brown cotton
· Drops Loves You 6, color 104

2 safety eyes, size 6mm
Stuffing

2.5-
3mm

ABBREVIATIONS

Chain stitch (ch)
Slip stitch (sl st)
Single crochet (sc)
Double treble crochet (dtr)
- See page 264.
Increase (2i1)
Decrease (2»1)
Round (R)

Little Yellow Lion will measure
approx. 16in (40cm) in height.

NO NEED TO WORRY –
THERE'S NO DANGER AHEAD.
LITTLE YELLOW LION IS A
GENTLE GUY. HE'S JUST AS
CUDDLY AS A PET CAT AND
IF IT WAS UP TO HIM, HE'D BE
SCRATCHED BEHIND HIS EARS
ALL DAY LONG.

LITTLE
YELLOW LION

LEGS

· curry yellow yarn (make 2)
Stuff as you go!
R1: 6 sc in a magic ring = 6 sts
R2: (2i1) x 6 = 12 sts
R3: (3 sc, 2i1) x 3 = 15 sts
R4-7: sc around = 15 sts
R8: (4 sc, 2i1) x 3 = 18 sts
R9-12: sc around = 18 sts
R13: (2 sc, 2i1) x 6 = 24 sts
R14-15: sc around = 24 sts
Finish with a slip stitch. Break
the yarn and crochet the other
leg. Don't break the yarn on the
2nd leg but continue crocheting
the body.

BODY

· curry yellow yarn
Chain 5 and insert your hook in any
stitch on the first leg.
Crochet around that leg and continue
crocheting around both the chain
stitches and the legs. You can find
a description on page 266 on how to
join legs.
R16: 24 sc, 1 sc in each of the 5 chain
stitches, 24 sc, 1 sc in each of the 5
chain stitches = 58 sts
R17: (28 sc, 2i1) x 2 = 60 sts

R18: (9 sc, 2i1) x 6 = 66 sts
R19: (10 sc, 2i1) x 6 = 72 sts
R20: (11 sc, 2i1) x 6 = 78 sts
R21: (12 sc, 2i1) x 6 = 84 sts
R22-31: sc around = 84 sts
R32: (12 sc, 2»1) x 6 = 78 sts
R33-34: sc around = 78 sts
R35: (11 sc, 2»1) x 6 = 72 sts
R36-37: sc around = 72 sts
R38: (10 sc, 2»1) x 6 = 66 sts
R39-40: sc around = 66 sts
R41: (9 sc, 2»1) x 6 = 60 sts
R42-43: sc around = 60 sts
R44: (8 sc, 2»1) x 6 = 54 sts
R45-47: sc around = 54 sts
R48: (7 sc, 2»1) x 6 = 48 sts
R49-51: sc around = 48 sts
R52: (6 sc, 2»1) x 6 = 42 sts
R53-55: sc around = 42 sts
R56: (5 sc, 2»1) x 6 = 36 sts
R57-59: sc around = 36 sts
R60: (4 sc, 2»1) x 6 = 30 sts
R61-63: sc around = 30 sts
R64: (3 sc, 2»1) x 6 = 24 sts
R65-66: sc around = 24 sts
Finish with a slip stitch. Break
the yarn but leave enough
to sew the body and the
head together.

HEAD

· off-white yarn
R1: 6 sc in a magic ring = 6 sts
R2: (2i1) x 6 = 12 sts
R3: (1 sc, 2i1) x 6 = 18 sts
R4: (2 sc, 2i1) x 6 = 24 sts
R5: (3 sc, 2i1) x 6 = 30 sts
R6: (4 sc, 2i1) x 6 = 36 sts
R7: (5 sc, 2i1) x 6 = 42 sts
R8: (6 sc, 2i1) x 6 = 48 sts
R9: (7 sc, 2i1) x 6 = 54 sts
R10: (8 sc, 2i1) x 6 = 60 sts
R11: (9 sc, 2i1) x 6 = 66 sts
R12: (10 sc, 2i1) x 6 = 72 sts
R13-24: sc around = 72 sts
Insert your safety eyes at this
point. They should be placed
between rounds 14 and 15 and
with 5 sc between them.
R25: (10 sc, 2»1) x 6 = 66 sts
R26: (9 sc, 2»1) x 6 = 60 sts
R27: (8 sc, 2»1) x 6 = 54 sts
R28: (7 sc, 2»1) x 6 = 48 sts
R29: (6 sc, 2»1) x 6 = 42 sts
R30: (5 sc, 2»1) x 6 = 36 sts
R31: (4 sc, 2»1) x 6 = 30 sts
R32: (3 sc, 2»1) x 6 = 24 sts
Finish with a slip stitch and break
the yarn.

MUZZLE

· off-white yarn

R1: 6 sc in a magic ring = 6 sts
R2: (2i1) x 6 = 12 sts
R3: (1 sc, 2i1) x 6 = 18 sts
R4: (2 sc, 2i1) x 6 = 24 sts
R5: (3 sc, 2i1) x 6 = 30 sts
R6: (4 sc, 2i1) x 6 = 36 sts
R7-11: sc around = 36 sts
Finish with a slip stitch. Break the yarn but leave enough to sew the muzzle onto the head.

NOSE

· light brown yarn

R1: 6 sc in a magic ring = 6 sts
R2: (1 sc, 2i1) x 3 = 9 sts
R3: (2 sc, 2i1) x 3 = 12 sts
R4: (3 sc, 2i1) x 3 = 15 sts
R5: sc around = 15 sts
R6: (4 sc, 2i1) x 3 = 18 sts
Change to off-white yarn
R7-13: sc around = 18 sts
Finish with a slip stitch. Break the yarn but leave enough to sew the nose onto the muzzle.

EARS

· off-white yarn (make 2)

R1: 6 sc in a magic ring = 6 sts
R2: (2i1) x 6 = 12 sts
R3: sc around = 12 sts
R4: (1 sc, 2i1) x 6 = 18 sts

R5: sc around = 18 sts
R6: (2 sc, 2i1) x 6 = 24 sts
R7-9: sc around = 24 sts
Finish with a slip stitch. Break the yarn but leave enough to sew the ear onto the head.

MANE

· curry yellow yarn

R1: 6 sc in a magic ring = 6 sts
R2: (2i1) x 6 = 12 sts
R3: (1 sc, 2i1) x 6 = 18 sts
R4: (2 sc, 2i1) x 6 = 24 sts
R5: (3 sc, 2i1) x 6 = 30 sts
R6: (4 sc, 2i1) x 6 = 36 sts
R7: (5 sc, 2i1) x 6 = 42 sts
R8: (6 sc, 2i1) x 6 = 48 sts
R9: (7 sc, 2i1) x 6 = 54 sts
R10: (8 sc, 2i1) x 6 = 60 sts
R11: (9 sc, 2i1) x 6 = 66 sts
R12-15: sc around = 66 sts
R16: (1 sc, 1 dtr) x 33 = 66 sts
R17: sc around = 66 sts
R18: (1 sc, 1 dtr) x 33 = 66 sts
R19: sc around = 66 sts
R20: (1 sc, 1 dtr) x 33 = 66 sts
R21: sc around = 66 sts
R22: (1 sc, 1 dtr) x 33 = 66 sts
R23: sc around = 66 sts
Finish with a slip stitch. Break the yarn but leave enough to sew the hat onto the head.

ARMS

· off-white yarn (make 2)

R1: 6 sc in a magic ring = 6 sts
R2: (2i1) x 6 = 12 sts
R3: (2 sc, 2i1) x 4 = 16 sts
R4-6: sc around = 16 sts
Change to curry yellow yarn
R7-24: sc around = 16 sts
R25: (6 sc, 2»1) x 2 = 14 sts
R26-28: sc around = 14 sts
Finish with a slip stitch. Break the yarn but leave enough to sew the arm onto the body.

TAIL

· light brown yarn

Stuff as you go but only the tip of the tail!

R1: 6 sc in a magic ring = 6 sts
R2: 2i1, 5 sc = 7 sts
R3: 2i1, 6 sc = 8 sts
R4: 2i1, 7 sc = 9 sts
R5: 2i1, 8 sc = 10 sts
R6: 2i1, 9 sc = 11 sts
R7: 2i1, 10 sc = 12 sts
R8: (3 sc, 2i1) x 3 = 15 sts
R9: sc around = 15 sts
R10: (3 sc, 2»1) x 3 = 12 sts
R11: (2 sc, 2»1) x 3 = 9 sts
Change to curry yellow yarn
R12-39: sc around = 9 sts
Finish with a slip stitch. Break the yarn but leave enough to sew the tail onto the body.

ASSEMBLING

1.

Pin the nose to the muzzle and sew it on along the edge. Thread a needle with light brown yarn and attach the tip of the nose. Embroider a mouth. See picture A.

2.

Stuff the head and the muzzle. Pin the muzzle to the head, 3 rounds below the eyes. Sew the muzzle all the way around. See picture B.

3.

Place the mane onto the head and sew it all the way around. Sew the head and body together. Make sure to stuff the neck properly to keep the head from dangling.

4.

Stuff the arms but not all the way to the top. Sew them onto to each side of the body at the neck.

5.

Fold the ears and sew them onto the top of the head. They should be placed just behind the "knots" and with 6 stitches between them. See picture C.

6.

Sew the tail onto the back of the body, at round 29 from the feet. See picture D.

LITTLE
YELLOW LION

CLOWN OF THE DAY

WHAT YOU WILL NEED

MATERIALS
14g of gray cotton
· Drops Safran, color 07

30g of dark blue cotton
· Drops Safran, color 09

25g of off-white cotton
· Drops Safran, color 18

30g of curry yellow cotton
· Drops Loves You 6, color 105

10g of white cotton
· Drops Safran, color 17

A small amount of petrol blue cotton
· Drops Safran, color 51

A small amount of black cotton
· Drops Safran, color 16

Stuffing

ABBREVIATIONS
Chain stitch (ch)
Slip stitch (sl st)
Single crochet (sc)
Increase (2i1)
Decrease (2»1)
Round (R)

Clown of The Day will measure
approx. 14in (35cm) in height.

2.5-3mm

CLOWN OF THE DAY
HAS ALWAYS KNOWN
THAT HE WANTED TO BE
A CLOWN. AT CLOWN
SCHOOL HE QUICKLY
LEARNED THAT HIS BLUE
NOSE IS SOMETHING
COMPLETELY UNIQUE AND
HE WEARS IT WITH PRIDE.

CLOWN OF THE DAY

LEGS

· gray yarn (make 2)
Stuff as you go!
R1: 6 sc in a magic ring = 6 sts
R2: (2i1) x 6 = 12 sts
R3: sc around = 12 sts
R4: (5 sc, 2i1) x 2 = 14 sts
R5-7: sc around = 14 sts
R8: (6 sc, 2i1) x 2 = 16 sts
R9-11: sc around = 16 sts
R12: (7 sc, 2i1) x 2 = 18 sts
R13-23: sc around = 18 sts
Finish with a slip stitch. Break
the yarn and crochet the other
leg. Don't break the yarn on the
2nd leg but continue crocheting
the body.

BODY

· gray yarn
Chain 9 and insert your hook in any
stitch on the first leg.
Crochet around that leg and continue
by crocheting around both the chain
stitches and the legs. You can find a
description on page 266 on how to
join legs.
R24: 18 sc, 1 sc in each of the 9 chain
stitches, 18 sc, 1 sc in each of the
9 chain stitches = 54 sts

R25: sc around = 54 sts
R26: (8 sc, 2i1) x 6 = 60 sts
R27: sc around = 60 sts
R28: (9 sc, 2i1) x 6 = 66 sts
R29-31: sc around = 66 sts
Change to dark blue yarn
R32-38: sc around = 66 sts
R39: (9 sc, 2»1) x 6 = 60 sts
R40-42: sc around = 60 sts
R43: (8 sc, 2»1) x 6 = 54 sts
R44-46: sc around = 54 sts
R47: (7 sc, 2»1) x 6 = 48 sts
R48-50: sc around = 48 sts
R51: (6 sc, 2»1) x 6 = 42 sts
R52-54: sc around = 42 sts
R55: (5 sc, 2»1) x 6 = 36 sts
R56-58: sc around = 36 sts
R59: (4 sc, 2»1) x 6 = 30 sts
R60-62: sc around = 30 sts
Finish with a slip stitch. Break
the yarn but leave enough
to sew the body and the
head together.

HEAD

· off-white yarn
R1: 6 sc in a magic ring = 6 sts
R2: (2i1) x 6 = 12 sts
R3: (1 sc, 2i1) x 6 = 18 sts
R4: (2 sc, 2i1) x 6 = 24 sts
R5: (3 sc, 2i1) x 6 = 30 sts

R6: (4 sc, 2i1) x 6 = 36 sts
R7: (5 sc, 2i1) x 6 = 42 sts
R8: (6 sc, 2i1) x 6 = 48 sts
R9: (7 sc, 2i1) x 6 = 54 sts
R10: (8 sc, 2i1) x 6 = 60 sts
R11: (9 sc, 2i1) x 6 = 66 sts
R12: (10 sc, 2i1) x 6 = 72 sts
R13-25: sc around = 72 sts
R26: (10 sc, 2»1) x 6 = 66 sts
R27: (9 sc, 2»1) x 6 = 60 sts
R28: (8 sc, 2»1) x 6 = 54 sts
R29: (7 sc, 2»1) x 6 = 48 sts
R30: (6 sc, 2»1) x 6 = 42 sts
R31: (5 sc, 2»1) x 6 = 36 sts
R32: (4 sc, 2»1) x 6 = 30 sts
Finish with a slip stitch and break
the yarn.

ARMS

· off-white yarn (make 2)
Stuff as you go!
R1: 6 sc in a magic ring = 6 sts
R2: (2i1) x 6 = 12 sts
R3-6: sc around = 12 sts
Change to dark blue yarn
R7-41: sc around = 12 sts
Finish with a slip stitch. Break the
yarn but leave enough to sew the
arm onto the body.

NOSE

· petrol blue

R1: 6 sc in a magic ring = 6 sts
R2: (2i1) x 6 = 12 sts
R3: (1 sc, 2i1) x 6 = 18 sts
R4: (2 sc, 2i1) x 6 = 24 sts
R5: (3 sc, 2i1) x 6 = 30 sts
R6-9: sc around = 30 sts
R10: (3 sc, 2»1) x 6 = 24 sts
Finish with a slip stitch. Break the yarn but leave enough to sew the nose onto the head.

HAIR

· curry yellow yarn (make 2)
Stuff as you go!

R1: 6 sc in a magic ring = 6 sts
R2: (2i1) x 6 = 12 sts
R3-5: sc around = 12 sts
R6: (1 sc, 2i1) x 6 = 18 sts
R7: (2 sc, 2i1) x 6 = 24 sts
R8-11: sc around = 24 sts
R12: (2 sc, 2»1) x 6 = 18 sts
R13: (2 sc, 2i1) x 6 = 24 sts
R14: (3 sc, 2i1) x 6 = 30 sts
R15: (4 sc, 2i1) x 6 = 36 sts
R16-17: sc around = 36 sts
R18: (4 sc, 2»1) x 6 = 30 sts
R19: (3 sc, 2»1) x 6 = 24 sts
R20: (3 sc, 2i1) x 6 = 30 sts
R21: (4 sc, 2i1) x 6 = 36 sts

R22: (5 sc, 2i1) x 6 = 42 sts
R23-29: sc around = 42 sts
R30: (5 sc, 2»1) x 6 = 36 sts
R31: (4 sc, 2»1) x 6 = 30 sts
Finish with a slip stitch. Break the yarn but leave enough to sew the hair onto the head.

SUSPENDERS

· black yarn (make 4)

R1: 6 sc in a magic ring = 6 sts
Finish with a slip stitch. Break the yarn but leave enough to sew the suspender onto the body.
Don't break the yarn on two of the circles but continue making the strap.
Chain 50 and sew the strap onto the other circle. Make sure that your row of chain stitches fits your clown. You might have to crochet a few more or less chain stitches.

SWIMMING RING

· white yarn
Chain 18 and join to the 1st chain forming a ring.

R1-4: sc around = 18 sts
Change to bordeaux red yarn
R5-9: sc around = 18 sts
Change to white yarn
R10-14: sc around = 18 sts
Continue by changing between red and white stripes until the swimming ring has 21 stripes in total.
Make each stripe 5 rounds except on the first and last stripe.
The last stripe consists of only 1 round of white to make the most invisible seam.
Finish with a slip stitch but leave enough to sew the ends together.

ASSEMBLING

1.
Stuff the head. Embroider 2 crosses as eyes. They should be placed from round 13 to round 16 and with 4 sc between them. Stuff the nose and sew it on below the eyes. See picture A.

2.
Stuff the hair pieces. Pin them to the head to make sure they are placed correctly. Sew them on 6 rounds from the top. See picture B.

3.
Sew the head and the body together. Make sure to stuff the neck properly to keep the head from dangling.

4.
Stuff the arms but not all the way to the top. Sew them onto each side of the body by the neck.

5.
It's now time to attach the suspenders. Sew the button on, right where the pants change to the color blue. Let the row of chain stitches stretch over the shoulder and sew the other button on at the back of the body. Please make sure the row of chain stitches don't twist. See picture C.

6.
Stuff the swimming ring but not too tightly. Sew the swimming ring together at the ends and put it on the clown. See picture D.

MR. STRONG

WHAT YOU WILL NEED

MATERIALS
65g of off-white cotton
· Drops Safran, color 18

35g of bordeaux cotton
· Drops Loves You 6, color 110

30g of black cotton
· Drops Safran, color 16

7g of gray cotton
· Drops Safran, color 07

Stuffing
Black sewing thread

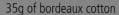
2.5-3mm

ABBREVIATIONS
Chain stitch (ch)
Slip stitch (sl st)
Single crochet (sc)
Half double crochet (hdc)
Double crochet (dc)
Increase (2i1)
Decrease (2»1)
Round (R)
Row (RW)

Mr. Strong will measure
approx. 12in (30cm) in height.

BEING THE STRONG MAN
OF A CIRCUS IS NOT
JUST LIFTING WEIGHTS
AND BEING TOUGH. EVERY
TIME LITTLE HAPPY
CIRCUS ARRIVES AT A
NEW TOWN, MR. STRONG
HELPS TO RAISE THE
BIG CIRCUS TENT.

MR. STRONG

LEGS

· off-white yarn (make 2)
Stuff as you go!
R1: 6 sc in a magic ring = 6 sts
R2: (2i1) x 6 = 12 sts
R3: (1 sc, 2i1) x 6 = 18 sts
R4-19: sc around = 18 sts
Finish with a slip stitch. Break the yarn and crochet the other leg. Don't break the yarn on the 2nd leg but continue crocheting the body.

BODY

· off-white yarn
Chain 15 and insert your hook in any stitch on the first leg. Crochet around that leg and continue by crocheting around both the chain stitches and the legs. You can find a description on page 266 on how to join legs.

R20: 18 sc, 1 sc in each of the 15 chain stitches, 18 sc, 1 sc in each of the 15 chain stitches = 66 sts
R21-40: sc around = 66 sts
R41: (9 sc, 2»1) = 60 sts
R42-43: sc around = 60 sts
R44: (8 sc, 2»1) x 6 = 54 sts
R45-46: sc around = 54 sts
R47: (7 sc, 2»1) x 6 = 48 sts
R48-49: sc around = 48 sts
R50: (6 sc, 2»1) x 6 = 42 sts
R51-52: sc around = 42 sts
R53: (5 sc, 2»1) x 6 = 36 sts
R54-56: sc around = 36 sts
R57: (4 sc, 2»1) x 6 = 30 sts
R58-60: sc around = 30 sts
Finish with a slip stitch. Break the yarn but leave enough to sew the body and the head together.

HEAD

· off-white yarn
R1: 6 sc in a magic ring = 6 sts
R2: (2i1) x 6 = 12 sts
R3: (1 sc, 2i1) x 6 = 18 sts
R4: (2 sc, 2i1) x 6 = 24 sts
R5: (3 sc, 2i1) x 6 = 30 sts
R6: (4 sc, 2i1) x 6 = 36 sts
R7: (5 sc, 2i1) x 6 = 42 sts
R8: (6 sc, 2i1) x 6 = 48 sts
R9: (7 sc, 2i1) x 6 = 54 sts
R10: (8 sc, 2i1) x 6 = 60 sts
R11: (9 sc, 2i1) x 6 = 66 sts
R12-22: sc around = 66 sts
R23: (9 sc, 2»1) x 6 = 60 sts
R24: (8 sc, 2»1) x 6 = 54 sts
R25: (7 sc, 2»1) x 6 = 48 sts
R26: (6 sc, 2»1) x 6 = 42 sts
R27: (5 sc, 2»1) x 6 = 36 sts
R28: (4 sc, 2»1) x 6 = 30 sts
Finish with a slip stitch and break the yarn.

HAIR

· black yarn
R1: 6 sc in a magic ring = 6 sts
R2: (2i1) x 6 = 12 sts
R3: (1 sc, 2i1) x 6 = 18 sts
R4: (2 sc, 2i1) x 6 = 24 sts
R5: (3 sc, 2i1) x 6 = 30 sts
R6: (4 sc, 2i1) x 6 = 36 sts
R7: (5 sc, 2i1) x 6 = 42 sts
R8: (6 sc, 2i1) x 6 = 48 sts
R9: (7 sc, 2i1) x 6 = 54 sts
R10: (8 sc, 2i1) x 6 = 60 sts
R11: (9 sc, 2i1) x 6 = 66 sts
R12-17: sc around = 66 sts
R18: 1 sc, 8 hdc, 34 sc, 22 hdc, 1 sl st = 66 sts
R19: 1 sc, 8 hdc, 33 sc, 23 hdc, 1 sl st = 66 sts

Finish with a slip stitch. Break the yarn but leave enough to sew the hair onto the head.

ARMS

· off-white (make 2)
R1: 6 sc in a magic ring = 6 sts
R2: (2i1) x 6 = 12 sts
R3-41: sc around = 12 sts
Finish with a slip stitch. Break the yarn but leave enough to sew the arm onto the body.

MOUSTACHE

· black yarn (make 2)
R1: 6 sc in a magic ring = 6 sts
R2: sc around = 6 sts
R3: 2i1, 5 sc = 7 sts
R4-5: sc around = 7 sts
R6: 2i1, 6 sc = 8 sts
R7: sc around = 8 sts
R8: 2i1, 7 sc = 9 sts
R9: sc around = 9 sts
R10: 2i1, 8 sc = 10 sts
R11: (2»1) x 5 = 5 sts
Finish with a slip stitch. Break the yarn but leave enough to sew the moustache together and onto the head.

SUIT
TROUSERS

· bordeaux red yarn (make 2)
Chain 19 and assemble to a ring.
R1-5: sc around = 19 sts
Finish with a slip stitch. Break the yarn and crochet the other trouser. Don't break the yarn on the 2nd trouser but continue crocheting the suit.

SUIT

· bordeaux red yarn

Chain 15 and insert your hook into any stitch on the first leg. Crochet around that leg and continue by crocheting around both the chain stitches and the trousers. You can find a description on page 266 on how to join legs.

R6: 19 sc, 1 sc in each of the 15 chain stitches, 19 sc, 1 sc in each of the 15 chain stitches = 68 sts

R7-26: sc around = 68 sts

R27: (9 sc, 2»1) x 6, 2 sc = 62 sts

Now it's time to crochet in rows. Turn each row with a chain stitch. Continue with the back of the suit.

SUIT
BACK

· bordeaux red yarn

Rw28: 1 sc in each of the next 6 sts = 6 sts

Rw29: 1 sc in each of the next 21 sts = 21 sts

Rw30: 2»1, 17 sc, 2»1 = 19 sts

Rw31: sc across = 19 sts

Rw32: 2»1, 15 sc, 2»1 = 17 sts

Rw33: sc across = 17 sts

Rw34: 2»1, 13 sc, 2»1 = 15 sts

Rw35: 2»1, 11 sc, 2»1 = 13 sts

Rw36: 2»1, 9 sc, 2»1 = 11 sts

Rw37: sc across = 11 sts

Rw38: 2 dc, 1 hdc, 5 sc, 1 hdc, 2 dc = 11 sts

Break the yarn and fasten off.

SUIT
STRAP

· bordeaux red yarn

Begin in the 12th sc from the back of the suit.

Rw1: 1 sc in each of the next 9 sc = 9 sts

Rw2: 2»1, 7 sc = 8 sts

Rw3: sc across = 8 sts

Rw4: 2»1, 6 sc = 7 sts

Rw5: sc across = 7 sts

Rw6: 2»1, 5 sc = 6 sts

Rw7: sc across = 6 sts

Rw8: 2»1, 4 sc = 5 sts

Rw9: sc across = 5 sts

Rw10: 2»1, 3 sc = 4 sts

Rw11: sc across = 4 sts

Rw12: 2»1, 2 sc = 3 sts

Rw13: sc across = 3 sts

Rw14: 2»1, 1 sc = 2 sts

Rw15-26: sc across = 2 sts

Rw27: 1 sc, 2i1 = 3 sts

Break the yarn but leave enough to sew the strap onto the back of the suit.

SUIT
SECOND STRAP

· bordeaux red yarn

Begin in the 2nd sc from the first strap.

Rw1: 1 sc in each of the next 9 sts = 9 sts

Rw2: 7 sc, 2»1 = 8 sts

Rw3: sc across = 8 sts

Rw4: 6 sc, 2»1 = 7 sts

Rw5: sc across = 7 sts

Rw6: 5 sc, 2»1 = 6 sts

Rw7: sc across = 6 sts

Rw8: 4 sc, 2»1 = 5 sts

Rw9: sc across = 5 sts

Rw10: 3 sc, 2»1 = 4 sts

Rw11: sc across = 4 sts

Rw12: 2 sc, 2»1 = 3 sts

Rw13: sc across = 3 sts

Rw14: 1 sc, 2»1 = 2 sts

Rw15-26: sc across = 2 sts

Rw27: 2i1, 1 sc = 3 sts

Break the yarn but leave enough to sew the strap onto the back of the suit. Sew the two straps and the back piece together and crochet a line of slip stitches all the way around the neck opening and the two armholes.

WEIGHT BAR

· black yarn

Stuff as you go!

R1: 6 sc in a magic ring = 6 sts

R2: (2i1) x 6 = 12 sts

R3: (1 sc, 2i1) x 6 = 18 sts

R4: (2 sc, 2i1) x 6 = 24 sts

R5: (3 sc, 2i1) x 6 = 30 sts

R6: (4 sc, 2i1) x 6 = 36 sts

R7-12: sc around = 36 sts

R13: (4 sc, 2»1) x 6 = 30 sts

R14: (3 sc, 2»1) x 6 = 24 sts

R15: (2 sc, 2»1) x 6 = 18 sts

R16: (1 sc, 2»1) x 6 = 12 sts

Change to gray yarn

R17-49: sc around = 12 sts

Change to black yarn

R50: (1 sc, 2i1) x 6 = 18 sts

R51: (2 sc, 2i1) x 6 = 24 sts

R52: (3 sc, 2i1) x 6 = 30 sts

R53: (4 sc, 2i1) x 6 = 36 sts

R54-60: sc around = 36 sts

R61: (4 sc, 2»1) x 6 = 30 sts

R62: (3 sc, 2»1) x 6 = 24 sts

R63: (2 sc, 2»1) x 6 = 18 sts

R64: (1 sc, 2»1) x 6 = 12 sts

R65: (2»1) x 6 = 6 sts

Finish with a slip stitch. Break the yarn but leave enough to sew the hole together. Sew the hole together by stitching through the front loop of the 6 sc and pull the yarn. Fasten off.

ASSEMBLING

1.

Stuff the head and sew the head and the body together. Make sure to stuff the neck properly to keep the head from dangling. Place the hair so he gets a side parting, and sew all the way around.

2.

Sew the moustache together at the middle and sew it onto the head. It should be placed between rounds 8 and 10 from the eyes. See picture A.

3.

Stuff the arms but not all the way to the top. Sew them onto each side of the body, 1 round below the neck.

4.

It's now time to make the chest hair. Thread a needle with black sewing thread and sew small pieces of thread around the chest. Cut the threads to make it look like small strings of hair. See picture B.

5.

Sew in the ends of the suit. See picture C.

6.

Dress Mr. Strong with his suit.

MR. STRONG

WALTER THE WALRUS

WHAT YOU WILL NEED

MATERIALS

85g of light brown cotton
· Drops Safran, color 22

5g off-white cotton
· Drops Safran, color 17

A scrap of beige cotton
· Drops Safran, color 18

A small amount of ice blue cotton
· Drops Safran, color 50

A small amount of of petrol blue cotton
· Drops Safran, 51

2 safety eyes, size 6mm
Stuffing

 2.5-3mm

ABBREVIATIONS
Chain stitch (ch)
Slip stitch (sl st)
Single crochet (sc)
Increase (2i1)
Decrease (2»1)
Round (R)

Walter the Walrus will measure
approx. 12in (30cm) in length.

WHEN WALTER THE
WALRUS ENTERS THE
CIRCUS ARENA, EVERY
PERSON IN THE AUDIENCE
IS IMPRESSED BY HIS
MANY TALENTS, WHICH
INCLUDE JUGGLING,
DANCING, CLAPPING, AND
CATCHING BALLS.

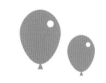

WALTER THE WALRUS

FINS

· light brown yarn (make 2)
R1: 6 sc in a magic ring = 6 sts
R2: (2i1) x 6 = 12 sts
R3: sc around = 12 sts
R4: (1 sc, 2i1) x 6 = 18 sts
R5-14: sc around = 18 sts
Finish with a slip stitch. Break the yarn and crochet the other fin. Don't break the yarn on the 2nd fin but continue crocheting the body.

BODY

· light brown yarn
Stuff as you go!
Chain 6 and insert your hook in any stitch on the first leg.
Crochet around that leg and continue by crocheting around both the chain stitches and the legs. You can find a description on page 266 on how to join legs.
R15: 18 sc, 1 sc in each of the 6 chain stitches, 18 sc, 1 sc in each of the 6 chain stitches = 48 sts
R16-22: sc around = 48 sts
R23: (7 sc, 2i1) x 6 = 54 sts
R24-26: sc around = 54 sts
R27: (8 sc, 2i1) x 6 = 60 sts
R28-30: sc around = 60 sts

R31: (9 sc, 2i1) x 6 = 66 sts
R32-33: sc around = 66 sts
R34: (10 sc, 2i1) x 6 = 72 sts
R35-36: sc around = 72 sts
R37: (11 sc, 2i1) x 6 = 78 sts
R38-39: sc around = 78 sts
R40: (12 sc, 2i1) x 6 = 84 sts
R41-42: sc around = 84 sts
R43: (13 sc, 2i1) x 6 = 90 sts
R44-66: sc around = 90 sts
R67: (13 sc, 2»1) x 6 = 84 sts
R68: sc around = 84 sts
R69: (12 sc, 2»1) x 6 = 78 sts
R70: sc around = 78 sts
R71: (11 sc, 2»1) x 6 = 72 sts
R72: (10 sc, 2»1) x 6 = 66 sts
R73: (9 sc, 2»1) x 6 = 60 sts
R74: (8 sc, 2»1) x 6 = 54 sts
R75: (7 sc, 2»1) x 6 = 48 sts
R76: (6 sc, 2»1) x 6 = 42 sts
R77: (5 sc, 2»1) x 6 = 36 sts
R78: (4 sc, 2»1) x 6 = 30 sts
R79: (3 sc, 2»1) x 6 = 24 sts
R80: (2 sc, 2»1) x 6 = 18 sts
R81: (1 sc, 2»1) x 6 = 12 sts
R82: (2»1) x 6 = 6 sts
Finish with a slip stitch. Break the yarn but leave enough to sew the hole together. Sew the hole together by stitching through the front loop of the 6 sc and pull the yarn. Fasten off.

MUZZLE

· light brown yarn
R1: 6 sc in a magic ring = 6 sts
R2: (2i1) x 6 = 12 sts
R3: (1 sc, 2i1) x 6 = 18 sts
R4: (2 sc, 2i1) x 6 = 24 sts
R5: (3 sc, 2i1) x 6 = 30 sts
R6: (4 sc, 2i1) x 6 = 36 sts
R7: (5 sc, 2i1) x 6 = 42 sts
R8: (6 sc, 2i1) x 6 = 48 sts
R9: (7 sc, 2i1) x 6 = 54 sts
R10-15: sc around = 54 sts
Finish with a slip stitch. Break the yarn but leave enough to sew the muzzle onto the head.

TUSKS

· white yarn (make 2)
R1: 6 sc in a magic ring = 6 sts
R2: sc around = 6 sts
R3: 2i1, 5 sc = 7 sts
R4: sc around = 7 sts
R5: 2i1, 6 sc = 8 sts
R6: sc around = 8 sts
R7: 2i1, 7 sc = 9 sts
R8-12: sc around = 9 sts
Finish with a slip stitch. Break the yarn but leave enough to sew the tusk on below the muzzle.

EYES
· white yarn (make 2)
R1: 6 sc in a magic ring = 6 sts
R2: (2i1) x 6 = 12 sts
R3: (1 sc, 2i1) x 6 = 18 sts
R4-5: sc around = 18 sts
Insert your safety eyes at this point. They should be placed in the center of the eye.
R6: (1 sc, 2»1) x 6 = 12 sts
Finish with a slip stitch. Break the yarn but leave enough to sew the eye onto the head.

FRONT FLIPPERS
· light brown yarn (make 2)
R1: 6 sc in a magic ring = 6 sts
R2: (2i1) x 6 = 12 sts
R3: (1 sc, 2i1) x 6 = 18 sts
R4: (2 sc, 2i1) x 6 = 24 sts
R5: (3 sc, 2i1) x 6 = 30 sts
R6-9: sc around = 30 sts
R10: (3 sc, 2»1) x 6 = 24 sts
R11-17: sc around = 24 sts
Finish with a slip stitch. Break the yarn but leave enough to sew the front flipper onto the body.

FISH
· light gray yarn
Stuff as you go!
R1: 6 sc in a magic ring = 6 sts
R2: (2i1) x 6 = 12 sts
R3: (1 sc, 2i1) x 6 = 18 sts
R4-9: sc around = 18 sts
Insert your safety eyes at this point. They should be placed on each side and between rounds 5 and 6.
R10: (1 sc, 2»1) x 6 = 12 sts
R11-12: sc around = 12 sts
Fold the fish, crochet the edge together and continue by crocheting in rows.
Rw13: sc across = 6 sts, turn with two chain stitches
Rw14: (in the same stitch, 1 dc, 1 sc) x 6 = 12 sts
Break the yarn and fasten off.

BALL
· ice blue yarn
Stuff as you go!
R1: 6 sc in a magic ring = 6 sts
R2: (2i1) x 6 = 12 sts
Change to petrol blue yarn
R3: (1 sc, 2i1) x 6 = 18 sts
R4: (2 sc, 2i1) x 6 = 24 sts
Change to ice blue yarn
R5: (3 sc, 2i1) x 6 = 30 sts
R6: (4 sc, 2i1) x 6 = 36 sts
Change to petrol blue yarn
R7: (5sc, 2i1) x 6 = 42 sts
R8: sc around = 42 sts
Change to ice blue yarn
R9-10: sc around = 42 sts
Change to petrol blue yarn
R11-12: sc around = 42 sts
Change to ice blue yarn
R13-14: sc around = 42 sts
Change to petrol blue yarn
R15: (5 sc, 2»1) x 6 = 36 sts
R16: (4 sc, 2»1) x 6 = 30 sts
Change to ice blue yarn
R17: (3 sc, 2»1) x 6 = 24 sts
R18: (2 sc, 2»1) x 6 = 18 sts
Change to petrol blue yarn
R19: (1 sc, 2»1) x 6 = 12 sts
R20: (2»1) x 6 = 6 sts
Finish with a slip stitch. Break the yarn but leave enough to sew the hole together. Sew the hole together by stitching through the front loop of the 6 sc and pull the yarn. Fasten off.

ASSEMBLING

1.

Pin the muzzle to the head to make sure it's placed correctly and sew it on. Stuff the muzzle before sewing all the way around.
See picture A.

2.

Sew the eyes on, just above the muzzle. The eyes should be attached so closely that they touch each other. Don't stuff the eyes.
See picture B.

3.

Stuff the tusks – tweezers might be handy. Sew them onto the lower side of the muzzle with 5 sc between them. Cut 20 pieces of beige yarn for the beard. They should be approx. 6in (15cm) long. Divide the pieces of yarn into 2 groups. Sew or crochet 10 pieces of yarn on, in front of each tusk. See picture C.
Stuff the front flippers and pin them to each side of the body.

4.

They should be placed 6 rounds from the muzzle. Before sewing them on, please make sure that your walrus can stand, resting on the flippers.
Make sure to stuff them a bit more before sewing all the way around. See picture D.

WALTER THE
WALRUS

GARLAND

WHAT YOU WILL NEED

MATERIALS

6g of curry yellow cotton
· Drops Loves You 6, color 105

6g of coral cotton
· Drops Loves You 6, color 109

6g of sea green cotton
· Drops Loves You 6, color 112

6g of light gray cotton
· Drops Loves You 6, color 103

6g of coal gray cotton
· Drops Loves You 6, color 118

A small amount of off-white cotton
· Drops Loves You 6, color 101

OR

6g of light pink cotton
· Drops Safran, color 01

6g of pink cotton
· Drops Safran, color 02

6g of coral cotton
· Drops Safran, color 13

6g of ice blue cotton
· Drops Safran, color 50

6g of petrol blue cotton
· Drops Safran, color 51

A small amount of off-white cotton
· Drops Safran, color 18

2.5-3mm

ABBREVIATIONS
Chain stitch (ch)
Slip stitch (sl st)
Single crochet (sc)
Decrease (2»1)
Row (RW)

GARLAND

The garland is crocheted in rows. Each row is turned with a chain stitch.

Chain 23. Starting in the 2nd chain stitch from the hook.

Rw1: sc across = 22 sts
Rw2: 2»1, 18 sc, 2»1 = 20 sts
Rw3: sc across = 20 sts
Rw4: 2»1, 16 sc, 2»1 = 18 sts
Rw5: sc across = 18 sts

Rw6: 2»1, 14 sc, 2»1 = 16 sts
Rw7: sc across = 16 sts
Rw8: 2»1, 12 sc, 2»1 = 14 sts
Rw9: sc across = 14 sts
Rw10: 2»1, 10 sc, 2»1 = 12 sts
Rw11: sc across = 12 sts
Rw12: 2»1, 8 sc, 2»1 = 10 sts
Rw13: sc across = 10 sts
Rw14: 2»1, 6 sc, 2»1 = 8 sts
Rw15: sc across = 8 sts
Rw16: 2»1, 4 sc, 2»1 = 6 sts
Rw17: sc across = 6 sts

Rw18: 2»1, 2 sc, 2»1 = 4 sts
Rw19: sc across = 4 sts
Rw20: (2»1) x 2 = 2 sts
Rw21: sc across = 2 sts
Rw22: 2»1 = 1 st

Don't break the yarn but continue crocheting around the garland, sc around. In the top two corners, crochet 3 sc in the same stitch. Finish with a slip stitch. Break the yarn and fasten off.

ASSEMBLING

I've placed the pennants in the following order:

· Curry, coral, sea green, light grey, jeans blue and coal
· Light pink, pink, coral, ice blue and petrol blue

With off-white yarn, chain 50. Sc in each stitch at the top of the first pennant. Don't break the yarn, but chain 10, and continue with a sc in each stitch at the top of the next pennant.

Continue like this to the end and finish off by chaining 50.

POPCORN

WHAT YOU WILL NEED

MATERIALS
Off-white cotton
· Drops Safran, color 18

 2.5-3mm

ABBREVIATIONS
Chain stitch (ch)
Slip stitch (sl st)
Single crochet (sc)
Half double crochet (hdc)
Double crochet (dc)
Increase (2i1)
Decrease (2»1)
Round (R)

POPCORN

· **off-white yarn**
R1: 6 sc in a magic ring = 6 sts
R2: (2i1) x 6 = 12 sts
R3-4: sc around = 12 sts
R5: (2»1) x 6 = 6 sts
R6: (in the same stitch; 1 hdc, 1 dc, 1 hdc),
1 sl st x 3 = 12 sts
Break the yarn and fasten off.

THANK YOU

It's a strange feeling writing the last page of a book. The last page of my first book, that is. My first book! I've groped in the dark and tried my way. The result has made it all worth it and it's with great pride (and some anxiety) that I'm passing the book along to you. I hope that you'll enjoy it.

This book would never have been realized if it wasn't for a lot of people supporting me along the way.

First of all, I would like to thank my amazing family. An eternal support from my sister, Louise Nielsen who has been with me all the way from idea to execution. My mother, Lise Nielsen who always makes sure I stay realistic. My father, Jørgen Madsen who never fails a challenge and helps me to bring all of my projects to life. Thank you all so very much.

Thank you to my amazing team of test crocheters who are behind me. It wouldn't be possible without any of you. You always stand ready to help me. Thank you so much to Susan Seloy, Camilla Vig, Annemarie Pedersen, Tina Gullberg, Kamilla Jensen, and Maria Linderod Bülow.

Thank you so much to Christina Bundgaard for editing all of my pictures. You have spent numerous hours on my book and it means the world to me. I've learned so much from you and I hope to learn even more in the future.

Janni Flammild, thank you. Thank you for keeping me sharp and the text in my patterns accurate and for spotting all of my mistakes. I trust you completely and utterly.

A special thanks to Yarnliving.com for supplying all of the yarn used to make this book. And equally as important, thank you for a great cooperation.

Last but not least, thank you to Kandrups Bogtrykkeri, Louise Klit Thomsen, and Thomas Thomsen. I've been welcomed with professionalism, positivity, and warmth. Thank you for meeting all of my expectations and even more. I will definitely use your services for any future projects.

SPONSORS AND SUPPLIERS

YARNLIVING.COM
Yarn, crochet hooks

EBAY
Safety eyes

SOSTRENE GRENE
Accessories

PANDURO HOBBY
Feathers, accessories

IKEA
Stuffing

SEWANDSO
Yarn, crochet hooks

Index

A SEWANDSO BOOK
© F&W Media International, Ltd and Little Happy Crochet 2019

SewandSo is an imprint of F&W Media International, Ltd
Pynes Hill Court, Pynes Hill, Exeter, EX2 5AZ, UK

F&W Media International, Ltd is a subsidiary of F+W Media, Inc
10151 Carver Road, Suite #200, Blue Ash, OH 45242, USA

Text and Designs © IraRott, Inc, Carolina Guzman Benitez and Tine Nielsen 2019
Layout and Photography © F&W Media International, Ltd and Little Happy Crochet 2019

First published in the UK and USA in 2019
Previously published as *Crochet Animal Rugs* (2018), *Snuggle & Play Crochet* (2017) and *Little Happy Circus* (2017). *Little Happy Circus* was originally published in Denmark by Little Happy Crochet.

Iryna MacGarvey (Ira Rott), Carolina Guzman Benitez and Tine Nielsen have asserted their right to be identified as authors of this work in accordance with the Copyright, Designs and Patents Act, 1988.

A catalogue record for this book is available from the British Library.

ISBN-13: 978-1-4463-0752-6 paperback

Printed in China by RR Donnelley for:
F&W Media International, Ltd
Pynes Hill Court, Pynes Hill, Exeter, EX2 5AZ, UK

10 9 8 7 6 5 4 3 2 1

Content Director: Ame Verso
Acquisitions Editor: Sarah Callard
Managing Editor: Jeni Hennah
Project Editors: Carolyne Voaden and Lynne Rowe
Proofreaders: Cheryl Brown and Jane Trollope
Design Manager: Anna Wade
Designers: Sarah Rowntree, Sam Staddon, Lisa Fordham, Ali Stark and Kandrups Bogtrykkeri
Art Direction: Prudence Rogers and Sarah Rowntree
Photographers: Jason Jenkins, Ira Rott, Tine Nielsen and Louise Nielsen
Photo Editor: Christina Bundgaard Photography
Production Manager: Beverley Richardson

Yarn for *Little Happy Circus* supplied by Yarnliving.com

F&W Media publishes high quality books on a wide range of subjects.
For more great book ideas visit: www.sewandso.co.uk

Layout of the digital edition of this book may vary depending on reader hardware and display settings.